西方文化简明教程

主　编　刘春芳　高兆金
副主编　杨银玲　李岩峰　张军燕

天津大学出版社
TIANJIN UNIVERSITY PRESS

图书在版编目（CIP）数据

西方文化简明教程/刘春芳，高兆金主编. —天津：天津大学出版社，2013.6（2020.12 重印）
ISBN 978-7-5618-4716-9

Ⅰ. ①西… Ⅱ. ①刘… ②高… Ⅲ. ①西方文化－教材 Ⅳ. ①G11

中国版本图书馆 CIP 数据核字（2013）第 133412 号

出版发行 天津大学出版社
地　　址 天津市卫津路 92 号天津大学内（邮编：300072）
电　　话 发行部：022-27403647
网　　址 publish.tju.edu.cn
印　　刷 北京虎彩文化传播有限公司
经　　销 全国各地新华书店
开　　本 148mm×210mm
印　　张 10.125
字　　数 360 千
版　　次 2013 年 6 月第 1 版
印　　次 2020 年 12 月第 4 次
定　　价 28.00 元

编　委　会

主　编：刘春芳　高兆金

副主编：杨银玲　李岩峰　张军燕

编　者：王　瑜　王　莉　朱晓静

倪爱霞　刘　雪　王　雪

《西方文化简明教程》导读

文化是一个极为宽泛的概念，文化的学习就是对一种代代相传的总体行为模式的了解过程。由于这种总体行为模式涵盖的历史深厚，涉及社会中的不同层级和不同方面，因此会使学生产生庞杂而无处下手的感觉。其实，文化本身应该是丰富生动、五彩缤纷的，研习文化是一个充满惊喜和快乐的过程。英国人类学家爱德华认为："文化是一个错综复杂的整体，它包括知识、信仰、艺术、法律、道德、习俗以及作为社会成员的人所获得的其他一切能力和习惯。"换言之，对文化的了解和掌握是通过一个社会不同层面的表现来获取的，这些层面可分为有形和无形两个部分，有形文化指的是人们的行为方式，包括语言、习俗等，也包括特定的文化产品，如文学、艺术、音乐等。而无形的层面则包括人的价值取向、信仰和道德观等。西方从地理环境到历史发展与我们的民族文化存在着巨大差异，因而生长出的文化也与我们迥异，作为一个生活在国际化、信息化和数码化时代的青年学生，极有必要对西方文化进行深入了解。唯有如此，才能在文化交融的时代保持清醒的头脑。

对于西方文化史的学习，有以下几个问题需要注意。

一是克服迷茫感，抓住西方文化史的发展脉络。《西方文化简明教程》包含的内容很丰富。纵向上讲，包括希伯来文明、古希腊文明、罗马文明、文艺复兴……一直到西方当代文化；横向上讲，包括哲学、思想、文学、艺术等各个层面的内容。学生们在学习时有时会感到迷茫和困惑，面对崭新的文化思想和浩瀚的知识产生力不从心之感。在这里，我希望以一个小小的比喻来解决大家的困惑，我们可以尝试把西方文化史的发展比做一个人的成长过程，这样我们就剥离了西方文化史的神秘抽象之感，形成生动而具体的认识。马克思曾说，“希腊是人类的正常儿童”，也就是说，希腊文化中所表现出来的随心所欲、张扬纵性的特点恰如小小的孩童，凡事以自己的所欲所求为中心，很少考虑外在规范与社会价值体系。沿着这种思路思考下去，想哭就哭、想闹就闹的孩童时期很快便会进入深受家长与老师管束的时期，我们可以把这个时期比做神学思想统治一切、人性备受压制的中世纪。长期的压制导致对人性的渴望与追求，因此当人逐渐成熟，对自我逐渐肯定并进行歌颂，相应的历史就是进入了以人文主义思想为主要特点的文艺复兴时期。这个时期对人性的颂扬是极其热烈的，人是“宇宙的精华、万物的灵长”就是这一时期的人性宣言。文艺复兴虽高扬人性的大旗开创了人类历史的崭新一页，但是这一时期也存在着热烈有余而理性思考不足的青春期般的特点。在此基础上的人的发展与成长越发成熟与理性，西方文化史也进入了以理性为主要特点的时代，理性的发展导致人能够不断地成功、不断地征服，从而进一步印证人的理性之伟大，这便是以理性为核心，以科技发展为主要成就的启蒙主义时期。理性的思索与理性的行为模式虽然使人取得了外在的不断成功，但却使人内心的情感世界逐渐失落与衰微，于是，渴盼激情的人们便发起了一场以情感为内核的思想革命，即浪漫主义大张旗鼓地在欧洲各国出现。之后，经历过激情变奏的人的发展进入了更为冷静、更为现实的中年时期，这便是西方文化史上的现实主义时期。这是一个浪漫的理想逐渐褪色，对现实的认识和思考更为客观的时期。如果没有意外的事件，西方本来可以沿着这条冷静而客观的道路渐渐前行，然而令人震惊的是，西方历史上却发生了令所有人精神崩溃的两次世界大战，残酷的战争摧毁了人们对未来的期待、对信仰的依赖以及对人间善与美的追求的信心。由此，西方的思想界承受了前所未有的打击。"上帝死了"等令人震惊的话语将西方世界宁静的状态打破，当代西方文化由此充满了对人性的怀疑、对人类未来的怀疑、对世界发展的不信任等黑色与荒诞的因素，当代西方文化没有在物质丰富的背景下走向丰盈与完满，反而越发支离破碎。这种境遇像不像一个中年人虽然拥有无尽财富，却因心灵无处皈依而感到落寞与孤独呢？以人的一生发展来比喻西方文化史的发展虽有不全面之处，但是希望这个比喻能帮助大家理清西方文化史发展的主要脉络，围绕这个脉络而出现的事件与人物大都具有某些共同的特点。在此基础上，对西方文化史的学习便能更加清晰、更加有的放矢。

二是对西方文化的学习要有文化比较的视野。多年的教学经验使我感到，我们的青年学生在面对与中华文化迥异的西方文化时常常有两种反应。一种思想是对西方文化甚为崇拜，从而对中国文化产生轻视之感。深受中国文化浸润的我们，面对与我们有着很多差异的西方文化，尤其是这种文化所取得的科技成就及物质的巨大发展，常常会对我们自身的文化产生质疑。为什么我们的文化没有创造如此辉煌的成就？这种观点形成的根源是对中华文化的理解不深、对西方文化的了解也不够。文化的形成有其独特的背景，中华文化的悠久历史与传统包含着西方文化所没有的智慧。中华文化从来就不以科技发展为其重要目标，而是以滋养内心、培养人格为其重要指向。在这些文化氛围的影响下，中国文化中的优秀人物大都有着良好的教养与高贵的人格，而非德行欠佳而只有一技之长之人。西方注重个性的文化氛围固然造就了其近代科技的发展，但也由于西方文化中单向的竞争思想与个性张扬思想，造就了不断征服、不断掠夺的性格底蕴，导致当今世界被战争阴云威胁，西方人自己的内心也因失落了精神依托而被无助感和荒诞感所笼罩。西方当代文化面临困境，正是由于西方过于强调科学精神而忽略了人文气质。我们学习西方文化，就是要了解其发展脉络、发生背景，学习其擅长理性思维、投身科技发展的科学精神，也要批判其忽略人文意蕴和高尚情操的价值取向。另一种思想则是由于对中国文化极其热爱，因而拒绝学习和了解西方文化，认为西方文化不足以和中国文化相提并论。这种思想的根源也是由于没有深入了解这两种文化。中国文化固然博大精深，充满智慧，但不能因此否认西方文化自身的价值，或者因此就对西方文化嗤之以鼻。西方文化与中国文化孕育发展的背景截然不同，其形成的文化思想也有着巨大差异。学习西方文化中的优点，避免其不完善的地方，才是对中国文化最好的热爱方式。"鸵鸟"政策本质上是一种懦弱心态的表现。宽容并支持差异性的存在，并在相互尊重的基础上相互学习、取长补短才是最佳的策略。

三是文化比较要注意避免草率下结论，片面得出孰优孰劣的结论。文化的学习就像打开了一扇大门，推开门后看到的是从未见过的五彩缤纷的花朵，正如郁金香与牡丹花难分美丑一样，这些花朵也难以从主观上判断好坏。正确的学习态度是了解差异、比较差异，不断进行深入的学习与研究。如果碰到什么问题和困难，最好的办法是与老师和同学沟通，同时阅读大量的文献资料，从而形成更加全面、更加深刻的认识，而非简单地对文化现象下结论。

以上是综合多年来的教学经验与体会，针对《西方文化简明教程》的学习中出现的一些问题所给予的一些解释。本教材试图对西方文化的发展脉络和精粹进行清晰的梳理和简明的陈述，目的是深化当前大学通识课的教育，使学生真正能领会西方文化史的思想要义。本书有以下三个特点。

第一，为使学生对西方文化史的发展脉络产生较为清晰的认识，本书将分为三大部分。根据西方文化史的简单划分，可以将其分为古希腊、罗马时期，中世纪时期和现代时期。本书即依据这种非常明了的划分进行编排。第一篇为古希腊、罗马时期，重点讲述古希腊和古罗马时期的文化，中世纪时期将包括基督教的发展和中世纪的思想文化特色。从文艺复兴至当代，统称为现代时期，西方文化步入了现代意义上的发展。这个时期包括文艺复兴、17 世纪革命、巴洛克艺术、启蒙主义、浪漫主义、现实主义及现代主义几个章节。这样的划分一改对西方文化史只有详细梳理的各个章节，缺乏体现大致脉络的阶段划分，从而避免使学生陷入各个年代文化现象的迷阵当中，失去了对西方文化发展的整体把握。

第二，本书每篇英文课文之前都有比较系统的中文介绍，帮助学生在学习西方文化之前形成对文化精髓的良好认知。这些介绍是授课者多年来对文化教学心得与体会的集中体现，是对西方文化史内在机制的简要陈述和独特评说。我们知道，文化史本质上就是人的发展史和文明史。在此意义上，人类文明史是一部物质文化和精神文化的发展史。作为意识形态的表现形式和社会文明的重要载体，文化具有知识培养和情操陶冶的功用。西方文化，是一个大文化的概念，包括哲学、思想、艺术、文学、音乐、制度、技术乃至社会生活和科学领域，可以说是西方文明的概括。若没有对这些领域所体现出来的普遍特点的综合论述，便难以把握这部庞杂的文明发展史。一般来说，西方文化中的西方，从地域上讲，主要指欧洲，18 世纪以来开始包括北美洲的美国和加拿大。从内容上讲，其源头主要由希腊的理性和艺术、希伯来的宗教和罗马的法律组成，其主流则是中世纪文化、文艺复兴、宗教改革、科学革命、启蒙运动、美国独立战争、法国大革命、工业革命、现代哲学思潮、现代主义、后现代……共同汇合而成，这一切构成了西方文化的源和流。对这些发展思潮、发展阶段的内在属性和基本思想的阐释，能够使学生建立起比较全面的认识。

第三，本书的章节划分以授课进度为主要依据，内容主次分明，语言简洁流畅。在课本的使用中，教师们可根据授课计划进行统筹安排。一般来说，第一部分占据全部课时的四分之一，中世纪部分也占据四分之一的课时，剩下的部分则由现代部分组成，因为现代部分包含的历史跨度虽然不如前两个部分长，但所包含的知识结构和信息量却是巨大的。而且，现代部分所蕴涵的西方文化发展的本质问题、走向问题、与中国文化的融合问题都是我们在授课中关注的焦点，因此其占据的课时量大约为总课时量的二分之一。

第四，教学手段应在以本课本为依据的基础上，尽量多样化，充分运用现代化教学手段，使本课程的教学不但信息量丰富，而且生动有趣。由于本书具有提纲挈领的特点，对每个历史阶段的介绍均重点突出，语言生动简洁，非常符合学生对通识课程的基本需求。而在教学中，可根据课本的内容，进行一些教学方法的改进与探索。由于篇幅所限，本书的图片并不多，在授课时可通过更多的图片展示来生动地阐释西方文化，如对西方典型建筑、著名绘画作品的介绍可运用该方法。其次，对于西方文化史的重大事件、重要人物，几乎均可找到相应的影视作品，一些作品早已成为永恒的经典。在课堂教学中，可为学生播放一些片段，激发学生的学习兴趣，并推荐一些能拓展学生知识面的影片与资料供其课后观看，在课堂上进行讲述与评论。再次，西方文化史的学习离不开对文化现象、文化问题、中西方文化比较与融合等问题的探讨。因此，对文化热点问题的讨论也是本课程教学的一项基本内容。问题的讨论可通过多种形式实现，使课堂教学更加丰富多彩。

总之，《西方文化简明教程》是一本系统介绍西方文化的书籍。西方是一个不同寻常的社会，是经过数千年的发展整合形成的。它的文化既表现出一致性，又呈现出复杂性和多彩性。《西方文化简明教程》在对西方文化进行探寻时，着重对它的起源、它的形成、它的发展、它的面貌特征进行了有特色的概述。其内容包括组成西方文化源头的希腊理性和艺术、希伯来宗教、罗马法律以及汇合成西方文化之流的中世纪文化、文艺复兴、宗教改革、科学革命、启蒙运动……本书在较为完整地展示西方文化的内涵和发展历程的同时，特别注意突显贯穿其中并推动西方文明进程、对人类社会进步产生深远影响的思想、运动和成就。西方文化的重要方面如历史、社会形态、思想（如哲学思想、文艺思潮、文艺理论等）、影响社会发展的科学成就、与文学密切关联和相互影响的艺术等无不包含其中。阅读本书无疑将扩大视野，有助于对西方世界的了解。特别的视野、高度的概括、独特的评说构成了《西方文化简明教程》的基本特色。希望本书的出版能为通识课程的教育增添一抹亮色，为推进青年学生对西方文化的全面了解做出贡献，为在此基础上对中国文化的深入了解、中西文化的发展走向等问题的探讨提供思路。

刘春芳

2013 年 3 月

Contents

Contents

Division I

Greek and Roman Culture

古希腊文化主要包括古希腊神话、古希腊战争及古希腊文学艺术。古希腊文化作为古典文化的代表，在西方乃至世界都占有极其重要的地位。爱琴海文明虽迟于古埃及文明、古巴比伦文明、古希伯来文明和古印度文明，但其影响却更为巨大。换言之，上述文明正淘汰于历史长河之中，而古希腊文化精神却未被湮没。其灿烂的古希腊文学反映了欧洲从氏族社会向奴隶制社会过渡时期的现实生活，特别体现了古代世界的人们对战争与和平、人与自然之间的关系的思考。古希腊时代显赫的英雄行为和社会历史的重大变迁都在文学作品中得以深刻的体现。这些文学作品不仅为整个西方文学的发展奠定了基调，也为人们研究古希腊世界的历史与社会提供了丰富的文献资料。

古希腊文明与中华文明不同，它是由海洋孕育的。由于其最初发源地是爱琴海一带以及邻近的希腊半岛，因此农耕并不发达，但航海业却比较发达。因此希腊地区同其他地区，特别是同埃及和西亚各国有着广泛的商业、文化联系。早在古希腊文明诞生之前，在西亚两河流域的峡谷里就连绵不断地产生了苏美尔文明、巴比伦文明和亚述文明。那里已经具备了较先进的书写、冶金、纺织等手工艺术，数学、天文学、建筑学也达到相当高的水平。地处北非的埃及，在工业、农业、科学、文学艺术方面也创造了古代罕见的奇迹。这一切都对希腊文化产生了深刻影响。希腊人从古老的东方文化中吸收了丰富的营养以滋润自己，希腊文学也具有显著的东方色彩。

由于海洋文化的滋养，希腊民族没有形成囿于家园的心理，从本质上讲，临海的生活环境也没有他们可以依附并通过农业生产繁衍生息的条件。在与自然的搏斗中，古希腊民族形成了强调开拓进取，强调征服占有的外向型文化特点。为了更好的生存环境，他们需要利用自己的头脑与武力去斗争，因此西方文化中擅长理性分析、逻辑思辨的思维模式逐渐形成，强调个人能力和征服欲望的文化底蕴也逐渐形成。从个性张扬、纵情随欲的古希腊神话中，这些特点便可见一斑。这些神之间的斗争不断，个性突出，神与神之间的恩怨纠葛体现了生动的古希腊文化场景。而希腊神话中相当精密的体系性和完整性，也体现出希腊人精神与理性的思维特点。因此，我们可以说古希腊文学表现了古希腊人对宇宙、自然与人生的理解与思考，其中蕴涵着他们较为原始的精神、心理、情感和文化。外部世界的神秘莫测，大自然的不可驾驭，人生的变幻无常，也使他们形成了带有宗教宿命论色彩的“命运观”。在文学中，命运对人具有绝对的控制性和不可改变性，人必须服从命运的安排，但人又可以在命定的范围内发挥最大的才干与潜能，随心所欲地去做自己的事。被命运所诅咒的俄狄浦斯便是极好的例子，他尽管充满智慧，拥有强大的能力，但却最终无法逃脱命运的魔咒。这也许是希腊人对于失败的人性解说。然而，俄狄浦斯虽遭受命运折磨，却未体现出丝毫的退让与懦弱。他最后选择刺瞎双眼流放天涯，便是人的最高尊严的表现。面对命运的不幸，人所选择的不是逃避和哭泣，而是主动承受痛苦，勇敢面对。

古希腊中的神和人都具有自由奔放、独立不羁、狂欢取乐、享受人生的个体本位意识，而在困难面前又表现出艰苦卓绝、百折不挠的精神。威力无穷的命运给古希腊人带来了困惑与恐惧，也培养了他们的自我意识和个体精神。此外，他们在与命运抗争中激发出了蓬勃的生命活力。古希腊文学正是在描写人对现世价值的追寻、人与命运的矛盾和抗争中展示的人性的活泼与美丽，表现了人类童年时期的自由、乐观与浪漫。生命意识、人本意识和自由观念是古希腊文学的基本精神，也成为日后西方文学与文化的基本内核。其深远的影响力和长久的生命力似乎只有中华文明方可比拟。

当希腊化的文明正在地中海东部沿岸盛行之时，一个新的强国在西方兴起了。古代罗马兴起于意大利半岛，与希腊毗邻。公元前5

世纪希腊古典文化高度繁荣之时，罗马还是一个刚刚步入文明的城邦。随着罗马的对外扩张，罗马文化的影响也越来越大。意大利有一个好战的城市，它开始打出一条通向世界帝国的道路，这就是古罗马。古罗马对古希腊人的征服，开启了希腊精神征服地中海的时代。古罗马对古希腊的征服是历史上最富戏剧化的一场斗争。古罗马在政治上的确战胜了希腊，但对古希腊的文化却几乎全盘接收。古罗马神话中的故事与人物，除却一些神的名字上有所改变之外，就是希腊神话的翻版。古罗马对古希腊文化的继承，反证出古希腊文化的璀璨与辉煌。可以说，罗马文化与希腊文化有着千丝万缕的历史联系。无论在建筑、宗教、科学、哲学，还是在文学、艺术等方面都可以看到希腊文化的影响和印记，都是对希腊文化的继承和发展，但同时它在这些方面的成就却又比希腊更胜一筹。

罗马人在对地中海的统治中融合了希腊文明的精神，把希腊精神转换成了罗马的政治统治形式，形成了罗马法的原则。罗马法不仅仅在当时罗马社会生活中发挥了极为重要的作用，而且在历史上形成了欧洲法律的基础。罗马的共和政体及立宪政体同时成为资产阶级初登政治舞台时与封建贵族分享权力的先例。罗马帝国的威名和疆域也成为后世强权主义、扩张主义和帝国主义所仰慕的先例。因此，不论是在历史上还是在地域上，罗马都处在古代文明向近代文明过渡、近代文明同欧洲文明混合的大路口，成为西方文明源头上的一个重要的组成部分。在整个西方文明史上，它起着承前启后、继往开来的作用。

总之，“辉煌的希腊，伟大的罗马”，这是人们对古希腊罗马文化特点的高度概括。古希腊和古罗马这两大文明是西方文化的摇篮，是世界文化史上两座永恒的丰碑，是西方人所津津乐道的光辉时代。勤劳的古希腊和罗马人民用他们的智慧给我们创造了一个个令人叹为观止的杰作，留给我们一个无论是文化史上还是艺术史上都难以超越的高度。罗马文化是西方古典文化的重要组成部分，更在希腊文化基础之上根据本国社会、经济、政治发展的需要，创造了自己独特的文化，为世界文化增添了新的内容。

Chapter 1 Ancient Greece

1 Greek Mythology

1.1 The Beginning of Greek Mythology

In ancient Greece, some people began telling stories to explain the mysteries of life. Over much time, the stories grew rich and imaginative. The storytellers actually wove in their customs, beliefs and theories about life, death, and the wonders of nature. The myths were about gods and goddesses, fearful monsters, brave heroes, and mysterious beauties.

According to mythology, the gods and goddesses looked and acted like human. They married each other. They laughed, loved, quarrelled and fought with each other. But they were immortal. They lived forever because a fluid called ichor — not blood — flowed through their veins.

The mightiest of the gods and goddesses lived in a golden palace on Olympus — a high mountain, the top was hidden by clouds. They feasted an ambrosia and nectar — the food and drink of the gods. And whenever they wished, they could change shape and speed down to earth to mingle with the mortals. The awesome Olympians earned their thrones on Olympus. They fought a fierce battle and won.

This is the story of how it happened.

In the very beginning, there was a dark space named Chaos and

Gaea. The Earth, grew out of this dark space and later Gaea gave birth to Uranus, the Sky. Uranus rained down on young Gaea, and plants, animals, and rivers appeared. Gaea became Mother Earth, mother of all living things — and mother of the first gods. Gaea and Uranus had many children. Their first born were the twelve giant Titans, six girls and six boys. Later, more children were born. Three were the mighty Cyclopes — strong, one-eyed giants. Three were the Hecatoncheires — monsters each with a hundred arms and fifty heads. Uranus hated the Cyclopes and the Hecatoncheires, because they were ugly. He threw them into Tartarus — the deepest pit in the Underworld.

Gaea was furious. She urged the Titans to overthrow their father and rescue their brothers. Only the youngest, Cronus, was brave enough. He attacked Uranus with a sickle and banished him from the Earth. Cronus replaced his father as Lord of the Universe. But he was cruel and did not free his brothers from Tartarus. Cronus married his sister Rhea, and they had many children. But Cronus was afraid that one of them might overthrow him just as he had done to his father. So as each child was born, he swallowed it. Rhea was horrified. When the youngest was born, she tricked Cronus. She hid the baby Zeus in a distant cave, so Cronus would not find him. Rhea then gave Cronus a stone wrapped in a blanket. He swallowed that instead — the blanket and all.

Hidden away, Zeus was raised by gentle woodland nymphs and a nymph-goat named Amaltheia, who fed him honeyed milk. When the baby cried, the Curetes — Zeus' guards — clashed their weapons to hide the sound. Zeus grew into the strongest of all the gods and married Metis, a Titan's daughter. Rhea was still angry with her husband and wanted Zeus to depose him. But Metis, the Goddess of Prudence, was wise. She said

Zeus needed help, for Cronus had the Titans on his side. Rhea found a way. With her help, Metis gave Cronus a drink she promised would make him undefeatable.

Instead, it made Cronus throw up the stone and his unharmed children — Hestia, Demeter, Hera, Hara, Hades, and Poseidon. They were reunited, and gratefully joined their brother. Zeus freed their uncles from Tartarus, and together they prepared to fight the Titans. The Cyclopes, who were great builders and smiths, made the weapons. They armed Zeus with a thunderbolt that shook the universe. They made Poseidon a trident that could split the seas. They gave Hades a helmet of darkness that made him invisible to his enemies. For ten years war raged between the old gods and the new gods. At last Cronus and the Titans were defeated and thrown into Tartarus, to be guarded forever by their hundred-armed brothers.

Mother Earth was finally at peace. Rule of the universe was divided among the three brothers. Zeus was declared King of the Gods, and God of Heaven and Earth. Poseidon became God of the Sea, and Hades God of the Underworld.

1. 2 The 12 Main Gods and Goddesses of Olympus

Zeus: King of the Gods
God of Heaven and Earth
Son of Cronus and Rhea

Hera: Goddess of Marriage and Childbirth
Daughter of Cronus and Rhea

Hephaestus: God of Fire and Blacksmiths
Son of Zeus and Hera

Aphrodite: Goddess of Love and Beauty

Eros: God of Love

Ares: God of War
Son of Zeus and Hera

Poseidon: God of Sea and Earthquakes
Son of Cronus and Rhea

Athena: Goddess of Wisdom and Arts and Crafts
Daughter of Zeus and Metis

Hermes: Messenger of Zeus
Herald of the Gods
Son of Zeus and the nymph Maia

Artemis: Goddess of the Moon, Wildlife, Hunting, and Chastity
Daughter of Zeus and the goddess Leto
Twin sister of Apollo

Apollo: God of the Sun, Music, Poetry, Archery, Healing, and Prophecy
Son of Zeus and goddess Leto
Twin brother of Artemis

Hades: God of the Underworld
Son of Cronus and Rhea

Demeter: Goddess of the Harvest, Grain, and Fertility
Daughter of Cronus and Rhea
Mother of Persephone

Dionysus: God of Wine and Vegetation
Son of Zeus and the mortal princess Semele

Hestia: Goddess of the Hearth
Daughter of Cronus and Rhea

2 The Trojan War

2.1 The Background Mythology

Paris was the youngest son of Priam and Hecuba. When he was born, it was foretold that he would be the cause of the downfall of Troy, as told in a dream of Hecuba. He was sent out of Troy in hopes that the message would be false. He went to Mount Ida in order to be a shepherd.

Eris, the goddess of discord, was not invited to the wedding of Peleus and Thetis. She came anyway, and she threw a golden apple into the middle of the wedding. Inscribed on the apple was a message. It read "To the fairest". Immediately, the apple was claimed by Hera, Athena and Aphrodite. They all asked Zeus to decide on who should receive the apple. Zeus knew how much trouble he would be in if he decided on one, because the other two would have grave revenge. So Zeus descended to Mount Ida where Paris was farming and asked him to be the Judge. Paris, being a mortal, could not decide. However, each of the three goddesses decided to make it easier for him. They would each offer him gifts, and he would get the gifts from the goddess he chose.

Hera offered Paris power. She offered to give him all of Asia, and great power. He thought this offer was great, but he decided to hear the other offers first before deciding.

Athena offered him great wisdom, and great luck in battle. He would be the best strategist in the world. He loved this idea, but he waited to hear Aphrodite's offer.

Aphrodite offered him two things. The first was his body, and the second was the love of the most beautiful woman in the world, Helen. Since Paris' first love was women, he decided to pick Aphrodite's offer.

Hera and Athena vowed vengeance.

Paris soon went home to Troy after that, and with Aphrodite's help, he managed to send a fleet of ships, break into Menelaus' palace in Greece and kidnap Helen. He also took a lot of treasure with him.

As Helen was the most beautiful woman in the world, all of her suitors were the most powerful people in Greece. In order for peace to be kept when Helen chose a suitor, all other suitors must vow to keep Helen as the wife of whom she chose. So when Helen chose Menelaus, all of the other suitors had to agree that if anyone tried to kidnap her, they would try to get her back. So, when Paris kidnapped her, all of Greece declared war on the city of Troy.

2.2 The Setting of Trojan War

Time of action: About 3,200 years ago in recorded history's infancy, when humankind's imagination peopled the known world with great heroes and villains and nature reflected the mood of the gods inhabiting the mountaintops, the seas, the forests, and the unseen worlds above and below. Homer fashioned the *Iliad*, the story of the Trojan War, about 600 years after the war ended. The story is a mixture of fact, legend, and myth.

Place of Action: The walled city of Troy and the surrounding plains in northwestern Anatolia, a region that is part of modern-day Turkey. Anatolia is west of Greece (across the Aegean Sea) and north of Egypt (across the Mediterranean Sea).

2.3 The Process of Trojan War

Relationships of the Characters:

Achaean	Trojan
Leader: Agamemnon Agamemnon's brother: Menelaus Menelaus' wife: Helen Heroes: Achilles Odysseus Ajax Diomedes Philoctetes (own Heracles' bow) Patroclus (Achilles' cousin)	King: Priam Prince: Hector Paris (second husband of Helen) Princess: Briseis (Achilles' concubine) Heroes: Aeneas (son of Aphrodite) Pandaros (killed by Diomedes)

Ten years have passed since the Greek armies arrived in Asia to lay waste Troy and win back their honor. Yet in all those years, neither side has gained enough advantage to force a surrender. The Greeks remained encamped outside the walls of the city, their nighttime fires mocking the glittering firmament while their generals plot stratagems and their warriors hone weapons.

Among the Greek leaders, bloodstained and hardened to war, were Agamemnon, the commander-in-chief; Menelaus, king of Sparta and brother of Agamemnon; Odysseus, king of Ithaca and a military genius of unparalleled cunning. With sword and spear, with rocks and fists, the Greeks fought the Trojans — led by the godlike Hector, their mightiest warrior, and Aeneas, a war machine second only to Hector on the Trojan side — to a standoff.

In time, the Greeks believed, they would prevail. They had right on their side after all. But even more important, they had Achilles. He was the greatest warrior ever to walk the earth — fierce, unrelenting, and unconquerable. But in the tenth year of the great war, Achilles refused to fight after Agamemnon insulted him. The rift between them opened after Agamemnon and Achilles captured two maidens while raiding the region around Troy. Agamemnon's prize was Chryseis, the daughter of a priest of the god Apollo. For Achilles, there was the beautiful Briseis, who became his slave mistress. Unfortunately for the Greeks, the headstrong king then ordered his men to seize Briseis as a replacement for his lost prize. Achilles was outraged. But rather than venting his wrath with his mighty sword, he retired from battle, vowing never again to fight for his countrymen.

On his behalf, his mother, the sea nymph Thetis, importuned Zeus, king of the gods, to turn the tide of war in favor of the Trojans. Such a reversal would be fitting punishment for Agamemnon.

Then Nestor, a wise old king of three score and ten, advised Agamemnon to make peace with Achilles. The proud commander, now repentant and fully acknowledging his unjust treatment of Achilles, accepted the advice and pledged to restore Briseis to Achilles. Told that all wrongs against him would be righted, Achilles — still smoldering with anger — spurned the peace-making overture. His wrath was unquenchable. However, Patroclus, unable to brook the Trojan onslaught against his countrymen, borrowed the armor of Achilles and, at the next opportunity, entered the battle disguised as Achilles. The stratagem worked for a while as Patroclus chopped and hacked his way through the Trojan ranks. But eventually Hector's spear felt brave Patroclus with no small help from meddlesome Apollo. The Trojan hero celebrated the kill with an audacious coup de grâce: He removed and put on Achilles' armor. Grievously saddened by the death of his friend and outraged at the brazen behavior of Hector, wrathful Achilles — with a new suit of armor forged in Olympus by Hephaestus at the behest of Achilles' mother, Thetis — agreed to rejoin the fight at long last.

The next day, Achilles ruled the battlefield with death and destruction, cutting a swath of terror through enemy ranks. Trojan blood mulched the fields. Limbs lay helter-skelter, broken and crooked, as fodder for diving raptors. Terrified, the Trojans fled to the safety of Troy and its high walls — all of them, that was, except Hector. Foolishly, out of his deep sense of honor and responsibility as protector of Troy, he stood his ground. In a fairy tale about a noble hero with an adoring wife and son, Hector would surely have won the day against a vengeful, all-devouring foe. His compatriots — and the gallery of sons and daughters and wives peering down from the Trojan bulwarks — would surely have crowned him king. But in the brutal world of Achilles — whose ability to disembowel and decapitate was a virtue — Hector suffered a humiliating death. After Achilles chased and caught him, he easily slew him, then strapped his carcass to his chariot and dragged him around the walls of Troy. Patroclus had been avenged, the Greeks had reclaimed battlefield supremacy, and victory seemed imminent.

However, old Priam, the king of Troy and the father of Hector, showed that Trojan valor had not died with Hector. At great risk to himself, he crossed the battlefield in a chariot and presented himself to Achilles to claim the body of his son. But there was no anger in Priam's heart. He understood the ways of wars and warriors. He knew that Achilles, the greatest of the Greek soldiers, had no choice but to kill his son, the greatest of the Trojan warriors. Humbly, Priam embraced Achilles and gave him his hand. Deeply moved, Achilles welcomed Priam and ordered an attendant to prepare Hector's body.

The *Iliad* ended here. Homer's audience was aware of the outcome of the war: the defeat and destruction of Troy by the Greeks. When Troy fell, so did Achilles — from the wound of arrow shot by Paris and guided by the god Apollo.

2.4 Trojan Horse

The key and final plan was to make a great wooden horse, which was suggested by smart Odysseus and guided by Athena. This was a hollow wooden horse, which kind of animal was sacred to the Trojans, inside which many soldiers were hidden. At the same time, the rest of the army burned their own camp and sailed back for Tenedos on purpose. When the Trojans saw all of this, they believed that the Greeks were gone out of fear and the war was over. Therefore, they dragged the horse, the sacred animal, inside the city. On midnight, the hidden soldiers from inside the horse emerged, killed the guards and opened the gate of Troy. The Acheans entered the city and killed the sleeping population. It led to the fall of Troy.

King Priam: killed

Queen Hecuba, princess Cassandra (公主), princess Andromache (王妃): slaves

Helen and Menelaus: reconciling (和好如初) and vanishing in the west

Aeneas (son of Aphrodite): wandering from land to land for a long time and becoming the founder of the Roman race

Agamemnon: murdered by his wife, who was later murdered by her son, Orestes

Odysseus: going through untold hardships, contending with wind and wave

3 Homer's Epic

3.1 Homer

Homer is the author of the *Iliad* and the *Odyssey*, and is revered as the greatest of ancient Greek epic poets. These epics lie at the beginning of the Western canon of literature, and have had an enormous influence on the history of literature.

When he lived, he was unknown. Herodotus estimated that Homer lived 400 years before Herodotus' own time, which would place him at around 850 BC; while other ancient sources claimed that he lived much nearer to the supposed time of the Trojan War, in the early 12th century BC. Modern researchers appear to place Homer in the 7th or 8th century BC. Some Ancient Lives depicted Homer as a wandering minstrel, who walked as far as Chalkis to sing at the funeral games of Amphidamas. We are given the image of a "blind, begging singer who hangs around with little people: shoemakers, fisherman, potters, sailors, elderly men in the gathering places of harbor towns".

The formative influence played by the Homeric epics in shaping Greek culture was widely recognized, and Homer was described as the teacher of Greece. Homer's works, which are about fifty percent speeches, provided models in persuasive speaking and writing that were emulated throughout the ancient and medieval Greek worlds. Fragments of Homer account for nearly half of all identifiable Greek literary papyrus finds.

3.2 *Iliad*

The *Iliad* (sometimes referred to as the *Song of Ilion* or *Song of Ilium*) is an epic poem in dactylic hexameters, traditionally attributed to Homer. Set during the Trojan War, the ten-year siege of the city of Troy (Ilium) by a coalition of Greek states, it tells of the battles and events during the weeks of a quarrel between King Agamemnon and the warrior Achilles.

Although the story covers only a few weeks in the final year of the war, the *Iliad* mentions or alludes to many of the Greek legends about the siege; the earlier events, such as the gathering of warriors for the siege, the cause of the war, and related concerns tend to appear near the beginning. Then the epic narrative takes up events prophesied for the future, such as Achilles' looming death and the sack of Troy, prefigured and alluded to more and more vividly, so that when it reaches an end, the poem has told a more or less complete tale of the Trojan War. The *Iliad* is paired with something of a sequel, the *Odyssey*, also attributed to Homer.

Along with the *Odyssey*, the *Iliad* is among the oldest extant works of Western literature, and its written version is usually dated to around the 8th century BC. In the modern vulgate (accepted version), the *Iliad* contains 15,693 lines; it is written in Homeric Greek, a literary amalgam of Ionic Greek and other dialects.

3.3 *Odyssey*

The *Odyssey* is one of two major ancient Greek epic poems attributed to Homer. It is, in part, a sequel to the *Iliad*. It is believed to have been composed near the end of the 8th century BC, somewhere in Ionia, the Greek coastal region of Anatolia.

The poem mainly centers on the Greek hero Odysseus (or Ulysses, as he was known in Roman myths) and his long journey home following the fall of Troy. It took Odysseus ten years to reach Ithaca after the ten-year Trojan War. In his absence, it was assumed he had died, and his wife Penelope and son Telemachus must deal with a group of unruly suitors, whose aim was to persuade Penelope to marry one of them, all the while enjoying the hospitality of Odysseus' household and eating up his wealth. She had remained faithful to Odysseus. Prince Telemachus, Odysseus' son, wanted desperately to throw them out but didn't have the confidence or experience to fight them. Unknown to the suitors, Odysseus was still alive.

The *Odyssey* was written in a poetic dialect of Greek — a literary amalgam of Aeolic Greek, Ionic Greek, and other Ancient Greek dialects — and comprises 12,110 lines of dactylic hexameter. Among the most noteworthy elements of the text are its non-linear plot, and the influence on events of choices made by women and serfs, besides the actions of fighting men. In the English language as well as many others, the word odyssey has come to refer to an epic voyage.

4 Greek Philosophy

4.1 Socrates

Socrates (469 – 399 BC), a Greek philosopher, profoundly affected Western philosophy through his influence on Plato. Born in Athens, he received the regular elementary education in literature, music, and gymnastics. Later he familiarized himself with the rhetoric and dialectics of the Sophists, the speculations of the Ionian philosophers, and the general culture of Periclean Athens. Initially, Socrates followed the craft of his father. According to a former tradition, he executed a statue group of the three Graces, which stood at the entrance to the Acropolis until the 2nd century. In the Peloponnesian War with Sparta he served as an infantryman with conspicuous bravery at the battles of Potidaea during 432 –430 BC, Delium in 424 BC, and Amphipolis in 422 BC. Socrates believed in the superiority of argument over writing and therefore spent the greater part of his mature life in the marketplace and public places of Athens, engaging in dialogue and argument with anyone who would listen or who would submit to interrogation. Socrates was reportedly unattractive in appearance and short of stature but was also extremely hardy and self-controlled. He enjoyed life immensely and achieved social popularity because of his ready wit and a keen sense of humor that was completely devoid of satire or cynicism.

Socrates' contribution to philosophy was essentially ethical in character. Belief in a purely objective understanding of such concepts as justice, love, and virtue, and the self-knowledge that he inculcated, were the basis of his teachings. He believed that all vice is the result of ignorance, and that no person is willingly bad; correspondingly, virtue is knowledge, and those who know the right will act rightly. His logic placed particular emphasis on rational argument and the quest for general definitions, as evidenced in the writings of his younger contemporary and pupil, Plato, and of Plato's pupil, Aristotle. Through the writings of these philosophers, Socrates profoundly affected the entire subsequent course of Western speculative thought.

4.2 Plato

Plato (428? -347 BC), Greek philosopher, is one of the most

creative and influential thinkers in Western philosophy. In 387 BC Plato founded the Academy in Athens, an institution often described as the first European university. It provided a comprehensive curriculum, including such subjects as astronomy, biology, mathematics, political theory, and philosophy. Aristotle was the Academy's most prominent student. The concluding years of his life were spent lecturing at the Academy and writing. He died at about the age of 80 in Athens in 348 or 347 BC.

Plato's writings were in dialogue form; philosophical ideas were advanced, discussed, and criticized in the context of a conversation or debate involving two or more persons. The earliest collection of Plato's works includes 35 dialogues and 13 letters. The authenticity of a few of the dialogues and most of the letters has been disputed.

At the heart of Plato's philosophy is his theory of Forms, or Ideas. Ultimately, his view of knowledge, his ethical theory, his psychology, his concept of the state, and his perspective on art must be understood in terms of this theory.

The Republic, Plato's major political work, is concerned with the question of justice and therefore with the questions "what is a just state" and "who is a just individual?" The ideal state, according to Plato, is composed of three classes. The economic structure of the state is maintained by the merchant class. Security needs are met by the military class, and political leadership is provided by the philosopher-kings. A particular person's class is determined by an educational process that begins at birth and proceeds until that person has reached the maximum level of education compatible with interest and ability. Those who complete the entire educational process become philosopher-kings. They are the ones whose minds have been so developed that they are able to grasp the

Forms and, therefore, to make the wisest decisions. Indeed, Plato's ideal educational system is primarily structured so as to produce philosopher-kings.

Plato divides the human soul into three parts: the rational part, the will, and the appetites. The just person is the one in whom the rational element, supported by the will, controls the appetites. An obvious analogy exists here with the threefold class structure of the state, in which the enlightened philosopher-kings, supported by the soldiers, govern the rest of society.

Plato's influence throughout the history of Western philosophy has been monumental. Neoplatonism, founded by the 3rd-century philosopher Plotinus, was an important later development of Platonism. During the Renaissance, the primary focus of Platonic influence was the Florentine Academy, founded in the 15th century near Florence. In England, Platonism was revived in the 17th century by Ralph Cudworth and others who became known as the Cambridge Platonists. Plato's influence extended into the 20th century. The British philosopher Alfred North Whitehead once paid tribute to him by describing the history of philosophy as simply "a series of footnotes to Plato".

4.3 Aristotle

Aristotle (384 – 322 BC) was a Greek philosopher and polymath, a student of Plato and teacher of Alexander the Great. His writings cover many subjects, including physics, metaphysics, poetry, theater, music, logic, rhetoric, linguistics, politics, government, ethics, biology, and zoology. Together with Plato and Socrates (Plato's teacher), Aristotle is one of the most important founding figures in Western philosophy.

Aristotle's writings were the first to create a comprehensive system of Western philosophy, encompassing morality, aesthetics, logic, science, politics, and metaphysics.

Aristotle's views on the physical sciences profoundly shaped medieval scholarship, and their influence extended well into the Renaissance, although they were ultimately replaced by Newtonian physics. In the zoological sciences, some of his observations were confirmed to be accurate only in the 19th century. His works contain the earliest known formal study of logic, which was incorporated in the late 19th century into modern formal logic. In metaphysics, Aristotelianism had a profound influence on philosophical and theological thinking in the Islamic and Jewish traditions in the Middle Ages, and it continued to influence Christian theology, especially the scholastic tradition of the Catholic Church. Aristotle was well known among medieval Muslim intellectuals and revered as "The First Teacher". His ethics, though always influential, gained renewed interest with the modern advent of virtue ethics. All aspects of Aristotle's philosophy continue to be the object of active academic study today. Though Aristotle wrote many elegant treatises and dialogues (Cicero described his literary style as "a river of gold"), it is thought that the majority of his writings are now lost and only about one-third of the original works have survived.

More than twenty-three hundred years after his death, Aristotle remains one of the most influential people who ever lived. He contributed to almost every field of human knowledge then in existence, and he was the founder of many new fields. According to the philosopher Bryan Magee, "it is doubtful whether any human being has ever known as much as he did". Aristotle was the founder of formal logic, pioneered the study of zoology, and left every future scientist and philosopher in his debt through his contributions to the scientific method. Despite these achievements, the influence of Aristotle's errors is considered by some to have held back science considerably. Bertrand Russell notes that "almost every serious intellectual advance has had to begin with an attack on some Aristotelian doctrine". Russell also refers to Aristotle's ethics as "repulsive", and calls his logic "as definitely antiquated as Ptolemaic astronomy". Russell notes that these errors make it difficult to do historical justice to Aristotle, until one remembers how large of an advance he made upon all of his predecessors.

4.4 Epicureanism

Epicurus (341 – 270 BC) was an ancient Greek philosopher as well as the founder of the school of philosophy called Epicureanism.

Epicurus believed that pleasure is the greatest good. But the way to attain pleasure was to live modestly and to gain knowledge of the workings of the world and the limits of one's desires. This led one to attain a state of tranquility (ataraxia) and freedom from fear, as well as absence of bodily pain (aponia). The combination of these two states is supposed to constitute happiness in its highest form.

Epicurus' philosophy is based on the theory that all good and bad derive from the sensations of pleasure and pain. What is good is what is pleasurable, and what is bad is what is painful. Pleasure and pain are ultimately, for Epicurus, the basis for the moral distinction between good and evil. If pain is chosen over pleasure in some cases it is only because it leads to a greater pleasure. Although Epicurus has been commonly misunderstood to advocate the rampant pursuit of pleasure, he was actually after the absence of pain (both physical and mental, i. e. suffering) — a state of satiation and tranquility that was free of the fear of death and the retribution of the gods. When we do not suffer pain, we are no longer in need of pleasure, and we enter a state of perfect mental peace.

Epicurus explicitly warned against overindulgence because it often leads to pain. For instance, Epicurus warned against pursuing love too ardently. He defended friendships as ramparts for pleasure and denied them any inherent worth. He also believed that death was not to be feared. When a man dies, he does not feel the pain of death because he no longer is and he therefore feels nothing. Therefore, as Epicurus famously said, "death is nothing to us." When we exist death is not, and when death exists we are not. All sensation and consciousness ends with death and therefore in death there is neither pleasure nor pain. The fear of death arises from the belief that in death there is awareness.

From this doctrine arose the Epicurean epitaph: Non fui, fui, non sum, non curo (I was not; I was; I am not; I do not care) — which is inscribed on the gravestones of his followers and seen on many ancient gravestones of the Roman Empire.

The "Epicurean paradox" is a version of the problem of evil. It is a trilemma argument (God is omnipotent, God is good, but Evil exists); or more commonly seen as in this quote:

Is God willing to prevent evil, but not able?

Then he is not omnipotent.

Is he able, but not willing?

Then he is malevolent.

Is he both able and willing?

Then whence cometh evil?

Is he neither able nor willing?

Then why call him God?

5 Greek Drama

5.1 Aeschylus

Aeschylus (525/524 – 456/455 BC) is the first of the three ancient Greek tragedians whose plays can still be read or performed. He is often described as the father of tragedy. According to Aristotle, he expanded the number of characters in plays to allow for conflicts amongst them, whereas previously characters had interacted only with the chorus.

Only seven of his estimated seventy to ninety plays have survived into modern times, and there is a longstanding debate about his authorship of one of these plays, *Prometheus Bound*. Fragments of some other plays have survived in quotes and more continue to be discovered on Egyptian papyrus, often giving us surprising insights into his works.

He was a deep, religious thinker. No poet has ever presented evil in such stark and tragic terms, yet he had an exalted view of Zeus, whom he celebrated with a grand simplicity reminiscent of David's *Psalms*, and a faith in progress or the healing power of time. The main plays written by him are as follows:

The Persians

The earliest of his plays to survive is *The Persians*, performed in 472 BC and based on experiences in Aeschylus' own life, specifically the Battle of Salamis. It is unique among surviving Greek tragedies in that it describes a recent historical event.

Seven against Thebes

Seven against Thebes, which was performed in 467 BC, has the contrasting theme of the interference of the gods in human affairs. It also marks the first known appearance in Aeschylus' works of a theme which would continue through his plays, that of the polis (the city) being a key development of human civilization.

The Suppliants

Aeschylus continued his emphasis on the polis with *The Suppliants* in 463 BC (Hiketides), which pays tribute to the democratic undercurrents running through Athens in advance of the establishment of a democratic government in 461 BC.

The Oresteia

The only complete (save a few missing lines in several spots) trilogy of Greek plays by any playwright still extant is the *Oresteia* (458 BC); although the satyr play that originally followed it, Proteus, is lost except for some fragments. The trilogy consists of *Agamemnon*, *The Libation Bearers* (*Choephoroi*), and *The Eumenides*. Together, these plays tell the bloody story of the family of Agamemnon, King of Argos.

Agamemnon

Agamemnon describes Agamemnon's death at the hands of his wife Clytemnestra, who was angry at his sacrifice of their daughter Iphigenia and his keeping of the Trojan prophetess Cassandra as a concubine. Cassandra enters the palace even though she knows she will be murdered by Clytemnestra, knowing that she cannot avoid her fate. The ending of the play includes a prediction of the return of Orestes, son of Agamemnon, who will seek to avenge his father.

The Libation Bearers

The Libation Bearers continues the tale, opening with Orestes' arrival at Agamemnon's tomb. At the tomb, Electra meets Orestes, who has returned from exile in Phocis, and they plan revenge upon Clytemnestra and her lover Aegisthus.

Prometheus Bound

The play consists mostly of static dialogue, as throughout the play the Titan Prometheus is bound to a rock as punishment from the Olympian Zeus for providing fire to humans. The play closes with Zeus sending Prometheus into the abyss because Prometheus refuses to divulge the secret of a potential marriage that could be Zeus' downfall.

5.2 Sophocles

Sophocles (497 – 406 BC) is one of three ancient Greek tragedians whose plays have survived. Sophocles wrote 123 plays during the course of his life, but only seven have survived in a complete form: *Ajax*, *Antigone*, *The Women of Trachis*, *Oedipus the King*, *Electra*, *Philoctetes* and *Oedipus at Colonus*. The most famous tragedies of Sophocles feature *Oedipus* and *Antigone*: they are generally known as the Theban plays, although each play was actually a part of a different tetralogy, the other members of which are now lost. Sophocles influenced the development of the drama, most importantly by adding a third actor, thereby reducing the importance of the chorus in the presentation of the plot. He also developed his characters to a greater extent than earlier playwrights such as Aeschylus. Most of Sophocles' plays show an undercurrent of early fatalism and the beginnings of Socratic logic as a mainstay for the long tradition of Greek tragedy.

Oedipus the King

It was the second of Sophocles' three Theban plays to be produced, but it comes first in the internal chronology, followed by *Oedipus at*

Colonus and then *Antigone*. *Oedipus Rex* chronicles the story of Oedipus, a man who becomes the king of Thebes who was destined from birth to murder his father Laius and marry his mother Jocasta. The play is an example of a classic tragedy; noticeably containing an emphasis on Oedipus' own faults contributing to the tragic hero's downfall, as opposed to having fate be the sole cause.

The protagonist of the tragedy is the son of King Laius and Queen Jocasta of Thebes. After Laius learns from an oracle that "he is doomed to perish by the hand of his own son", he tightly binds the feet of the infant together with a pin and orders Jocasta to kill the infant. Hesitant to do so, she orders a servant to commit the act for her. Instead, the servant takes the baby to a mountain top to die from exposure. A shepherd rescues the infant and names him Oedipus (or "swollen feet"). The shepherd carries the baby with him to Corinth, where Oedipus is taken in and raised in the court of the childless King Polybus of Corinth as if he were his own.

On the road to Thebes, he meets Laius, his true father. Unaware of each other's identities, they quarrel over whose chariot has right-of-way. King Laius moves to strike the insolent youth with his scepter, but Oedipus throws him down from the chariot and kills him, thus fulfilling part of the oracle's prophecy. He kills all but one of the other men.

Shortly after, Oedipus solves the riddle of the Sphinx, which has baffled many a diviner: "What is the creature that walks on four legs in the morning, two legs at noon, and three in the evening?" To this Oedipus replies, "Man" (who crawls on all fours as an infant, walks upright later, and needs a walking stick in old age), and the distraught Sphinx throws herself off the cliffside. Oedipus' reward for freeing the kingdom of Thebes from her curse is the kingship and the hand of Queen Dowager

Jocasta, his biological mother. The prophecy is thus fulfilled, although none of the main characters know it. Everything is at last revealed, and Oedipus curses himself and fate. The play laments how even a great man can be felled by fate.

5.3 Euripides

Euripides (480 – 406 BC) was one of the three great tragedians of classical Athens. Some ancient scholars attributed ninety-five plays to him but according to the Suda it was ninety-two at most. Of these, eighteen or nineteen have survived complete and there are also fragments, some substantial, of most of the other plays. Euripides is identified with theatrical innovations that have profoundly influenced drama down to modern times, especially in the representation of traditional, mythical heroes as ordinary people in extraordinary circumstances. This new approach led him to pioneer developments that later writers adapted to comedy, some of which were characteristic of romance. Yet he also became "the most tragic of poets", focusing on the inner lives and motives of his characters in a way previously unknown. He was also unique among the writers of ancient Athens for the sympathy he demonstrated towards all victims of society, including women. Euripides was the first one to introduce women on the stage, not as heroines but as they are in actual life.

For the tragedians of later times Euripides was the absolute model and pattern, and equally so for the poets of the new comedy. Diphilus called him the "Golden Euripides," Among the Romans, too, he was held in high esteem, serving as a model for tragedy.

Medea

The *Medea* tells the story of the jealousy and revenge of a woman betrayed by her husband. She left home and father for Jason's sake, and he, after she had borne him children, forsook her, Medea murdered the bride and then slew her own children in revenge. Jason, who had come to punish the murderess of his bride, heard that his children had perished too, and Medea rebelled in the anguish of her faithless husband.

6 Greek Sculpture and Architecture

6.1 Sculpture: Venus de Milo

Aphrodite of Milo, better known as the Venus de Milo, is an ancient Greek statue and one of the most famous works of ancient Greek sculpture. Created sometime between 130 and 100 BC, it is believed to depict Aphrodite, the Greek goddess of love and beauty (Venus to the Romans). It is a marble sculpture, slightly larger than life size at 203 cm high. The arms and original plinth were lost following the discovery. From an inscription that was on its plinth, it is thought to be the work of Alexandros of Antioch. The Venus de Milo statue was praised dutifully by many artists and critics as the epitome of graceful female beauty.

6.2 Architecture

Greek life was dominated by religion and so it is not surprising that the temples of ancient Greece were the biggest and most beautiful. They also had a political purpose as they were often built to celebrate civic power and pride, or offer thanksgiving to the patron deity of a city for success in war.

The Greeks developed three architectural systems, called orders, each with their own distinctive proportions and detailing. The Greek orders are: Doric, Ionic, and Corinthian.

Doric

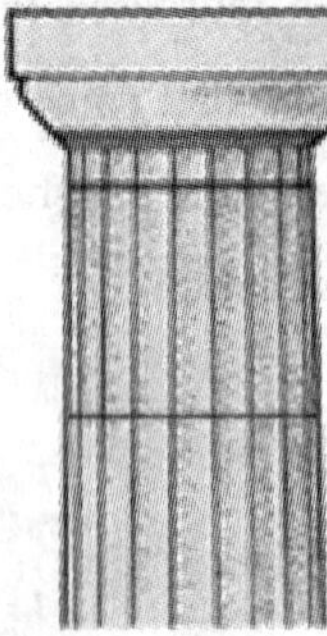

The Doric style is rather sturdy and its top (the capital), is plain. This style was used in mainland Greece and the colonies in southern Italy and Sicily.

Ionic

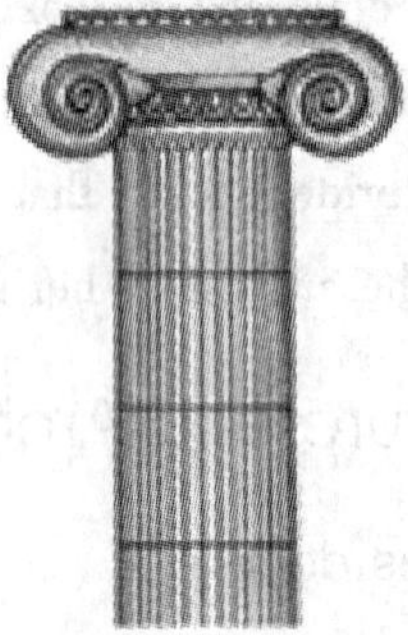

The Ionic style is thinner and more elegant. Its capital is decorated with a scroll-like design (a volute). This style was found in eastern Greece and the islands.

Connthian

The Corinthian style is seldom used in the Greek world, but often seen on Roman temples. Its capital is very elaborate and decorated with acanthus leaves.

Questions for Discussion

1. Please name the important Chinese gods and goddesses.

2. What are the features of Chinese mythology?

3. Discuss the differences between the Greek myth and the Chinese myth.

4. What do you know about Greek and Roman Mythology? What kind of influence does it cast on Western art, literature and social customs? Could you please give some examples, like famous paintings, novels, essays, proverbs, word expressions related to Greek and Roman myths?

5. Could you please explain the meaning of the following expressions after you have read the story: an Apple of Discord, Achilles' Heel, Trojan Horse.

6. In class, we will have a story relay based on the article you have read plus your own imagination. One student will tell part of the story in his/her own words followed by another student. Anyone who is stuck in the middle will be asked to give a performance as punishment.

7. Which factors do you think contribute to the breakout of the Trojan War? Some people argue that it is Helen that triggers this great war. Do you agree with it?

Chapter 2 Ancient Rome

Ancient Roman civilization was a thriving one and the history of Rome was long. Beginning with the foundation of the city of Rome on the Italian peninsula in the 8th century BC, it grew into one of the largest empires in ancient times. In its approximately 1,200 years of existence, Roman civilization changed from a monarchy to an aristocratic republic, and then to an increasingly autocratic empire. The Romans are still remembered today, including names such as Julius Caesar, Cicero, Augustus, etc. Ancient Roman society contributed greatly to government, law, politics, engineering, art, literature, architecture, technology, warfare, religion, language, society and more in the western world.

For centuries, the city of Rome symbolized civilization. The Romans were industrious and determined in character. They thought themselves as appointed rulers of the world, who had a mission to spread Roman culture from the north of England to Africa, from Spain to India. They romanized the territories conquered, and spread the ideas they had drawn from other peoples. Through the Romans, Greek art and literature were handed down into the western tradition. Because one of the Roman emperors decided to adopt it as the official religion of the Empire, Christianity got a rapid spread. However, the Romans were modest about their achievements. They believed that their strengths lay in good government and military skills rather than in other fields like arts and intellectual attainments. Today, we admire not only the superior quality of Roman roads, sewers, and aqueducts, but also their sculpture, drama, music, and lyric poetry, needless to say philosophy and military arts. One last thing to remember about the Romans is their ability and genius to absorb and combine foreign ideas and then create something new out of them.

1 Founding Myths

1.1 Aeneas

According to the myth, after the fall of city of Troy, Prince Aeneas led a group of Trojans on a sea voyage to found a new Troy, since the original was destroyed in the outcome of the outcome of the Trojan War. After a long time in rough seas, they landed at the banks of the Tiber River. Not long after they landed, the men wanted to take to the sea again, but the women who were traveling with them did not want to leave. One woman, named Roma, suggested that the women burn the ships out at sea to prevent them from leaving. At first, the men were angry with Roma, but they soon realized that they were in the ideal place to settle. They named the settlement after the woman who torched their ships.

This legend was recounted by the Roman poet Virgil on his classical poem *Aeneid*.

1.2 Romulus and Remus

Besides the Greek myth, there also goes an Italian myth of Romulus and Remus, who, taken as historical figures would have been born around 771 BC. According to the legend, they were the twin sons of the Rhea Silvia and Mars, the god of war. Because of a prophecy that they would overthrow their murderous uncle, they were, in the manner of many mythological heroes, abandoned at birth; in this case, they were left on the Tiber River by servants who took pity on the infants, despite their orders. The twins were nurtured by a she-wolf until a shepherd named Faustulus found and took Romulus and Remus as his sons. When Remus and Romulus became adults, they decided to establish a city; however, they quarrelled, and Romulus killed his brother. Thus Rome began with a fratricide, a story that was later taken to represent the city's history of internecine political strife and bloodshed.

2 The Domain of Ancient Rome

The truth is the city of Rome grew from settlements around a ford on the river Tiber, a crossroad of traffic and trade. According to archaeological evidence, the village of Rome was probably founded sometime in the 8th century BC, though it may go back as far as the 10th century BC, by members of the Latin tribe of Italy.

In its approximately twelve centuries of existence, through conquest and assimilation, it came to dominate Southern Europe, Western Europe, Asia Minor, North Africa, parts of Northern Europe, and parts of Eastern Europe. Rome was preponderant throughout the Mediterranean region and was one of the most powerful entities of the ancient world.

2.1 Brief History

In its approximately 1,200 years of existence, Roman civilization changed from a monarchy to an aristocratic republic, and then to an increasingly autocratic empire:

The Monarchy (753 – 510 BC), ruled by kings;

The Republic (509 – 31 BC), democratic government first developed and then collapsed;

The Empire (31 – 476 AD), ruled, at least in theory, by one man — the Emperor.

2.1.1 The Monarchy (753 – 510 BC)

The Roman Kingdom was the period of the ancient Roman civilization characterized by a monarchical form of government of the city of Rome and its territories.

Nearly no written records about the Roman Kingdom survive, and the histories about it were written during the Republic and Empire and are largely based on legend. However, the history of the Roman Kingdom began with the city's founding, traditionally dated to 753 BC with settlements around the Palatine Hill along the river Tiber in Central Italy, and ended with the overthrow of the kings and the establishment of the Republic in about 509 BC.

According to legend, in Rome's first centuries it was ruled by a succession of seven kings. The kings, excluding Romulus, who according to legend held office by virtue of being the city's founder, were all elected by the people of Rome to serve for life, with none of the kings relying on military force to gain or keep the throne.

The insignia of the kings of Rome were twelve lictors wielding the fasces bearing axes, the right to sit upon a Curule chair, the purple Toga Picta, red shoes, and a white diadem around the head. Of all these insignia, the most important was the purple toga.

2.1.2 The Republic (509 – 31 BC)

The Roman Republic was the period of the ancient Roman civilization when the government operated as a republic. It began with the overthrow of the Roman monarchy, traditionally dated around 509 BC, and its replacement by a government headed by two consuls, elected annually by the citizens and advised by a senate. A complex constitution gradually developed, centered on the principles of a separation of powers and checks and balances. Except in times of dire national emergency, public offices were limited to one year, so that, in theory at least, no single individual could dominate his fellow citizens.

During the first two centuries of its existence the Republic expanded through a combination of conquest and alliance, from central Italy to the entire Italian peninsula. By the following century it included North Africa, the Iberian Peninsula, Greece, and what is now southern France. Two centuries after that, towards the end of the 1st century BC, it included the rest of modern France, and much of the eastern Mediterranean. By this time, Roman politics was dominated by a small number of Roman leaders. During a series of civil wars, the Roman republic was dying with nothing but a name left, turning into an empire.

2. 1. 3 The Empire (31 BC – 476 AD)

In 27 BC, Octavian became the sole Roman leader. His leadership brought the zenith of the Roman civilization, which lasted for two centuries. In that year, he took the name Augustus. That event is usually taken by historians as the beginning of Roman Empire.

The first two centuries of the Empire were a period of unprecedented stability and prosperity known as the "Pax Romana" (Roman Peace). It reached its greatest expanse during the reign of Trajan (98 – 117 AD). In the 3rd century, the Empire underwent a crisis that threatened its existence, but was reunified and stabilized. Christians rose to power in the 4th century, during which time a system of dual rule was developed in the

Latin West and Greek East. After the collapse of central government in the West in the 5th century, the eastern half continued as what would later be known as the Byzantine Empire.

Because of the Empire's vast extent and long endurance, the institutions and culture of Rome had a profound and lasting influence on the development of language, religion, architecture, philosophy, law, and forms of government in the territory it governed, particularly in Europe, and by means of European expansionism throughout the modern world.

3 Significant Figures and Events

3.1 Caesar and the First Triumvirate

The First Triumvirate was the political alliance of Gaius Julius Caesar, Marcus Licinius Crassus, and Gnaeus Pompeius Magnus.

The First Triumvirate had no official status whatsoever; its overwhelming power in the Roman Republic was strictly unofficial influence, and was in fact kept secret for some time as part of the political machinations of the Triumvirs themselves. It was formed in 60 BC and lasted until Crassus' death in 53 BC.

Gaius Julius Caesar (100 – 44 BC) was a Roman general and statesman and a distinguished writer of Latin prose. He played a critical role in the events that led to the end of the Roman Republic and the creation of the Roman Empire. He was also deemed to be one of the greatest military commanders of history.

In 60 BC, Caesar, Crassus and Pompey formed a political alliance that was to dominate Roman politics for several years. Caesar's conquest of Gaul, completed by 51 BC, extended Rome's territory to the English Channel and the Rhine.

These achievements granted Caesar unmatched military power and threatened the position of Pompey and the Senate. After the Gallic Wars, the Senate ordered Caesar to lay down his military command and return to Rome. Caesar refused, thus was accused of treason. Caesar marked his defiance in 49 BC by crossing the Rubicon with a legion to march on Rome. Upon crossing the Rubicon, Caesar, according to Plutarch and Suetonius, is supposed to have quoted a sentence in Greek, "The die is cast." to manifest his resolution. With this step, he entered Italy at the head of his army in defiance and began his long civil war against Pompey and the Senate. The phrase is still used today to mean that events have passed a point of no return that something inevitably will happen. Civil war resulted, from which he emerged as the unrivaled leader of Rome.

After assuming control of the government, Caesar began a program of social and governmental reforms, including the creation of the Julian calendar. He centralized the bureaucracy of the Republic and was eventually proclaimed "dictator in perpetuity".

3.2 The Assassination of Julius Caesar

Toward the later stages of his rule, Caesar came to recognize his need for greater autonomy, authority, and a freedom of action in the name of Rome and the empire. He came into direct confrontation with the Roman Senate. His ambition caused fear and hatred. Some of the senators plotted a conspiracy to assassinate Caesar. The conspirators had a variety of economic, political, or personal motivations for carrying out the assassination. Many were afraid that Caesar would soon resurrect the monarchy and declare himself king. Others feared loss of property or prestige as Caesar carried out his land reforms in favor of the landless classes.

On the Ides of March of 44 BC, the conspirators staged a game of gladiatorial sport at Pompey's theatre. According to Plutarch, as Caesar arrived at the Senate, a senator Tillius Cimber presented him with a petition to recall his exiled brother. The other conspirators crowded round to offer their support. In the crowd, senator Casca produced his dagger and made a glancing thrust at the dictator's neck. Within moments, the entire group, including Brutus, whom Caesar loved as his own son, was striking out at the dictator. Caesar attempted to get away, but, blinded by blood, he tripped and fell; the men continued stabbing him as he lay defenseless on the lower steps of the portico. Around 60 or more men participated in the assassination. Caesar was stabbed 23 times.

The dictator's last words are a contested subject among scholars and historians and people alike. One saying goes as that Caesar's last words were the Greek phrase, "You too, child?" in English to Brutus.

After the assassination, all the conspirators fled the city after Caesar's death in fear of retaliation. The civil war that followed destroyed what was left of the Republic. A new series of civil wars broke out, and the constitutional government of the Republic was never restored. Caesar's adopted heir, later known as Augustus, rose to sole power, and the era of the Roman Empire began.

3.3 The Second Triumvirate

The Second Triumvirate is the name historians give to the official political alliance of Octavian (later known as Augustus), Marcus Aemilius Lepidus, and Mark Antony, formed on 26 November 43 BC and marked the end of the Roman Republic. The Triumvirate existed for two five-year terms, covering the period 43 – 33 BC.

After the assassination of Caesar, Mark Antony formed an alliance with Caesar's adopted son and great-nephew, Gaius Octavian. Along with Marcus Lepidus, they formed an alliance known as the Second Triumvirate. After defeating their enemies who assassinated Caesar, the Triumvirate divided the Roman Republic between themselves and ruled as military dictators with overwhelming power. The Triumvirate was eventually torn apart under the competing ambitions of its members: Lepidus was driven into exile and stripped of his position, and Antony committed suicide with his love, Cleopatra, following his defeat at the Battle of Actium by Augustus in 31 BC.

In 29 BC, Octavian returned to Rome as the unchallenged master of the Empire and later accepted the title of Augustus— "Exalted One". Octavian, having restyled himself "Augustus" in 27 BC, remained as the sole master of the Roman world, and became the first Roman "emperor".

3.4 Gaius Augustus

Augustus (63 BC – 14 AD) was the founder of the Roman Empire and its first Emperor, ruling from 27 BC until his death in 14 AD. Born into an old, wealthy, and influential family, Augustus was adopted posthumously by his maternal great-uncle Gaius Julius Caesar following Caesar's assassination. Together with Mark Antony and Marcus Lepidus, he formed the Second Triumvirate to defeat the assassins of Caesar.

After the demise of the Second Triumvirate, Augustus retained his autocratic power over the Republic as a military dictator. By law, Augustus held a collection of powers granted to him for life by the Senate, including supreme military command. He rejected monarchical titles, and instead called himself "First Citizen". The resulting constitutional framework became known as the Principate, the first phase of the Roman Empire.

The reign of Augustus initiated an era of relative peace known as "Pax Romana" (Roman Peace). Despite continuous wars or imperial expansion, the Mediterranean world remained at peace for more than two centuries. Augustus dramatically enlarged the Empire. Beyond the frontiers, he secured the Empire with a buffer region of client states, and made peace with the Parthian Empire through diplomacy. He reformed the Roman system of taxation, developed networks of roads with an official courier system, established a standing army, created official police and fire-fighting services for Rome, and rebuilt much of the City during his reign.

Augustus died in 14 AD at the age of 75. He may have died from natural causes, though there were unconfirmed rumors that his wife Livia poisoned him.

3.5 Cleopatra

Cleopatra (69 - 30 BC) was the last pharaoh of Ancient Egypt. Being clever and ambitious, she gradually seized the controlling power of Egypt. She was most known for her relationship with two significant figures of Ancient Rome — Julius Caesar and Mark Antony.

It was said that Cleopatra had herself rolled up in a carpet and smuggled secretly into the palace to meet with Caesar. In this way, she became Caesar's mistress and used Caesar's power to restore Cleopatra to her throne. After the assassination of Caesar, Cleopatra plunged herself in the Roman civil war and was frustrated. Mark Antony, as one of the triumvirs, summoned Cleopatra to swear her loyalty to Rome. It was said that Cleopatra arrived in great state and so charmed Antony. Later Antony actually married her.

Relations between Antony and Octavian finally broke down in 33 BC and war arose. In 31 BC, Antony was defeated. Cleopatra took flight with her ships at the height of the battle and Antony followed her. It was said that Cleopatra killed herself by inducing a cobra to bite herself after Antony's suicide.

With her wit and beauty, the fate of Cleopatra tangled with the two great Roman figures and the fate of Rome as well. In a famous aphorism, Blaise Pascal once observed, "Had Cleopatra's nose been shorter, the face of the world would have changed." In other words, if Cleopatra had been less beautiful, Caesar and Antony would not have fallen in love with her, and the course of history would have been fatefully altered. And "Cleopatra's nose" became a famous historical hypothesis to show the many possibilities of historical changes.

3.6 Spartacus

Spartacus (109 – 71 BC) was a Thracian gladiator, who was one of the slave leaders in the Third Servile War, a major slave uprising against the Roman Republic. Little is known about Spartacus beyond the events of the war. According to the differing sources, Spartacus either was an auxiliary from the Roman legions later condemned to slavery, or a captive taken by the legions. Spartacus was trained at the gladiatorial school.

In 73 BC, Spartacus was among a group of gladiators plotting an escape. The plot was betrayed but about 70 men fought their way free from the school, and seized several wagons of gladiatorial weapons and armor.

The escaped slaves defeated a small force sent after them, plundered the region surrounding Capua, recruited many other slaves into their ranks, and eventually retired to a more defensible position on Mount Vesuvius.

Once free, the escaped gladiators chose Spartacus and two Gallic slaves — Crixus and Oenomaus — as their leaders. They spent the winter of 73 - 72 BC training, arming and equipping their new recruits, and expanding their raiding territory. At first, due to the absence of Roman Army, Spartacus and his men won several battles. But with the return of the main force of Roman Republic, in 71 BC the final battle saw the defeat of Spartacus. On the battle, Spartacus was killed but his body was never found. 6,000 survivors of the revolt were captured by the Roman legions and crucified.

Spartacus' struggle, interpreted by some as an example of oppressed people fighting for their freedom against a slave-owning oligarchy, has been an inspiration to many political thinkers. It has also been featured in literature, television, and film.

3.7 Constantine the Great

During the 3rd century BC, Roman Empire fell into a crisis of separation. In order to heal the empire from the crisis, a new form of government was established: the Tetrarchy. The Empire was divided among four emperors, two in the West and two in the East.

Constantine was Roman Emperor from 306 to 337. He was well known for being the first Roman emperor to convert to Christianity, enforcing the Christian faith. Therefore, he began the Christianization of the Empire and of Europe — a process concluded by the Catholic Church in the Middle Ages.

In 324 he defeated the other three emperors of the tetrarch, and controlled all the empire. To celebrate his victories and Christianity's relevance, he rebuilt Byzantium and renamed it Nova Roma ("New Rome"); but the city soon gained the informal name of Constantinople ("City of Constantine"). The city served as a new capital for the Empire.

3.8 The Fall of Roman Empire

After Constantine's rule, the empire's deterioration became more evident and entered into a critical stage. Christian values, which were centered in a heaven in an afterlife, were responsible for making Romans less warlike and not so willing to risk their lives for the country, which was in total opposition to the old and traditional Roman values.

Years after Constantine, the Empire was divided into the Eastern Roman Empire and the Western Roman Empire. In 476, barbarians killed the emperor of the Western Roman Empire. Having lasted for about 1,200 years, the rule of Rome in the west ended. The Eastern Empire survived for almost 1,000 years until 1453, and became the most stable Christian realm during the Middle Ages.

4 Roman Literature

4.1 The Rise of Latin Literature

Roman military expansion made Latin the dominant language of the Italian peninsula and ultimately spread the tongue throughout the Mediterranean world. Beginning around the 3rd century BC, as the direct ancestor of many languages of modern Europe, Latin became an important medium for conveying distinctive concepts in scholarship and religion. Since then, Latin literature took two centuries to become a dominant literature of Ancient Rome.

Formal Latin literature began in 240 BC that a Roman audience first saw a Latin version of a Greek play. The adaptor was Livius Andronicus (? –200 BC). He was a Greek who had been brought to Rome as a prisoner of war in 272 BC. Andronicus translated Homer's Greek epic the *Odyssey* into an old type of Latin verse called *Saturnian*. Initiated by him, writers began to rewrite the Greek plays into Latin version or composed plays, comedies especially, in Latin on Greek models. On that account he is regarded as the father of Roman drama and of Latin literature in general. All men of letters, such as Cicero and Horace, during the subsequent Classical Latin period, considered Livius Andronicus the originator of Latin literature. He is the earliest Roman poet whose name is known. His influence even reached Shakespeare.

4. 2 The Golden Age

Latin literature was at its height from 81 BC to 17 AD. This period began with the first known speech of Cicero and ended with the death of Ovid and it is regarded as the golden age of Latin literature.

4. 2. 1 The Age of Cicero

Marcus Cicero (106 –43 BC) was a Roman philosopher, statesman, orator and consul and was a major political figure in the last years of the Republic, he was best known as one of Rome's greatest orators and prose stylists.

Cicero influenced the Latin language immensely. He has been traditionally considered the master of Latin prose, with praise such as Cicero was "not the name of a man, but of eloquence itself". He is credited with transforming Latin from a modest utilitarian language into a versatile literary medium capable of expressing abstract and complicated thoughts with clarity. Cicero also introduced the Romans to the chief schools of Greek philosophy and created a Latin philosophical vocabulary.

Along with Cicero, Julius Caesar himself was one of the outstanding historical writers of Cicero's time. Caesar wrote commentaries on the Gallic and civil wars in a straightforward style to justify his actions as a general.

4. 2. 2 The Augustan Age

The emperor Augustus took a personal interest in the literary works produced during his years of power from 27 BC to 14 AD. This period is sometimes called "the Augustan Age" of Latin literature.

Virgil (70 – 19 BC) is traditionally ranked as one of Rome's greatest poets and is known for three major works of Latin literature, the *Eclogues*, the *Georgics*, and the epic *Aeneid*. The pastoral *Eclogues*, the *Georgics*, perhaps are the most beautiful poems ever written about country life.

Virgil's *Aeneid* has been considered the national epic of ancient Rome from the time of its composition to the present day. Modeled after Homer's *Iliad* and *Odyssey*, the *Aeneid* is an epic poem describing the events that led to the creation of Rome. Virgil told how the Trojan hero Aeneas became the ancestor of the Roman people. In the *Aeneid*, the Trojan prince Aeneas was destined by the gods in his enterprise of founding a new Troy. After reaching Italy, Aeneas, who wanted to marry Lavinia, was forced to wage war with her former suitor, Turnus. According to the poem, the Alban kings were descended from Aeneas, and thus, Romulus, the founder of Rome, was his descendant.

Virgil's works have had wide and deep influence on Western literature, most notably on the *Divine Comedy* of Dante. Although Virgil died before he could put the finishing touches on his poem, it was soon recognized as the greatest works of Latin literature.

Virgil's friend Horace (65 – 8 BC), author of *Epodes*, *Odes*, *Satires*, and *Epistles*, was the leading Roman lyric poet during the time of Augustus. His works show Horace crafted elegant hexameter verses and iambic poetry. The perfection of the *Odes* in content, form, and style has charmed readers for hundreds of years. The *Satires* and *Epistles* discuss ethical and literary problems in an urbane, witty manner. *The Art of Poetry* greatly influenced later poetic theories. It stated the basic rules of classical writing as the Romans understood and used them.

Ovid (43 BC – 17/18 AD) is considered a master of the elegiac couplet, and is traditionally ranked alongside Virgil and Horace as one of the three canonic poets of Latin literature. Ovid's greatest work, the *Metamorphoses* weaves various myths into a fast-paced, fascinating story and is regarded as his most ambitious and popular works. The works consists of almost 250 different myths which are the transformations of Greek and Roman mythology and set within a loose mytho-historical framework. Each myth is set outdoors where the mortals are often vulnerable to external influences. Ovid was a witty writer who excelled in creating lively and passionate characters. The *Metamorphoses* was the best-known source of Roman mythology throughout the Middle Ages and the Renaissance. It inspired many poets, painters, and composers.

5 Religion and Philosophy

5.1 The Greek Influence

The presence of Greeks on the Italian peninsula and the spread of Greek culture greatly influenced Roman culture. They introduced some religious practices that became as fundamental as the cult of Apollo. The

Romans looked for common ground between their major gods and those of the Greeks, adapting Greek myths and iconography for Latin literature and Roman art. Etruscan religion was also a major influence, particularly on the practice of augury, since Rome had once been ruled by Etruscan kings.

Imported mystery religions, which offered initiates salvation in the afterlife, were a matter of personal choice for an individual, practiced in addition to carrying on one's family rites and participating in public religion. The mysteries, however, involved exclusive oaths and secrecy, conditions that conservative Romans viewed with suspicion as characteristic of "magic", conspiracy, and subversive activity.

5.2 Religion

Roman religion was practical and contractual, depending on knowledge and the correct practice of prayer, ritual, and sacrifice, not on faith or dogma. The priesthoods of public religion were held by members of the elite classes. Priests married, raised families, and led politically active lives. Julius Caesar became Pontifex Maximus before he was elected consul.

For ordinary Romans, religion was a part of daily life. Each home had a household shrine at which prayers and libations to the family's domestic deities were offered. Neighborhood shrines and sacred places such as springs and groves dotted the city. People who passed a cult place might make a vow or a fruit offering, or merely sit for a while. The Roman calendar was structured around religious observances. In the Imperial era, as many as 135 days of the year were devoted to religious festivals and games. Women, slaves, and children all participated in a range of religious activities. Some public rituals could be conducted only by women, and women formed what is perhaps Rome's most famous priesthood, the state-supported Vestal Virgins, who tended Rome's sacred hearth for centuries, until disbanded under Christian domination.

5.3 Roman Deities

People of ancient Roman acknowledged that immortal gods ruled all realms of the heavens and earth. There were gods of the upper heavens, gods of the underworld and a myriad of lesser deities between. Some evidently favored Rome because Rome honored them.

Basically speaking, the Roman gods are the Latin version of Greek gods, however, ancient Romans assigned them different tasks. The gods represented distinctly the practical needs of daily life. At every stage of daily life like plowing or sowing invoked a separate deity and the name of each deity being regularly derived from the verb for the operation.

Jupiter, the most powerful of all gods consistently personified the divine authority of Rome's highest offices, internal organization and external relations. Janus and Vesta guarded the door and hearth, the Lares protected the field and house, Pales the pasture, Saturn the sowing, Ceres the growth of the grain, Pomona the fruit, and Consus and Ops the harvest. Even the majestic Jupiter, the ruler of the gods, was honored for the aid his rains might give to the farms and vineyards. In his more encompassing character, through his weapon of lightning, he was considered director of human activity. By his widespread domain, Jupiter was also considered the protector of the Romans in their military activities beyond the borders of their own community. Prominent in early times were the gods Mars and Quirinus, who were often identified with each other.

Mars was a god of war; he was honored in March and October. Quirinus was the patron of the armed community in time of peace.

5.4 The Rise of Christianity

In the wake of the Republic's collapse, state religion had adapted to support the new regime of the emperors. Augustus, the first Roman emperor, directed a vast program of religious revivalism and reform. People had to vow their loyalty to the emperor, otherwise would be regarded as treason. This led to the Rome's conflict with Christianity, whose followers were prosecuted.

From the 2nd century onward, the Christian Church Fathers began to condemn the diverse religions practiced throughout the Empire collectively as "pagan". In the early 4th century, Constantine the Great became the first emperor to convert to Christianity, launching the era of Christian hegemony. In 391 under Theodosius I, Christianity became the official state church of the Roman Empire. Heretics as well as non-Christians were subject to exclusion from public life or persecution, but Rome's original religious hierarchy and many aspects of its ritual influenced Christian forms, and many pre-Christian beliefs and practices survived in Christian festivals and local traditions.

5.5 Philosophy

Philosophy gained a significant boost in 155 BC, when Athens sent to Rome an embassy composed of the heads of three major philosophical schools: Carneades the Skeptic, Critolaus the Peripatetic, and Diogenes the Stoic, in which stoicism are the most influential one.

5. 5. 1 Stoicism

Stoicism is a school of Hellenistic philosophy founded in Athens in the early 3rd century BC. The Stoics taught that destructive emotions resulted from errors in judgment, and that a sage, or person of moral and intellectual perfection, would not suffer such emotions.

Stoics believed it is virtuous to maintain a will that is in accord with nature. Because of this, the Stoics presented their philosophy as a way of life, and they thought that the best indication of an individual's philosophy was not what a person said but how he behaved.

A distinctive feature of Stoicism is its cosmopolitanism: All people are manifestations of the one universal spirit and should live in brotherly love and readily help one another. They held that external differences such as rank and wealth are of no importance in social relationships. Instead they advocated the brotherhood of humanity and the natural equality of all human beings.

Stoicism became the most influential school of the Greco-Roman world, and produced a number of remarkable writers and personalities, such as Cato the Younger and Epictetus.

5. 5. 2 Stoicism and Christianity

The major difference between the two philosophies is Stoicism's pantheism, in which God is never fully transcendent but always immanent. God as the world-creating entity is personalized in Christian thought, but Stoicism equates God with the totality of the universe, which was deeply contrary to Christianity. Also, Stoicism, unlike Christianity, does not posit a beginning or end to the universe, nor does it assert that the individual continues to exist beyond death.

Stoicism was later regarded by the Fathers of the Church as a "pagan philosophy". Nonetheless, some of the central philosophical concepts of Stoicism were employed by the early Christian writers, including the terms "logos", "virtue", "spirit", and "conscience". Besides borrowing terminologies, both Stoicism and Christianity encourage people to depress inferior emotions such as lust, envy and anger, so that the higher possibilities of one's humanity can be awakened and developed.

6 Roman Law and Constitution

6.1 Roman Law

Roman law is the legal system of ancient Rome, and the legal developments comprising more than a thousand years of jurisprudence from the *Twelve Tables* (439 BC) to the *Corpus Juris Civilis* (the *Justinian Code* 529 AD). The historical importance of Roman law is reflected by the continued use of Latin legal terminology in legal systems influenced by it.

The major divisions of the law of ancient Rome consisted of *Citizen Law*, *Law of Nations* and *Natural Law*. The *Citizen Law* was the body of common laws that applied to Roman citizens. The *Law of Nations* was the body of common laws that applied to foreigners, and their dealings with Roman citizens. *Natural law* is the body of laws that were considered common to all beings.

The first legal text is the *Law of the Twelve Tables*, dating from mid-5th century BC. It was proposed that the law should be written, in order to prevent magistrates from applying the law arbitrarily. After eight years of political struggle, the plebeian social class convinced the patricians to send a delegation to Athens to copy the Laws of Solon. In 451 BC, according to the traditional story, ten Roman citizens (decemvirate) were chosen to record the laws and were given absolute power. Finally, the *Law of the*

Twelve Tables was approved by the people's assembly. The largest part of the tables contained specific provisions designed to change the then-existing customary law.

The *Corpus Juris Civilis* (*Body of Civil Law*) is a collection of fundamental works in jurisprudence, issued from 529 to 534 by the order of Justinian I, Eastern Roman Emperor. It is also sometimes referred to as the "Code of Justinian". During the Middle Ages, interest in it revived. This revived Roman law, in turn, became the foundation of law in all civil law jurisdictions.

6.2 The Roman Constitution

Initially, Rome was ruled by kings, who were elected from each of Rome's major tribes in turn. The exact nature of the king's power is uncertain. At least in military matters, the king's authority was likely absolute. He was also the head of the state religion. In addition to the authority of the King, there were three administrative assemblies: the Senate, which acted as an advisory body for the King; the Curiate Assembly, which could endorse and ratify laws suggested by the King; and the Roman Assemblies, which was an assembly of the priestly college that could assemble the people to bear witness to certain acts, hear proclamations, and declare the feast and holiday schedule for the next month.

In the Republic, the Senate held great authority, and it was technically only an advisory council. However, as the Senators were individually very influential, it was difficult to accomplish anything against the collective will of the Senate. New Senators were chosen from among the most accomplished patricians by Censors, who could also remove a Senator from his office if he was found "morally corrupt"; a charge that could include bribery or embracing one's wife in public.

The Republic had no fixed bureaucracy, and collected taxes through the practice of tax farming. Government positions such as quaestor, aedile, or praefect were funded from the office-holder's private finances. To prevent any citizen from gaining too much power, new magistrates were elected annually and had to share power with a colleague. For example, under normal conditions, the highest authority was held by two consuls. In an emergency, a temporary dictator could be appointed.

In the early Empire, the pretense of a republican form of government was maintained. The Roman Emperor was portrayed as only a Princeps, or "First Citizen", and the Senate gained legislative power and all legal authority previously held by the popular assemblies. However, the rule of the Emperors became increasingly autocratic, and the Senate was reduced to an advisory body appointed by the Emperor.

7 Roman Art

A distinctive Roman art developed from the fusion of Italic and Greek traditions. Architecture, sculpture, and painting flourished in Rome and beyond. Sculpture was perhaps considered as the highest form of art by Romans, but figure painting was also very highly regarded.

7.1 Roman Painting

Roman painting styles show Greek influences. Several examples of Roman painting have been found at Pompeii, which show that painting had been an important part of ordinary life.

Roman painting provides a wide variety of themes: animals, still life, scenes from everyday life, portraits, and some mythological subjects. During the Hellenistic period, it evoked the pleasures of the countryside and represented scenes of shepherds, herds, rustic temples, rural mountainous landscapes and country houses. In the late empire, after 200 AD, Christian themes gradually began to domain the theme of painting.

7.2 Sculpture

Roman sculpture started from copying the most famous Greek works, but later developed its own style. The strengths of Roman sculpture are in portraiture.

Portraiture is a dominant genre of Roman sculpture, growing perhaps from the traditional Roman emphasis on family and ancestors; the entrance hall of a Roman elite house displayed ancestral portrait busts. "Augustus of Prima Porta", the 2.04 m high marble stature of Augustus Caesar, is probably the most famous Roman statue.

Advancements were also made in relief sculptures, usually depicting Roman victories. Trajan Column is a Roman triumphal column that commemorates Roman emperor Trajan's victory in the Dacian Wars. It is located in Trajan's Forum, completed in 113. The column is most famous for its spiral base relief, which artistically describes the epic wars between the Romans and Dacians (101 - 102 and 105 - 106). Its design has inspired numerous victory columns, both ancient and modern.

7.3 Roman Architecture

Ancient Roman architecture adopted certain aspects of Ancient Greek architecture, creating a new architectural style. And in the area of architecture that Roman art produced its greatest innovations. The use of new materials like the use of concrete made not only massive buildings but new styles such as arches, vaults, and domes possible.

During the reign of Trajan (98 – 117 AD) and Hadrian (117 – 138 AD), the Roman Empire reached its greatest extent as well as its artistic glory. It was achieved through massive building programs of monuments, meeting houses, gardens, aqueducts, baths, palaces, pavilions, and temples. Outstanding examples of dome construction include the Pantheon, the Baths of Diocletian, and the Baths of Caracalla. The Pantheon is the best preserved temple of ancient times with an intact ceiling featuring an open "eye" in the center. The height of the ceiling exactly equals the interior diameter of the building, creating an enclosure that could contain giant sphere.

Roman buildings were then built in the commercial, political, and social grouping known as a forum, with the Forum Romanum being the most famous. The greatest arena in the Roman world, the Colosseum, was completed around 80 AD at the far end of that forum. It held over 50,000 spectators, had retractable fabric coverings for shade, and could stage massive spectacles including huge gladiatorial contests and mock naval battles.

The Romans first adopted the arch from the Greeks, and implemented it in their own building. An arch is a very strong shape as no single spot holds all the weight and is still used in architecture today. The arch is seen in aqueducts, especially in many surviving examples, such as the Pont du Gard, the aqueduct at Segovia and the remains of the Aqueducts of Rome itself. Their survival is testimony to the durability of their materials and design.

7.4 Roman City: Pompeii

Pompeii was an ancient city in southern Italy, southeast of Naples. Founded in the 6th or early 5th century BC, it was a Roman colony by 80 BC. Later it became a prosperous port and resort boasted noted villas, temples, theaters and baths.

Though Pompeii was destroyed by an eruption of Mount Vesuvius in 79, its ruins were incredibly well-preserved and were rediscovered in 1748. Some idea of the character of provincial daily life can be gained from the excavations at Pompeii and the other cities around the Bay of Naples.

7.5 Roman Citizen Life

Roman music was largely based on Greek music, and played an important part in many aspects of Roman life. No matter in the Roman military or in religious rituals, music was used at almost all public ceremonies.

Ancient Rome is also notorious for the popular and cruel entertainment-gladiatorial combats. Gladiators fought either to death or to "first blood" with a variety of weapons in different scenarios. Sometimes, foreign animals were combined with gladiatorial combat. A prisoner or gladiator, armed or unarmed, was thrown into the arena and an animal was released. Most of the losers would be killed, sometimes the brave ones would be "spared" with the gestures of the audience.

Ancient Rome is the progenitor of Western civilization. The customs, religion, law, technology, architecture, political system, military, literature, languages, alphabet, government and many factors and aspects of western civilization are all inherited from Roman advancements. The rediscovery of Roman culture revitalized Western civilization, playing a role in the Renaissance and the Age of Enlightenment.

Questions for Discussion

1. Did Romans basically just rename the gods of the Greeks? Was it a way of incorporating the culture — or why did they do it?

2. How to judge the constitution of Roman Republic? And what are the differences between the implications of the so-called "democracy" and those of the modern ones?

3. Why did Caesar say, "The die is cast"?

4. How do you understand the assassination of Julius Caesar?

5. How did the Roman Empire divide into two halves — the West Roman Empire and the East Roman Empire?

6. How do you understand elements of slavery, gladiator and Legion 9 in the Roman culture?

7. What does the saying "All roads lead to Rome" signify?

Division II

The Middle Ages

中世纪（The Middle Ages）（约公元476年—公元1453年），是从西罗马帝国的覆灭直到文艺复兴时期的开始。在整个欧洲历史发展过程中，中世纪（主要是西欧）其实是一个较为普通的过渡时期，它是从由罗马帝国统治的古典时代到文艺复兴时期的一个过渡，也是由欧洲封建制度占统治地位到资本主义思想觉醒的一段时期。“中世纪”一词是15世纪后期的人文主义者开始使用的。这个时期的欧洲没有一个强有力的政权来统治。封建割据带来频繁的战争，造成科技和生产力发展停滞，人民生活在毫无希望的痛苦中，所以中世纪或者中世纪早期在欧美普遍被称作“黑暗时代”，传统上认为这是欧洲文明史上发展比较缓慢的时期。有历史学家这样评判中世纪：“公元500年至1 500年，被看成是人类进步征途中一个漫长而毫无目标的迂回时代——穷困、迷信、黯淡的一千年，将罗马帝国黄金时代和意大利文艺复兴新黄金时代分隔开来。”这样，中世纪的黑暗表象，也就完全地遮盖了中世纪的文化成就。

可以说，造成黑暗的中世纪印象主要有两个原因：一个是罗马帝国在分裂的过程中遭到日耳曼人的入侵，东罗马帝国长期采取防卫自保的政策，限制了文化创造的活力，使文化发展处于停滞状态；而西罗马帝国无力抵挡外来入侵而亡国，新的统治者日耳曼人还处于氏族阶段，在文化上远远落后于罗马人，于是出现了文化发展的空缺，从而与罗马帝国的黄金时代形成强烈的反差。另一个是基督教分裂之后出现长期纷争，东罗马帝国的统治者以政治手段来操纵与压制不同教派，使东正教沦为御用工具，失去了基督教的宗教独立；西罗马帝国灭亡以后的新统治者与天主教达成妥协，教皇国的建立加快了其世俗化的进程，远离了基督教的宗教本位，从而与意大利文艺复兴的新黄金时代形成强烈的反差。

然而，不可否认的是，中世纪并非是一个漆黑一团的历史时代，因为“经年累月的研究已经表明，中世纪社会仍在持续发生变化”，这就是“约在公元1 500年左右，中世纪时代结束时，欧洲的技术与政治以及经济的结构，已在世界上所有其他文明当中占有决定性的优势”。中世纪是西方文明发展史上不可或缺的时代。它在许许多多方面，都取得一定的成果，促进了文艺复兴的到来。首先，中世纪的欧洲政治经济制度，属于封建制度，但并不专制，包含着对自由的尊重，是近现代西方民主和自由观念的先声。在这种制度下，王国被分成一块块领地，分给一层一层的封臣们。领主与作为附庸的封臣们各有各的义务，也各有各的权利。由于王国的统治者的力量并不太强大，作为封臣的贵族的力量也不太弱小，这就在西方形成一种独立的财产，即权利和义务对等的观念。其次，中世纪在科学、文学、艺术、教育、技术等方面也有一定的贡献。中世纪的文学家和作品，如罗兰和奥利佛，尼贝龙根，以及关于亚历山大大帝的史诗等，都成为世界文学宝库的瑰宝。中世纪的音乐由于基督教而得到不同寻常的发展。中世纪创建了许多大学，不但教授神学课程，而且教授自然科学、修辞学、法学、逻辑学等人文课程。大学为学者们从事学术活动提供了更好的环境，成为欧洲学术活动的中心。中世纪后期，欧洲的建筑艺术出现了一种新形式，后人称之为“哥特式建筑”。这种建筑形式影响了欧洲几个世纪之久。最后，中世纪在宗教信仰上做出了可贵的探索，给后世积累了一笔极其宝贵的文化遗产。中世纪，人们对宗教信仰做出了艰苦卓绝的探索，持续时间之久，兴趣之专，思考之深，均是世界史所少见的。中世纪杰出宗教思想家如托马斯·阿奎那等，大大发展了古希腊罗马以来的政治学、伦理学、法学等学科的思想，这些思想是人类文明的瑰宝。正如有位学者所说，“从某种意义上说，中世纪是停滞的一千年，沉静的一千年，但同时也是充满了上帝之言、祈祷之声和人心祝福的一千年，是西方人走向内心、修炼趋圣的一千年。是他们为未来那个即将到来的更加激动人心的时代做充分准备、充分筹划的一千年”。

Chapter 1 Christianity

1 Introduction

The phrase "Middle Ages" has its origins in the fifteenth century. Scholars of the time — primarily in Italy — were caught up in an exciting movement of art and philosophy, and they saw themselves embarking on a new age that revived the long-lost culture of "classical" Greece and Rome. The time that intervened between the ancient world and their own was a "middle" age and, sadly, one they disparaged and from which they disassociated themselves.

The field of medieval studies is by its very nature "eurocentric". This does not mean that medievalists deny or ignore the significance of events that took place outside of what is today Europe during the medieval era. But the entire concept of a "medieval era" is a European one.

The medieval era might be also considered as the period of a time during which Europe became a geopolitical entity.

The most common time frame of the Middle Ages is approximately 500 - 1,500. Once, when political history defined the boundaries of the past, the date span of 476 to 1453 was generally considered the time frame of the medieval era. The reason for this is that each date marked the fall of an empire. In 476, the Western Roman Empire "officially" came to an end when the Germanic warrior Odoacer deposed and exiled the last emperor, Romulus Augustus. Instead of taking the title of emperor or acknowledging anyone else as such, Odoacer chose the title "King of Italy", and the western empire was no more. In 1453, the Eastern Roman Empire, Byzantine Empire, came to an end when its capital city of Constantinople fell to invading Turks.

Generally, the medieval era is divided into three periods: the Early Middle Ages, the High Middle Ages, and the Late Middle Ages. Like the Middle Ages itself, each of these three periods lacks hard and fast parameters.

The Early Medieval Era is sometimes still called the Dark Ages. This era is often considered to begin with the "fall of Rome" and end sometime in the 11th century. It encompasses the reigns of Charlemagne, Alfred the Great, and the Danish Kings of England; it saw frequent Viking activity, the Iconoclastic Controversy, and the birth and rapid expansion of Islam in Northern Africa and Spain. Over these centuries, Christianity spread throughout much of Europe, and the Papacy evolved into a powerful political entity.

The High Medieval Era is the period of time that seems to typify the Middle Ages best. Usually beginning with the 11th century, some scholars end it in 1300. The High Middle Ages saw such significant events as Norman conquests in Britain and Sicily, the earlier Crusades, the Investiture Controversy and the signing of the Magna Carta. By the end of the 11th century, nearly every corner of Europe had become Christianized (with the notable exception of much of Spain), and the Papacy, long established as a political force, was in constant struggle with some secular governments and alliance with others. This period is often what we think of when someone mentions "medieval culture." It is sometimes referred to as the "flowering" of medieval society, thanks to an intellectual renaissance in the 12th century, such notable philosophers as Pierre Abelard and Thomas Aquinas, and the establishment of such Universities as those in Paris, Oxford and Bologna. There was an explosion of stone castle-building, and the construction of some of the most magnificent cathedrals in Europe. In terms of material culture and political structure, the High Middle Ages saw medievalism at its peak. What we call feudalism today was firmly established in Britain and parts of Europe; trade in luxury items as well as staples flourished; towns were granted charters of privilege and even established anew by feudal lords with alacrity; and a well-fed population was beginning to burgeon. By the end of the thirteenth century, Europe was at an economic and cultural height, perched at the verge of a downturn.

The Late Middle Ages is the end of the Middle Ages which can be characterized as a transformation from the medieval world to the early modern one. It is often considered to begin in 1300, though some scholars look at the mid- to late-fifteenth century as the beginning of the end. Once again, the end is debatable, ranging from 1500 to 1650.

High medieval society had been characterized by corporation. The nobility, the clergy, the peasantry, the guilds — all were group entities that saw to the welfare of their members but put the welfare of the community, and their own community in particular. Now, as was reflected in the Italian Renaissance, a new regard for the value of the individual was growing. By no means was late medieval nor early modern society a culture of equality, but the seeds of the idea of human rights had been sown. Though famine and disease had always been a lurking presence, the Late

Medieval era saw the horrific results of both in abundance. The Black Death, preceded by famine and overpopulation, wiped out at least a third population of Europe and marked the end of the prosperity that had characterized the high medieval era. The Church, once so highly respected by the general populace, suffered reduced status when some of its priests refused to minister to the dying during the plague and sparked resentment when it enjoyed enormous profits in bequests from plague victims. More and more towns and cities were wresting control of their own governments from the hands of the clergy or nobility that had previously ruled them. And the reduction in population triggered economic and political changes that would never be reversed.

2 The Origin and Development of Christianity

Christianity is an Abrahamic religion based on the life and teachings of Jesus as presented in canonical gospels and other *New Testament* writings. It also considers the *Hebrew Bible*, which is known as the *Old Testament*, to be canonical. Adherents of the Christian faith are known as Christians. Christianity began as a Jewish sect in the mid-1st century. Originating in the Levant region of the Middle East (modern Israel and Palestine), it quickly spread to Syria, Mesopotamia, Asia Minor and Egypt. It grew in size and influence over a few centuries, and by the end of the 4th century had become the official state church of the Roman Empire, replacing other forms of religion practiced under the Roman rule. During the Middle Ages, most of the remainder of Europe was Christianized, with Christians also being a sometimes large religious minority in the Middle East, North Africa, Ethiopia and parts of India. Following the Age of Discovery, through missionary work and colonization,

Christianity spread to the Americas, Australasia, sub-Saharan Africa, and the rest of the world.

Worldwide, the three largest groups of Christianity are the Roman Catholic Church, the Eastern Orthodox Church, and the various denominations of Protestantism. The Roman Catholic and Eastern Orthodox patriarchates split from one another in the East-West Schism of 1054 AD, and Protestantism came into existence during the Protestant Reformation of the 16th century, splitting from the Roman Catholic Church.

As of the early 21st century, Christianity has approximately 2.2 billion adherents. Christianity represents about a third of the world's population and is the world's largest religion. Christianity is the state religion of several countries. Among all Christians, 37.5% live in the Americas, 25.7% in Europe, 22.5% in Africa, 13.1% in Asia, 1.2% in Oceania and 0.9% in the Middle East. Christianity has played a prominent role in the shaping of sub-Saharan African and Western civilization.

2.1 The Jews and Judaism

The Jews, also known as the Jewish people, are a nation originating in the Israelites or Hebrews of the Ancient Near East. The Jewish ethnicity, nationality, and religion are strongly interrelated, as Judaism is the traditional faith of the Jewish nation. Converts to Judaism, whose status as Jews within the Jewish ethnos is equal to those born into it, have been absorbed into the Jewish people throughout the millennia.

According to the Hebrew Bible, all Israelites descend from Abraham, Isaac and Jacob. Abraham was born in the Sumerian city and migrated to Canaan (commonly known as the Land of Israel) with his family.

However, Israelite culture did not overtake the region, but rather grew out of Canaanite culture.

2.2 Who Is a Jew?

According to traditional Jewish Law, a Jew is anyone born of a Jewish mother or converted to Judaism in accordance with Jewish Law. All mainstream forms of Judaism today are open to sincere converts, although conversion has traditionally been discouraged since the time of the Talmud. The conversion process is evaluated by an authority, and the convert is examined on his or her sincerity and knowledge. Converts are given the name "ben Abraham" or "bat Abraham" (son or daughter of Abraham). Traditional Judaism maintains that a Jew, whether by birth or conversion, is a Jew forever. Thus a Jew who claims to be an atheist or converts to another religion is still considered by traditional Judaism to be Jewish.

Judaism is the religion, philosophy and way of life of the Jewish people. A monotheistic religion originating in the Hebrew Bible (also known as the Tanakh) and explored in later texts such as the Talmud, Judaism is considered by religious Jews to be the expression of the covenantal relationship God established with the Children of Israel. Rabbinic Judaism holds that God revealed his laws and commandments to Moses on Mount Sinai in the form of both the Written and Oral Torah. Judaism claims a historical continuity spanning more than 3,000 years. Of the major world religions, Judaism is considered one of the oldest monotheistic religions. The Hebrews / Israelites were already referred to as "Jews" in later books of the Tanakh, with the term Jews replacing the title "Children of Israel". Judaism's texts, traditions and values strongly influenced later Abrahamic religions, including Christianity and Islam. Many aspects of Judaism have also directly or indirectly influenced secular Western ethics and civil law.

Judaism guides its adherents in both practice and belief, and has been called not only a religion, but also a "way of life," which has made drawing a clear distinction between Judaism, Jewish culture, and Jewish identity rather difficult.

3 Doctrines of Christianity

Though there are many important differences of interpretation and opinion of the Bible on which Christianity is based, Christians share a set of beliefs that they hold as essential to their faith.

3.1 Jesus

The mainstream Christian belief is that Jesus is the Son of God, fully divine and fully human and the savior of humanity. Because of this, Christians commonly refer to Jesus as Christ from Greek or Messiah from Hebrew.

Christians believe that Jesus is the Messiah prophesied in the Hebrew Bible. The foundation of Christian theology is expressed in the early Christian ecumenical creeds which contain claims predominantly accepted by followers of the Christian faith. These professions state that Jesus suffered, died, was buried, and was resurrected from the dead in order to grant eternal life to those who believe in him and trust him for the remission of their sins (salvation). They further maintain that Jesus bodily ascended into heaven where he rules and reigns with God the Father. Most denominations teach that Jesus will return to judge all humans, living and dead, and grant eternal life to his followers. He is considered the model of a virtuous life, and both the revealer and physical embodiment of God. Throughout history, in eras and places as diverse as the ancient Hellenic world, in Europe before and after The Age of Enlightenment in Islamic Spain and Portugal, in North Africa and the Middle East India, and China, or the contemporary United States and Israel, cultural phenomena have developed (that are in some sense characteristically Jewish) without being at all specifically religious. Some factors in this come from within Judaism, others from the interaction of Jews or specific communities of Jews with their surroundings, others from the inner social and cultural dynamics of the community, as opposed to from the religion itself. This phenomenon has led to considerably different Jewish cultures unique to their own communities, each as authentically Jewish as the next.

According to the Gospels of Matthew and Luke, Jesus was conceived by the Holy Spirit and born from the Virgin Mary. Little of Jesus' childhood is recorded in the canonical Gospels, however infancy Gospels were popular in antiquity. In comparison, his adulthood, especially the week before his death, is well documented in the Gospels contained within *the New Testament*. The Biblical accounts of Jesus' ministry include: his baptism, miracles, preaching, teaching, and deeds.

3.2 Ten Commandments

The Ten Commandments are a set of biblical principles relating to ethics and worship, which play a fundamental role in Judaism and most forms of Christianity. They include instructions to worship only God and to keep the Sabbath; Different groups follow slightly different traditions for interpreting and numbering them.

The Ten Commandments:

First

"I am The Lord your God, Who brought you out of the land of Egypt, out of the house of bondage. You shall have no other gods before Me."

Second

"You shall not make for yourself a graven image, or any likeness of anything that is in heaven above, or that is in the earth beneath, or that is in the water under the earth; you shall not bow down to them or serve them; for I The Lord your God am a jealous God, visiting the iniquity of the fathers upon the children to the third and the fourth generation of those who hate Me, but showing steadfast love to thousands of those who love Me and keep My Commandments."

Third

"You shall not take The Name of The Lord your God in vain; for The Lord will not hold him guiltless who takes His Name in vain."

Fourth

"Remember the Sabbath day, to keep it holy. Six days you shall labor, and do all your work; but the seventh day is a Sabbath to The Lord your God; in it you shall not do any work, you, or your son, or your daughter, your manservant, or your maidservant, or your cattle, or the sojourner who is within your gates; for in six days The Lord made heaven and earth, the sea, and all that is in them, and rested the seventh day; therefore The Lord blessed the Sabbath day and hallowed it."

Fifth

"Honor your father and your mother, that your days may be long in the land which The Lord your God gives you."

Sixth

"You shall not kill."

Seventh

"You shall not commit adultery."

Eighth

"You shall not steal."

Ninth

"You shall not bear false witness against your neighbor."

Tenth

"You shall not covet your neighbor's house; you shall not covet your neighbor's wife, or his manservant, or his maidservant, or his ox, or his ass, or anything that is your neighbor's."

3.3 Trinity

Trinity, an essential doctrine of mainstream Christianity, is defined as one God in three Persons. It refers to the teaching that the one God comprises three distinct, eternally co-existing persons; the Father, the Son (incarnate in Jesus Christ), and the Holy Spirit. Together, these three persons are sometimes called the Godhead, although there is no single term in use in Scripture to denote the unified Godhead. The three persons are distinct from another, and cannot be divided from one another in being or in operation.

According to this doctrine, God is not divided in the sense that each person has a third of the whole; rather, each person is considered to be fully God. The distinction lies in their relations, the Father being unbegotten; the Son being begotten of the Father; and the Holy Spirit proceeding from the Father and from the Son. Regardless of this apparent difference, the three persons are each eternal and all-powerful.

3.4 The End of the World

The end of things, whether the end of an individual life, the end of the age, or the end of the world, broadly speaking, is Christian eschatology, the study of the destiny of humans as it is revealed in the Bible. The major issues in Christian eschatology are the Tribulation, death and the afterlife, the Rapture, the Second Coming of Jesus, Resurrection of the Dead, Heaven and Hell, Millennialism, the Last Judgment, the end of the world, and the New Heavens and New Earth. Christians believe that the second coming of Christ will occur at the end of time after a period of severe persecution (the Great Tribulation). All who have died will be resurrected bodily from the dead for the Last Judgment. Jesus will fully establish the Kingdom of God in fulfillment of scriptural prophecies.

3.5 Death and Afterlife

Most Christians believe that human beings experience divine judgment and are rewarded either with eternal life or eternal damnation. This includes the general judgments at the Resurrection of the dead as well as the belief in a judgment particular to the individual soul upon physical death.

In Roman Catholicism, those who die in a state of grace, i. e. without any mortal sin separating them from God, but are still imperfectly purified from the effects of sin, undergo purification through the intermediate state of purgatory to achieve the holiness necessary for entrance into God's presence. Those who have attained this goal are called saints.

Some Christian groups believe that the human soul is not naturally immortal, and is unconscious during the intermediate state between bodily death and resurrection. These Christians also hold to the belief that the wicked, subsequent to the final judgment, will cease to exist rather than suffer everlasting torment.

4 *The Old Testament* and *the New Testament*

Bible is the name given to several collections of writings held sacred by the Jewish and Christian religions. It is also known as the Holy Scriptures. Both religions regard the Bible as inspired by God. They base many of their beliefs and customs on the teachings found in the Bible. The Bible is the most widely distributed book in history. It has also been translated more times, and into more languages than any other book.

The Jewish and Christian Bibles differ from each other in several ways. The Jewish Bible is commonly called the Hebrew Bible because most of it was written in Hebrew. It tells the story of Creation. It also contains information on pre-Israelite times and the history and religious life of ancient Israel from about 1300 BC to the 100 BC. The Hebrew Bible, which Christians call *the Old Testament*, forms the first part of the Christian Bible. The second part of the Christian Bible, *the New Testament*, was written in Greek. It covers about 100 years, from the birth of Jesus Christ to about 125 AD. Some Christian groups also include in *the Old Testament* additional originally Jewish writings that are not found in the Hebrew Bible. The individual writings collected in the Bible are known as books. The books that are officially accepted by any group as part of its Bible are called the canon.

Both the Jewish and the Christian Bibles view God as the supreme power behind the events they describe, though God's role may not always be apparent. The Bible does not define God or try to prove God's existence. Instead, it testifies to God's presence in history including, in the Christian Bible, the life of Jesus Christ and the development of the early church.

4.1 *The Old Testament*

The *Old Testament* is a Christian term for a collection of religious writings of ancient Israelis that form the major and first section of Christian Bibles, in contrast to the Christian *New Testament* which deals explicitly with the 1st century Christianity.

It contains 39 (Protestant) or 46 (Catholic) or more (Orthodox and other) books. The books can be broadly divided into the Pentateuch (meaning "five books": Genesis, Exodus, Leviticus, book of Numbers and Deuteronomy — make up the Torah, the story of Israel from the Genesis creation narrative to the death of Moses.), which tells how God selected Israel to be his chosen people; the history books telling the history of the Israelites from their conquest of Canaan to their defeat and exile in Babylon; the poetic and "wisdom" books dealing, in various forms, with questions of good and evil in the world; and the books of the biblical prophets, warning of the consequences of turning away from God. For the Israelites who were its original authors and readers these books told of their own unique relationship with God and their relationship with proselytes, but the overarching messianic nature of Christianity has led Christians from the very beginning of the faith to see *the Old Testament* as a preparation for *the New Testament*.

4.2 *The New Testament*

The New Testament is the second major division of the Christian biblical canon, the first division being *the Old Testament*. The contents of *the New Testament* deal explicitly with 1st century Christianity, although both the *Old* and *New Testament* are regarded, together, as sacred scripture. The *New Testament* has therefore frequently accompanied the spread of Christianity around the world, and both reflect and serve as a source for Christian theology. *The New Testament* has not only influenced religious, philosophical, and political movements in Christendom, but also left an indelible mark on its literature, art and music.

The *New Testament* is an anthology, a collection of Christian works written in the common Greek language of the first century, at different times by various writers, and canonically named for the early Jewish disciples of Jesus of Nazareth. In almost all Christian traditions today, *the New Testament* consists of 27 books. The original texts were written in the first and perhaps the second centuries of the Christian era. Interestingly, although *the Old Testament* canon is not uniform within Christianity, with e. g. Roman Catholics, Protestants, the Greek Orthodox Church, the Slavic Orthodox Churches, and the Armenian Orthodox Church differing as to which books are included, the twenty-seven-book canon of *the New Testament* has, since at least Late Antiquity, been almost universally recognized within Christianity. *The New Testament* consists of four narratives of the life, teaching, and death of Jesus, called "gospels"; a narrative of the Apostles' ministries in the early church, called the "Acts of the Apostles" and probably by the same author as the Gospel of Luke, which it continues; twenty-one letters, often called "epistles" in the biblical context, written by various authors and consisting mostly of Christian counsel, instruction, and conflict resolution; and an Apocalypse, the Book of Revelation.

5 Stories of the Bible

The Bible is often described as "the greatest book ever written." This is because of its unending significance and influence on people throughout the ages. No other book in history has impacted peoples and cultures like the Bible. So far, the Bible has been translated into 2,018 languages and every year more copies of the Bible are sold than any other single book.

The entire Bible was written over a period of 1,500 years from about 1450 BC to 100 AD. The Bible states that it was written through the divine inspiration of God. Its authors include more than 25 men from a variety of backgrounds including prophets, priests, fishermen, kings, tax collectors, and doctors.

The Bible covers a wide range of literary styles. It includes history, poetry, law, biography, prophecy, philosophy, science and inspirational reading. The major theme of the Bible, however, is God's relationship with man. Throughout the Bible, God expresses Himself to mankind through acts of protection, provision, love and judgment. The Bible also answers many important questions that men of all ages have asked such as, "Where have I come from?", "Where am I going?", "Why do I exist?", "What is truth?"

5.1 Stories from the Old Testament

5.1.1 Story Summary of the Creation of the World

The opening chapter of the Bible begins with these words, "In the beginning of creation, when God made heaven and earth, the earth was without form and void, with darkness over the face of the abyss, and a mighty wind that swept over the surface of the waters." Then God made heaven and earth when they were created.

Day 1 — God created light and separated the light from the darkness, calling light "day" and darkness "night."

Day 2 — God created an expanse to separate the waters and called it "sky."

Day 3 — God created the dry ground and gathered the waters, calling the dry ground "land," and the gathered waters "seas." On day three, God also created vegetation (plants and trees).

Day 4 — God created the sun, moon, and the stars to give light to the earth and to govern and separate the day and the night. These would also serve as signs to mark seasons, days, and years.

Day 5 — God created every living creature of the seas and every winged bird, blessing them to multiply and fill the waters and the sky with life.

Day 6 — God created the animals to fill the earth. On day six, God also created man and woman (Adam and Eve) in his own image to commune with him. He blessed them and gave them every creature and the whole earth to rule over, care for, and cultivate.

Day 7 — God had finished his work of creation and so he rested on the seventh day, blessing it and making it holy.

5. 1. 2 Noah's Ark

This is the story of Noah. Noah was a righteous man, the one blameless man of his time; he walked with God. He had three sons, Shem, Ham and Japheth. Now God saw that the whole world was corrupt and full of violence. In his sight the world had become corrupted, for all men had lived corrupt lives on earth. God said to Noah, "The loathsomeness of all mankind has become plain to me, for through them the earth is full of violence. I intend to destroy them, and the earth with them. Make yourself an ark with ribs of cypress; cover it with reeds and coat it inside and out with pitch. I intend to bring the waters of the flood over the earth to destroy every human being under heaven that has the spirit of life; everything on earth shall perish. But with you I will make a covenant, and you shall go into the ark, you and your sons, your wife and your sons' wives with you. And you shall bring living creatures of every kind into the ark to keep them alive with you. Two of each kind, a male and a female; two of every kind of bird, beast, and reptile, shall come to you to be kept alive. See that you take and store every kind of food that can be eaten; this shall be food for you and for them." Exactly as God had commanded him, so Noah did. Towards the end of seven days the waters of the flood came upon the earth. In the year when Noah was six hundred years old, on the seventeenth day of the second month, on that very day, all the springs of the great abyss broke through, the windows of the sky were opened, and rain fell on the earth for forty days and forty nights...

After forty days Noah opened the trap-door that he had made in the ark , and released a raven to see whether the water had subsided, but the bird continued flying to and fro until the water on the earth had dried up. Noah waited for seven days, and then he released a dove from the ark to see whether the water on the earth had subsided further. But the dove found no place where she could settle, and so she came back to him in the ark, because there was water over the whole surface of the earth. He waited another seven days and again released the dove from the ark. She came back to him towards evening with a newly plucked olive leaf in her beak. Then Noah knew for certain that the water on the earth had subsided still further. He waited yet another seven days and released the dove, but she never came back. And so it came about that, on the first day of the first month of his six hundred and first years, the water had dried up on the earth, and Noah removed the hatch and looked out of the ark. The surface of the ground was dry. By the twenty-seventh day of the second month the whole earth was dry. And God told Noah to come out of the ark with his family and all the creatures with him, so Noah did. Then Noah built an altar to the Lord. He took ritually clean beasts and birds of every kind, and offered whole-offerings on the altar. When the Lord smelt the soothing odor, he said within himself, "Never again will I curse the ground because of man, however evil his inclinations may be from his youth upwards. I will never again kill every living creature, as I have just done."

5. 1. 3 The Tower of Babel

Once upon a time all the world spoke a single language and used the same words. As men journeyed in the east, they came upon a plain in the land of Shinar and settled there. They said to one another, "Come, let us make bricks and bake them hard"; they used bricks for stone and bitumen for mortar. "Come," they said, "let us build ourselves a city and a tower with its top in the heavens, and make a name for ourselves; or we shall be dispersed all over the earth." Then the Lord came down to see the city and tower which mortal men had built, and he said, "Here they are, one people with a single language, and now they have started to do this; henceforward nothing they have a mind to do will be beyond their reach. Come, let us go down there and confuse their speech, so that they will not understand what they say to one another." So the Lord dispersed them from there all over the earth, and they left off building the city. That is why it is called Babel, because the Lord there made a babble of the language of the entire world; from that place the Lord scattered men all over the face of the earth.

5.1.4 The Beginnings of History

When the Lord God made earth and heaven, there was neither shrub nor plant growing wild upon the earth, because the Lord God had sent no rain on the earth; nor was there any man to till the ground. A flood used to rise out of the earth and water all the surface of the ground. Then the Lord God formed a man from the dust of the ground and breathed into his nostrils the breath of life. Thus the man became a living creature. Then the Lord God planted a garden in Eden away to the east, and there he put the man whom he had formed. the Lord God made trees spring from the ground, all trees pleasant to look at and good for food; and in the middle of the garden he set the tree of life and the tree of the knowledge of good and evil. There was a river flowing from Eden to water the garden, and when it left the garden it branched into four streams. The Lord God took the man and put him in the Garden of Eden to till it and care for it. He told the man, "You may eat from every tree in the garden, but not from the tree of the knowledge of good and evil; for on the day that you eat from it, you will certainly die." Then the Lord God said, "It is not good for the man to be alone. I will provide a partner for him." So God formed out of the ground all the wild animals and all the birds of heaven. He brought them to the man to see what he would call them, and whatever the man called each living creature, that was its name. Thus the man gave names to all cattle, to the birds of heaven, and to every wild animal; but for the man himself no partner had yet been found. And so the Lord God put the man into a trance, and while he slept, he took one of his ribs and closed the flesh over the place. The Lord God then built up the rib, which he had taken out of the man, into a woman. He brought her to the man, and the man said: "now this, at last-bone from my bones, flesh from my flesh! — this shall be called woman, for from man was this taken." That is why a man leaves his father and mother and is united to his wife, and the two become one flesh. Now they were both naked, the man and his wife, but they had no feeling of shame towards one another.

5. 1. 5 Man's First Sin

The serpent was craftier than any wild creature that the Lord God had made. He said to the woman, "Is it true that God has forbidden you to eat from any tree in the garden?" The woman answered the serpent, "We may eat the fruit of any tree in the garden, except for the tree in the middle of the garden; God has forbidden us either to eat or to touch the fruit of that; if we do, we shall die." The serpent said, "Of course you will not die. God knows that as soon as you eat it, your eyes will be opened and you will be like gods knowing both good and evil." When the woman saw that the fruit of the tree was good to eat, and that it was pleasing to the eye and tempting to contemplate, she took some and ate it. She also gave her husband some and he ate it. Then the eyes of both of them were opened and they discovered that they were naked; so they stitched fig-leaves together and made themselves loincloths.

The man and his wife heard the sound of the Lord God walking in the garden at the time of the evening breeze and hid from the Lord God among the trees of the garden. But the Lord God called to the man and said to him, "Where are you?" He replied, "I heard the sound as you were walking in the garden, and I was afraid because I was naked, and I hid myself." God answered, "Who told you that you were naked? Have you eaten from the tree which I forbade you?" The man said, "The woman you gave me for a companion, she gave me fruit from the tree and I ate it." Then the Lord God said to the woman, "What is this that you have done?" The woman said, "The serpent tricked me, and I ate." Then the Lord God said to the serpent: "Because you have done this you are accursed more than all cattle and all wild creatures. On your belly you shall crawl and dust you shall eat all the days of your life. I will put enmity between you and the woman, between your brood and hers. They shall strike at your head, and you shall strike at their heel." To the woman he said: "I will increase your labour and your goaning, and in labour you shall bear children. You shall be eager for your husband, and he shall be your master." And to the man he said: "Because you have listened to your wife and have eaten from the tree which I forbade you, the accursed shall be the ground on your account. With labour you shall win your food from it all the days of your life. It will grow thorns and thistles for you, none but wild plants for you to eat. You shall gain your bread by the sweat of your brow until you return to the ground; for from it you were taden. Dust you are, to dust you shall return." The man called his wife Eve because she was the mother of all who live. The Lord God made tunics of skins for Adam and his wife and clothed them. He said, "The man has become like one of us, knowing good and evil; what if he now reaches out his hand and takes fruit from the tree of life also, eats it and lives for ever?" so the Lord God drove him out of the Garden of Eden to till the ground from which he had been taken. He cast him out, and to the east of the Garden of Eden he stationed the cherubim and a sword whirling and flashing to guard the way to the tree of life. Later the symbolic meanings were added to characters in the story, such as the Forbidden Fruit and the Snake.

5. 2 Stories from *the New Testament*

5. 2. 1 The Birth of the Messiah

This is the story of the birth of the Messiah. Mary, his mother, was betrothed to Joseph; before their marriage she found that she was with child by the Holy Spirit. Being a man of principle, and at the same time wanting to save her from exposure, Joseph desired to have the marriage contract set aside quietly. He had resolved on this, when an angel of the Lord appeared to him in a dream. "Joseph son of David," said the angel, "do not be afraid to take Mary home with you as your wife. It is by the Holy Spirit that she has conceived this child. She will bear a son; and you shall give him the name Jesus (Saviour), for he will save his people from their sins." All this happened in order to fulfill what the Lord declared through the prophet: "The virgin will conceive and bear a son, and he shall be called Emmanuel", a name which means "God is with us". Rising from sleep Joseph did as the angel had directed him; he took Mary home to be his wife, but had no intercourse with her until her son was born. And he named the child Jesus.

Jesus was born at Bethlehem in Judaea during the reign of Herod. After his birth astrologers from the east arrived in Jerusalem, asking, "Where is the child who is born to be king of the Jews? We observed the rising of his star, and we have come to pay him homage." King Herod was greatly perturbed when he heard this; and so was the whole of Jerusalem. He called a meeting of the chief priests and lawyers of the Jewish people, and put before them the question: "Where is it that the Messiah is to be born?" "At Bethlehem in Judaea", they replied; and they referred him to the prophecy which reads: "Bethlehem in the land of Judah, you are far from least in the eyes of the rulers of Judah; for out of you shall come a leader to be the shepherd of my people Israel."

Herod next called the astrologers to meet him in private, and ascertained from them the time when the star had appeared. He then sent them on to Bethlehem, and said, "Go and make a careful inquiry for the child. When you have found him, report to me, so that I may go myself and pay him homage." They set out at the king's bidding; and the star which they had seen at its rising went ahead of them until it stopped above the place where the child lay. At the sight of the star they were overjoyed, entering the house, they saw the child with Mary his mother, and bowed to the ground in homage to him; then they opened their treasures and offered him gifts: gold, frankincense, and myrrh. And being warned in a dream not to go back to Herod, they returned home another way. After they had gone, an angel of the Lord appeared to Joseph in a dream, and said to him, "rise up, take the child and his mother and escape with them to Egypt, and stay there until I tell you; for Herod is going to search for the child to do away with him." So Joseph rose from sleep, and taking mother and child by night he went away with them to Egypt, and there he stayed till Herod's death. This was to fulfill what the Lord had declared through the prophet: "I called my son out of Egypt."

When Herod saw how the astrologers had tricked him he fell into a passion, and gave orders for the massacre of all children in Bethlehem and its neighborhood, of the age of two years or less, corresponding with the time he had ascertained from the astrologers. So the words spoken through Jeremiah the prophet were fulfilled: "A voice was heard in Rama, wailing and loud laments; it was Rachel weeping for her children, and refusing all consolation, because they were no more."

The time came that Herod died; and an angel of the Lord appeared in a dream to Joseph in Egypt and said to him, "Rise up, take the child and his mother, and go with them to the land of Israel, for the men who threatened the child's life are dead." So he rose, took mother and child with him, and came to the land of Israel. Hearing, however, that Archways had succeeded his father Herod as king of Judie, he was afraid to go there. And being warned by a dream, he withdrew to the region of Galilee; there he settled in a town called Nazareth. This was to fulfill the words spoken through the prophets: "He shall be called a Nazarene."

5.2.2 John the Baptist

About that time John the Baptist appeared as a preacher in the Judean wilderness; his theme was: "Repent; for the kingdom of Heaven is upon you!" It is of him that the prophet Isaiah spoke when he said, a voice crying aloud in the wilderness, "Prepare a way for the Lord; clear a straight path for him."

John's clothing was a rough coat of camel's hair, with a leather belt round his waist, and his food was locusts and wild honey. They flocked to him from Jerusalem, from all Judea, and the whole Jordan valley, and were baptized by him in the River Jordan, confessing their sins.

When he saw many of the Pharisees and Sadducees coming for baptism he said to them: "You vipers' blood! Who warned you to escape from the coming retribution? Then prove your repentance by the fruit it bears; and do not presume to say to yourselves, "We have Abraham for our telling you that God can make children for Abraham out of these stones here." Already the axe is laid to the roots of the trees; and every tree that fails to produce good fruit is cut down and thrown on the fire. I baptize you with water, for repentance; but the one who comes after me is mightier than I. I am not fit to take off his shoes. He will baptize you with the Holy

Spirit and with fire. His shovel is ready in his hand and he will winnow his threshing-floor, the wheat he will gather into his granary, but he will burn the chaff on a fire that can never go out."

Then Jesus arrived at the Jordan from Galilee, and came to John to be baptized by him. John tried to dissuade him. "Do you come to me?" he said; "I need rather to be baptized by you." Jesus replied, "Let it be so for the present; we do well to conform in this way with all that God requires." John then allowed him to come. After baptism Jesus came up out of the water at once, and at that moment heaven opened; he saw the Spirit of God descending like a dove to alight upon him; and a voice from heaven was heard saying, "This is my Son, my Beloved, on whom my favor rests."

5. 2. 3 The Temptation by Satan

Jesus was then led away by the Spirit into the wilderness, to be tempted by the devil. For forty days and nights he fasted, and at the end of them he was famished. The tempter approached him and said, "If you are the Son of God, tell these stones to become bread." Jesus answered, "Scripture says, 'Man cannot live on bread alone; he lives on every word that God utters.' "

The devil then took him to the Holy City and set him on the parapet of the temple. "If you are the Son of God," he said, "throw yourself down; for Scripture says, 'He will put his angels in charge of you, and they will support you in their arms, for fear you should strike your foot against a stone.' " Jesus answered him, "Scripture says again, 'You are not to put the Lord your God to the test.' "

Once again, the devil took him to a very high mountain, and showed him all the kingdoms of the world in their glory. "All these", he said, "I will give you, if you, will only fall down and do me homage." But Jesus said, "Begonia, Satan! Scripture says, 'You shall do homage to the Lord your God and worship him alone.' "

Then the devil left him; and angels appeared and waited on him.

5. 2. 4 The First Batch of Disciples

The next day again John was standing with two of his disciples when Jesus passed by. John looked towards him and said, "There is the Lamb of God." The two disciples heard him say this, and followed Jesus. When he turned and saw them following him, he asked, "What are you looking for?" They said, "Rabbi (which means a teacher), where are you staying?" "Come and see", he replied. So they went and saw where he was staying, and spent the rest of the day with him. It was then about four in the afternoon.

One of the two who followed Jesus after hearing what John said was Andrew, Simon Peter's brother. The first thing he did was to find his brother Simon. He said to him, "We have found the messiah which is the Hebrew for 'Christ' ". He brought Simon to Jesus, who looked at him and said, "You are Simon son of John. You shall be called Cephas (that is Peter, the Rock). "

The next day Jesus decided to leave for Galilee. He met Philip, who, like Andrew and Peter, came from Bedside, and said to him, "Follow me." Philip went to find Nathaniel, and told him, "We have met the man spoken of by Moses in the Law, and by the prophets: it is Jesus son of Joseph, from Nazareth." "Nazareth!" Nathaniel exclaimed, "can anything good come from Nazareth?" Philip said, "Come and see." When Jesus saw Nathaniel coming, he said, "Here is an Israelite worthy of the name; there is nothing false in him." Nathaniel asked him, "How do you come to know me?" Jesus replied, "I saw you under the fig-tree before Philip spoke to you." "Rabbi," said Nathaniel, "you are the Son of God; you are king of Israel." Jesus answered, "Is this the ground of your faith, that I told you I saw you under the fig-tree? You shall see greater things than that." Then he added, "In truth, in very truth I tell you all, you shall see heaven wide open, and God's angels ascending and descending upon the Son of Man."

5.2.5 To Turn Water into Wine

On the third day there was a wedding at Cana-in-Galilee. The mother of Jesus was there, and Jesus and his disciples were guests also. The wine gave out, so Jesus' mother said to him, "They have no wine left." He answered, "your concern, mother, is not mine. My hour has not yet come." His mother said to the servants, "Do whatever he tells you." There were six stone water-jars standing near, of the kind used for Jewish rites of purification; each held from twenty to thirty gallons. Jesus said to the servants, "Fill the jars with water", and they filled them to the brim. "Now draw some off", he ordered, "and take it to the steward of the feast." And they did so. The steward tasted the water now turned into wine, not knowing its source; though the servants who had drawn the water knew. He hailed the bridegroom and said, "Everyone serves the best wine first, and waits until the guests have drunk freely before serving the poorer sort; but you have kept the best wine till now."

Questions for Discussion

1. What are the three largest groups of Christianity?

2. What's the relationship between Judaism and Christianity?

3. Who were the Jews and what were their characteristics?

4. What are the doctrines of Christianity? Please try to understand the concepts of Jesus, Trinity and the Ten Commandments.

5. What are the differences between *the Old Testament* and *the New Testament*, and what are the different images of God in them?

6. Please retell the Bible stories in your own words.

Chapter 2 Byzantium

1 History

In 330 AD, the first Christian ruler of the Roman empire, Constantine the Great (306 - 337), transferred the ancient imperial capital from Rome to the city of Byzantium located on the easternmost territory of the European continent, at a major intersection of east-west trade. The emperor renamed this ancient port city Constantinople ("the city of Constantine") in his own honor; it was also called the "New Rome," owing to the city's new status as political capital of the Roman Empire. The Christian, ultimately Greek-speaking state ruled from that city would come to be called Byzantium by modern historians, although the empire's medieval citizens described themselves as "Rhomaioi", Romans, and considered themselves the inheritors of the ancient Roman Empire.

1.1 The Beginning of Byzantium

The first golden age of the empire, the Early Byzantine period, extends from the founding of the new capital into the 700s. Christianity replaced the gods of antiquity as the official religion of the culturally and religiously diverse state in the late 300s. The practice of Christian monasticism developed in the fourth century, and continued to be an important part of the Byzantine faith, spreading from Egypt to all parts of the empire.

In the Early Byzantine period, Byzantium's educated elite used Roman law, and Greek and Roman culture, to maintain a highly organized government centered on the court and its great cities. In later decades, urban decline and the invasions of the empire's western territories by Germanic tribes, especially in the fifth century, led to the diminishment of western centers including Rome, sacked in 410 by the Goths and in 455 by the Vandals. Despite the territorial gains of the emperor Justinian I in the sixth century, many of the empire's Italian provinces were overtaken by Lombards in the late 500s. In the 600s, Persian and Arab invasions devastated much of Byzantium's eastern territories.

1.2 The Middle Byzantium

The resolution of the Iconoclastic controversy in favor of the use of icons ushered in a second flowering of the empire, the Middle Byzantine period (843 – 1204). Greek became the official language of the Byzantine state and church, and Christianity spread from Constantinople throughout the Slavic lands to the north. Efforts to recover eastern territories lost to Arab armies in the seventh century, including Syria and Crete, met with some success early in the period. The Byzantine system of military governorship over themes (administrative divisions), existing from the seventh to twelfth centuries, provided administration for the state's distant and expanding territories.

1.3 The Period of the Latin Occupation

In 1204, armies of the Fourth Crusade invaded from western Europe, conquering the ancient Byzantine imperial capital and founding the "Latin Empire of Constantinople", while other imperial territories also fell to Crusader rule. The Crusader state in Constantinople was one of several in the thirteenth-century Levant, all under the spiritual authority of the pope as head of the Latin Church of Western Europe. This Crusader state lasted from 1204 until 1261, when Byzantine rule was reestablished in Constantinople and limited portions of the former Byzantine Empire were also retaken.

The Latin Occupation of 1204 – 1261 had a profound effect on the empire and the Byzantine peoples, causing major political fragmentation as well as the dislocation of Byzantine populations, especially the empire's nobility and ruling classes. New political capitals and Byzantine states "in exile" with competing rulers were founded on the periphery of the empire's former borders: in the west, in Arta, capital of the Despotate of Epirus; in the east, at Trebizond, capital of the Empire of Trebizond on the Black Sea; and at Nicaea, capital of the Kingdom of Nicaea, located in western Asia Minor bordering the Latin Empire in Constantinople on its eastern periphery. This last Byzantine state at Nicaea was to lead the expulsion of the Latins from Constantinople in 1261 and the reestablishment of Byzantine rule over the imperial city in the name of a new reigning dynasty, the Palaiologoi.

1.4 Late Byzantium

While the political boundaries of Late Byzantium under the Palaiologan emperors were drastically reduced from the expansive lands of the Early and Middle Byzantine periods, Byzantine religious influence still extended far beyond its borders. The focus of Byzantine power was now centered in Constantinople, and extended westward to northern and central Greece, and south into the Peloponnesos. In the east, the Byzantine Empire of Trebizond, which had flourished during the Latin Occupation, continued to exist as an independently ruled Byzantine territory in competition with the Palaiologan-ruled empire with its capital at Constantinople. The last Byzantine lands would be conquered by the Ottoman Turks in the mid-fifteenth century, with Constantinople taken in 1453, and Mistra and Trebizond in 1460. These Islamic conquests brought an end to an empire that endured more than 1,100 years after its first founding. Long after its fall, Byzantium set a standard for luxury, beauty, and learning that inspired the Latin West and the Islamic East.

2 Religion in Byzantium

Napoleon once said that if the world had a center, Istanbul would be it. Rarely does the physical world provide a more majestic confluence of land and water. As capital of the Roman Empire, Byzantium was the nucleus of the political world. After the city's fall in 1453, it simply became the center of another powerful empire. The people who lived here once regarded their city as the heart of a larger, invisible world filled with angels and demons where the words of soothsayers could hold as much sway as the will of emperors.

The Byzantine Empire had a major influence upon Orthodox Christianity. This was embodied in the Byzantine version of Christianity, which spread Orthodoxy and eventually led to the creation of the "Byzantine commonwealth" (a term coined by 20th-century historians) throughout Eastern Europe. Early Byzantine missionary work spread Orthodox Christianity to various Slavic peoples, where it still is a predominant religion. Such modern-day countries are Bulgaria, the Former Yugoslav Republic of Macedonia, Montenegro, Russia, Serbia, Romania, and Ukraine; of course, it has also remained the official religion of the Greeks via the uninterrupted continuity of the Greek Orthodox Church.

Byzantine Christianity also reflected Greek influence. Although Christianity had originated from Jewish sources, theologians sought to harmonize it with cultural Greek traditions, such as philosophy. Their reasoning was that a religion with Christian revelation and Greek reason would be especially appealing. As a result, Byzantine philosophers began extensive examination of religious questions from a philosophical point of view. They used philosophy to understand the nature of Jesus and the extent to which he could be both God and man. The debate at times was exceptionally technical, but demonstrated their efforts to understand Christian doctrine in terms of classical philosophy. The patriarch of Constantinople maintained a school that provided instruction in advanced theology. Thus, Byzantium built its own cultural and religious traditions on Classical Greek foundations, rather than on the Classical Latin foundations of the Western church. This difference would ultimately lead to a split of the two churches into the Roman Catholic and Greek Orthodox churches.

Robert Byron, one of the first 20th century Philhellenes, argued that the greatness of Byzantium lay in what he described as "the Triple Fusion": that of a Roman body, a Greek mind and an oriental and mystical soul.

2.1 The Byzantine Church

Byzantine Christianity was closely tied to the government, so much so that its emperors are often referred to as *caesaropapist*, supreme over both church and state. Constantine himself often intervened in Church matters. The Byzantine church was treated by the Emperors as a department of the state. They appointed the Patriarch of Constantinople (the highest church office in Byzantium and counterpart to the Pope in Rome). Patriarchs, bishops and priests were instructed to deliver sermons which supported imperial policy and encouraged obedience to the government. This was a source of conflict that often led to protests when the views of the government were not those of the populace.

2.2 Conflict between East and West

With the onset of Islam in the Middle East and southwest Asia, the influence of church Patriarchs in Jerusalem, Alexandria and Antioch declined, leaving only Rome and Constantinople as the central authorities of the Church. Even so, tensions developed between the Eastern and Western Churches. Although there were political and social differences between the two areas (one was Latinized, the other Greek) the two divided most severely over theological matters, including the Iconoclastic movement. Western theologians considered Icons as perfectly appropriate aids to devotion and resented the fact that Byzantine scholars claimed otherwise. The Iconoclasts resented Roman efforts to restore Icons in Byzantium. Later disagreements over form of worship and the precise wording of theological teachings (relatively minor in themselves) caused more dissension.

A further dividing issue was the extent of control exercised by Church authorities. Byzantine Patriarchs argued that that all Christian jurisdictions were autonomous; the Popes of Rome argued that they were the sole authority for all Christendom. The debate became so heated that in 1054, the patriarch in Constantinople and the Pope of Rome each excommunicated the other, and refused to recognize the other's church as properly Christian. This was the Great Schism of 1054. Although some efforts have been made at reconciliation, the two churches remain separate, with separate customs and rituals. The Eastern Church is the Greek Orthodox, and the Western the Roman Catholic.

3 Byzantine Literature

The finest Byzantine literary works were Hymns and devotionals. The other area where the Byzantines excelled was in practical writing. While rarely works of genius, a series of competent, diligent writers, both male and female, produced many works of practical value in the fields of public administration, military affairs, and the practical sciences. The early theological work of the Byzantines was important in the development of western thought. Historiography influenced later Russian chroniclers.

Most of the writing was in classical Greek. Vernacular literature developed much more slowly than in the west. There was little fiction, the best-known work being the epic poem *Digenis Acritas*, written in something approaching the vernacular. Much of the writing of the day was history, theology, biography, and hagiography. Many letters have survived some work-a-day correspondence, a few minor masterpieces, as well as a few large encyclopedic works, such as the huge Suda. Perhaps the Byzantine Empire's greatest contribution to literature was their careful preservation of the best works of the ancient world, as well as compilations of works on certain subjects, with certain revisions, most specifically in the fields of medicine and history.

4 Architecture of Byzantium

Byzantine Architecture was largely based around the Christian story and its heralds, and the importance of icons in Orthodox society. In terms of architecture, Byzantines emphasized the Dome, the arch and the Grecian cross layout. It is evidenced today in countless examples of old Byzantine Churches with their traditional mosaics depicting Saints and figures from the Bible. Its impact was such that it spawned a Neo-Byzantine architectural revival in later years. Byzantine Art was also important in this respect; its impact on Orthodoxy can be witnessed across southeast Europe, Russia, the Holy Land and parts of the Middle East, but also in those areas of Turkey where it was allowed to survive.

The golden age of Byzantine Architecture was under the rule of Justinian in 527 – 565. The style has a large dome in the middle of the structure. The dome has a unique form in that it rest on 4 massive pillars which are arranged in a square. The dome remained the main focus of the Byzantine Church for the remainder of the empire. The Eastern Orthodox preferred a low light, somber, and almost mysterious mood in their services.

Byzantine architecture made use of dome and the arch to a greater extent and often constructed churches in a square or octagonal shape. In the west, the shape was more rectangular and developed from the basilica.

Hagia Sophia (St. Sophia) was built at Constantinople (now Istanbul, Turkey) in the 6th century (532 – 537) under the direction of the Byzantine emperor Justinian I. By general consensus, it is the most important Byzantine structure and one of the world's great monuments.

Questions for Discussion

1. How was the Byzantine Empire named, and what were the characteristics of different stages?

2. How were and Islam established and how did they influence the culture of the Middle Ages?

3. What were the conflicts between the Eastern Church and the Western Church?

Chapter 3 The Middle Ages

1 History of the Middle Ages

1.1 What Is the Middle Ages?

The Middle Ages is the period of European history encompassing the 5th to the 15th centuries, normally marked from the collapse of the Western Roman Empire (the end of Classical Antiquity) until the beginning of the Renaissance and the Age of Discovery, the periods which ushered in the Modern Era. The medieval period thus is the mid-time of the traditional division of Western history into Classical, Medieval, and Modern periods; moreover, the Middle Ages usually is divided into the Early Middle Ages, the High Middle Ages, and the Late Middle Ages.

1.2 The Early Middle Ages

In the Early Middle Ages, depopulation, deurbanization, and barbarian invasions, which began in Late Antiquity, continued apace. The barbarian invaders formed new kingdoms in the remains of the Western Roman Empire. In the 7th century, North Africa and the Middle East, once part of the Eastern Roman Empire, became an Islamic Empire after the conquest by Muhammad's successors. Although there were substantial changes in society and political structures, the break with Antiquity was not complete. The Eastern Roman Empire — or Byzantine Empire — survived and remained a major power. Additionally, most of the new kingdoms incorporated many of the extant Roman institutions, while monasteries were founded as Christianity expanded in western Europe. In the 7th and 8th centuries, the Franks, under the Carolingian dynasty, established an empire covering much of western Europe; the Carolingian Empire endured until the 9th century, when it succumbed to the pressures of invasion — the Vikings from the north, the Magyars from the east, and the Saracens from the south.

1.3 The High Middle Ages

During the High Middle Ages, which began after 1000 AD, the population of Europe increased greatly as technological and agricultural innovations allowed trade to flourish and crop yields to increase. Manorialism — the organization of peasants into villages that owed rent and labor services to the nobles; and feudalism — the political structure whereby knights and lower-status nobles owed military service to their overlords, in return for the right to rent from lands and manors — were two of the ways society was organized in the High Middle Ages. Kingdoms became more centralized after the breakup of the Carolingian Empire. The Crusades, first preached in 1095, were military attempts, by western European Christians, to regain control of the Middle Eastern Holy Land from the Muslims, and succeeded long enough to establish Christian states in the Near East. Intellectual life was marked by scholasticism and the founding of universities, and the building of Gothic cathedrals, which was one of the outstanding artistic achievements of the High Middle Ages.

1.4 The Late Middle Ages

The Late Middle Ages were marked by difficulties and calamities, such as famine, plague, and war, which much diminished the population of western Europe; in the four years from 1347 through 1350, the Black Death killed approximately a third of the European population. Controversy, heresy, and schism within the Church paralleled the warfare between states, the civil war, and peasant revolts occurring in the kingdoms. Cultural and technological developments transformed European society, concluding the Late Middle Age and beginning the early modern period.

2 Feudalism

Feudalism was the dominant form of political organization in medieval Europe. It was a hierarchical system of social relationships where in a noble lord granted land known as a fief to a free man, who in turn swore fealty to the lord as his vassal and agreed to provide military and other services. A vassal could also be a lord, granting portions of the land he held to other free vassals; this was known as "subinfeudation," and often led all the way up to the king. The land granted to each vassal was inhabited by serfs who worked the land for him, providing him with income to support his military endeavors; in turn, the vassal would protect the serfs from attack and invasion.

Feudalism arose at a time when central governments were weak or nonexistent in Europe, and kings used the system to exert control over their subjects and secure military strength throughout their lands. In the absence of a strong monarchy and rule of law, the feudal relationship between the lord and his vassal was the glue that held medieval society together.

The Feudal System
Kings Give large land grants to Upper Lords called fiefs Give Protection Receive money, military service, and advice
Upper Lords Give land grants to Lesser Lords Give Protection Receive money, military service
Lesser Lords Give land grants to knights Receive money, military service
Knights Give land to peasants/serfs Receive crops, labor
Peasants/ Serfs Receive land to farm Pay with labor, crops

3 Castle

A castle (from Latin castellum) is a type of fortified structure built in Europe and the Middle East during the Middle Ages by nobility, which is usually considered to be the private fortified residence of a lord or noble. This is distinct from a palace, which is not fortified; from a fortress, which was not always a residence for nobility; and from a fortified settlement, which was a public defense — though there are many similarities among these types of construction.

A European innovation, castles originated in the 9th and 10th centuries, after the fall of the Carolingian Empire resulted in its territory being divided among individual lords and princes. These nobles built castles to control the area immediately surrounding them, and were both offensive and defensive structures; they provided a base from which raids could be launched as well as protection from enemies. Although their military origins are often emphasized in castle studies, the structures also served as centers of administration and symbols of power. Urban castles were used to control the local populace and important travel routes, and rural castles were often situated near features that were integral to life in the community, such as mills and fertile land.

Many castles were originally built from earth and timber, but had their defenses replaced later by stone. Early castles often exploited natural defences, and lacked features such as towers and arrowslits and relied on a central keep. In the late 12th and early 13th centuries, a scientific approach to castle defence emerged. This led to the proliferation of towers, with an emphasis on flanking fire. Many new castles were polygonal or relied on concentric defence — several stages of defence within each other that could all function at the same time to maximise the castle's firepower. These changes in defence have been attributed to a mixture of castle technology from the Crusades, such as concentric fortification, and inspiration from earlier defences such as Roman forts. Not all the elements of castle architecture were military in nature, and devices such as moats evolved from their original purpose of defence into symbols of power. Some grand castles had long winding approaches intended to impress and dominate their landscape.

Although gunpowder was introduced to Europe in the 14th century, it did not significantly affect castle building until the 15th century, when artillery became powerful enough to break through stone walls. While castles continued to be built well into the 16th century, new techniques to deal with improved cannon fire made them uncomfortable and undesirable places to live. As a result, true castles went into decline and were replaced by artillery forts with no role in civil administration, and country houses that were indefensible. From the 18th century onwards, there was a renewed interest in castles with the construction of mock castles, part of a romantic revival of Gothic architecture, but they had no military purpose.

4 Birth of Chivalry

Chivalry as an institution is to be considered from three points of view: the military, the social, and the religious.

4.1 Military Background

In the military sense, chivalry was the heavy cavalry of the Middle Ages which constituted the chief and most effective warlike force. The knight or chevalier was the professional soldier of the time; in medieval Latin, the ordinary word miles (soldier) was equivalent to "knight." This pre-eminence of cavalry was correlative with the decline of infantry on the battlefield. Four peculiarities distinguished the professional warrior: his weapons; his horse; his attendants, and his flag.

4.2 Social Background

The career of a knight was costly, requiring personal means in keeping with the station; for a knight had to defray his own expenses in an age when the sovereign had neither treasury nor war budget at his disposal. When land was the only kind of riches, each lord paramount who wished to raise an army divided his domain into military fiefs, the tenant being held to military service at his own personal expense for a fixed number of days (forty in France and in England during the Norman period). These fees, like other feudal grants, became hereditary, and thus developed a noble class, for whom the knightly profession was the only career. Knighthood, however, was not hereditary, though only the sons of a knight were eligible to its ranks. In boyhood they were sent to the court of some noble, where they were trained in the use of horses and weapons, and were taught lessons of courtesy. From the thirteenth century, the candidates, after they had attained the rank of squire, were allowed to take part in battles; but it was only when they had come of age, commonly twenty-one years, that they were admitted to the rank of knight by means of a peculiar ceremonial called "dubbing". Every knight was qualified to confer knighthood, provided the aspirant fulfilled the requisite conditions of birth, age, and training. Where the condition of birth was lacking in the aspirant, the sovereign alone could create a knight, as a part of his royal prerogative.

4.3 Religious Background

In the ceremonial of conferring knighthood the Church shared, through the blessing of the sword, and by the virtue of this blessing chivalry assumed a religious character. In early Christianity, although Tertullian's teaching that Christianity and the profession of arms were incompatible was condemned as heretical, the military career was regarded with little favor. In chivalry, religion and the profession of arms were reconciled. This change in attitude on the part of the Church dates, according to some, from the Crusades, when Christian armies were for the first time devoted to a sacred purpose. Even prior to the Crusades, however, an anticipation of this attitude is found in the custom called the "Truce of God". It was then that the clergy seized upon the opportunity offered by these truces to exact from the rough warriors of feudal times a religious vow to use their weapons chiefly for the protection of the weak and defenseless, especially women and orphans, and of churches.

Chivalry, in the new sense, rested on a vow; it was this vow which dignified the soldier, elevated him in his own esteem, and raised him almost to the level of the monk in medieval society. As if in return for this vow, the Church ordained a special blessing for the knight in the ceremony called in the Pontificale Romanum, "Benedictio novi militis." At first very simple in its form, this ritual gradually developed into an elaborate ceremony. Before the blessing of the sword on the altar, many preliminaries were required of the aspirant, such as confession, a vigil of prayer, fasting, a symbolical bath, and investiture with a white robe, for the purpose of impressing on the candidate the purity of soul with which he was to enter upon such a noble career. Kneeling, in the presence of the clergy, he pronounced the solemn vow of chivalry, at the same time often renewing the baptismal vow; the one chosen as godfather then struck him lightly on the neck with a sword (the dubbing) in the name of God and St. George, the patron of chivalry.

5 The Crusades

5.1 What were the Crusades?

The Crusades were a series of religiously sanctioned military campaigns waged by much of Latin Christian Europe, particularly the Franks of France and the Holy Roman Empire. The specific crusades to restore Christian control of the Holy Land were fought over a period of nearly 200 years, between 1095 and 1291.

The Crusades were fought mainly by Roman Catholic forces (taking place after the East-West Schism and mostly before the Protestant Reformation) against Muslims who had occupied the Near East since the time of the Rashidun Caliphate, although campaigns were also waged against pagan Slavs, pagan Balts, Jews, Russian and Greek Orthodox Christians, Mongols, Cathars, Hussites, Waldensians, Old Prussians, and political enemies of the various popes.

The Crusades originally had the goal of recapturing Jerusalem and the Holy Land from Muslim rule and were launched in response to a call from the Christian Byzantine Empire for help against the expansion of the Muslim Seljuk Turks into Anatolia.

The term is also used to describe contemporaneous and subsequent campaigns conducted through to the 16th century in territories outside the Levant usually against pagans, heretics, and peoples under the ban of excommunication for a mixture of religious, economic, and political reasons.

The Crusades had far-reaching political, economic, and social impacts, some of which have lasted into contemporary times. Because of internal conflicts among Christian kingdoms and political powers, some of the crusade expeditions were diverted from their original aim, such as the Fourth Crusade, which resulted in the sack of Christian Constantinople and the partition of the Byzantine Empire between Venice and the Crusaders.

The Sixth Crusade was the first crusade to set sail without the official blessing of the Pope. The Seventh, Eighth and Ninth Crusades resulted in Mamluk and Hafsid victories, as the Ninth Crusade marked the end of the Crusades in the Middle East.

5.2 The Impact of Crusades

The major results of the Crusades included cultural diffusion and an increase in trade. European interest in goods from the east was stimulated by returning Crusaders who brought back many things. As the Crusades ended, ships that were once used to carry soldiers to the Middle East now carried trade goods. Merchants from rich Italian city-states, such as Venice and Florence, dominated this trade.

Along the trade routes, trade fairs were established in towns with larger populations, or at major crossroads. Merchants and craftsman settled in these towns, and some grew to be cities of several thousand people. This fundamentally altered the way people lived in Europe, and marked the beginning of the end of feudalism as serfs began to pay their feudal obligations with cash instead of service. An economy based not on barter but on money emerged.

6 The Black Death

The Black Death was one of the most devastating pandemics in human history, peaking in Europe between 1348 and 1350. Although there were several competing theories as to the etiology of the Black Death, recent analysis of DNA from victims in northern and southern Europe indicates that the pathogen responsible was the Yersinia pestis bacterium, which causes the Bubonic plague, although these were different, previously unknown ancestral variants of those identified in the 20th century.

The Black Death is thought to have started in central Asia, before spreading west. The plague then travelled along the Silk Road and reached the Crimea by 1346. From there, it was probably carried by Oriental rat fleas living on the black rats that were regular passengers on merchant ships. Spreading throughout the Mediterranean and Europe, the Black Death is estimated to have killed more than one third of Europe's population. All in all, the plague reduced the world population from an estimated 450 million to between 350 and 375 million in the 14th century.

The aftermath of the plague created a series of religious, social and economic upheavals which had profound effects on the course of European history. It took 150 years for Europe's population to recover. The plague reoccurred occasionally in Europe until the 19th century.

7 Medieval Painting and Architecture

During the Middle Ages and Renaissance, painting was neither a leisure activity or something carried out by people who were somehow, differently, artistic. Most paintings came into existence solely because a patron (an individual or organization) approached and commissioned a painter to produce a work to meet a particular use. These uses might be for a fresco cycle to commemorate a saint on the walls of a church, for a painted crucifix to be placed over an altar or for a small painting of the Virgin and Child for private prayer.

The medieval artist was, for the most part, a skilled craftsman comparable to a carpenter or blacksmith — someone who had learned the skill of producing pictorial representations. While the names of some of these artists are known many did not sign their work. In fact few artists would work alone — fresco painting, applied to wet plaster on walls would require a plasterer to apply the plaster (intonaco) and perhaps others to build and adjust the staging that the artist would work from.

Painters who worked on wooden panels would need assistance in preparing the panel; especially in the case of a large painted cross or polyptych, and possibly in gilding their work. There were three types of painting during this period, namely, Fresco-wall painting, panel painting and shapes and types of panel. Those paintings mainly aimed to illustrate the subjects such as life of Christ — the Annunciation and Crucifixion.

7.1 Gothic Architecture

Gothic architecture is a style of architecture that flourished during the high and late medieval period. It evolved from Romanesque architecture and was succeeded by Renaissance architecture. Originating in the 12th century France and lasting into the 16th century, Gothic architecture was known during the period as "French work" (Opus Francigenum), with the term Gothic first appearing during the latter part of the Renaissance. Its characteristic features include the pointed arch, the ribbed vault and the flying buttress.

Gothic architecture is most familiar as the architecture of many of the great cathedrals, abbeys and churches of Europe. It is also the architecture of many castles, palaces, town halls, guild halls, universities and to a less prominent extent, private dwellings.

7.2 Characteristics of Gothic Churches and Cathedrals

In Gothic architecture, a unique combination of existing technologies established the emergence of a new building style. Those technologies were the ogival or pointed arch, the ribbed vault, and the flying buttress.

The Gothic style, when applied to an ecclesiastical building, emphasizes verticality and light. This appearance was achieved by the development of certain architectural features, which together provided an engineering solution. The structural parts of the building ceased to be its solid walls, and became a stone skeleton comprising clustered columns, pointed ribbed vaults and flying buttresses.

8 Medieval Literature

8.1 Historical Background

The Dark Ages is one of the terms used to describe nearly 1,000 years of history — a history that is often hard to understand due to a lack of surviving documents, and often is clouded by myth and legends. Western Europe was under the rule of hundreds of feudal lords and kings. Castles dominated the landscape, and entire cities were built behind protective walls.

The Roman Empire formally legalized Christianity during the 4th century, and soon afterward, the zeal and evangelism of practitioners spread this faith throughout Western Europe as far west as Ireland. The Church would be one of the most powerful medieval institutions, controlling publication of books and the making of laws. Much of medieval Europe's art and architecture has a direct connection to the Christian church.

Knights, soldiers, peasants and pilgrims marched along European roads and trails during the Crusades and brought back with them stories of differing cultures, and began to adopt their architecture, tales of Romance, and advances in medicine. Trade was both a blessing anda curse. Merchants began importing silks, cottons and rare spices from all over the known world. But these ships would also bring the horror that became known as the Black Death. The disease ravaged Asia, before wiping out nearly one-third of Western Europe.

Wars took their toll, from William the Conqueror's invasion of England in 1066, to the Hundred Year's War that ended in 1453; there were few years that didn't see battles raging in some part of Europe. This was an era of siege warfare — catapults, trebuchets, battering rams, and towers. Men fought hand-to-hand in the thousands in bloody conflicts using swords, axes, longbows, crossbows, stones and daggers. Medieval Europe saw some humanity-changing developments, such as Gutenberg's moveable types press in the middle of the 15th century. This would bring printed material to the masses, and improve communication between societies. Marco Polo would popularize the account of his voyage to the Orient, and intrigue Europeans about this exotic land. Through these centuries, Europe was slowly waking from a harsh slumber, and began to sow the seeds of a Renaissance.

The Middle Ages saw the beginnings of a rebirth in literature. Early medieval books were painstakingly hand-copied and illustrated by monks. Paper was a rarity, with vellum, made from calf's skin, and parchment, made from lamb's skin, were the media of choice for writing. Students learning to write used wooden tablets covered in green or black wax. A greatest number of books during this era were bound with plain wooden boards, or with simple tooled leather for more expensive volumes.

Wandering scholars and poets traveling to the Crusades learned of new writing styles. Courtly Love spawned a new interest in romantic prose. Troubadours sang in medieval courtyards about epic battles involving Roland, Arthur, and Charlemagne. Literature exploded from the universities as scholars began to question convention and write social commentary, as well as poetic fiction.

Language saw further development during the Middle Ages. Capital and lowercase letters were developed with rules for each. Books were treasures, rarely shown openly in a library, but rather, kept safely under lock and key. Finding someone who might loan you a book was a true friend. Some might rent out their books, while others, desperate for cash, might turn to the book as a valuable item to be pawned.

8.2 Medieval Masterpiece

La Chanson de Roland (*The Song of Roland*) remains one of the most studied medieval epic poems. This is the story of Roland, the nephew to Charlemagne, King of France. The army is dispatched to Spain to fight invading Moors in a quasi-crusade. As the victorious French army heads home, Roland, bringing up the rear, is attacked. He had been given a horn to sound in time of desperation, but he blows this horn too late for help to arrive. While the poem is far from historical truth, this tale remains one of the great examples of early French literature.

One of the greatest works in all of literature was penned in Italy during the Middle Ages. Dante Alighieri finished his *La Divina Commedia* (*The Divine Comedy*) in 1321. The first of the three volumes, the Inferno, is probably the best known and describes the afterlife for the wicked, where hell is comprised of nine descending circles and there is no forgiveness. The Ninth and lowest circle was reserved for Satan and betrayers of benefactors, kin, and country. Purgatorio and Paradiso, the remaining volumes of *La Divina Commedia*, continue Dante's journey through more of the afterlife.

Medieval England thrilled to the adventures of King Arthur and his knights. This king, who supposedly grew up near Cornwall, led his armies in battles against the Angles and Saxons. He called his warriors knights, hundreds of years before codes of chivalry would make this word commonplace. The first stories about Arthur were actually penned in French in a work called *La Morte d'Arthur* (*The Death of Arthur*).

Questions for Discussion

1. How did religions influence the culture of the Medieval Ages?

2. How did Chivalry of the middle ages influence the medieval literature, and how did it come into being?

3. How many people died from the Black Death, and what were the influence to the social development of the Middle Ages?

4. Why was the Middle Ages regarded as "Dark Ages", and was it really "dark"?

5. What was the style of the medieval architecture and what were other influences of this style?

6. How much do you know about the art style of the Middle Ages? And comment on the characteristics of the Middle Ages Literature.

Division III

Modern Times

为了使学生对西方文化史有一个简单而清晰的认识，本书在结构安排上将西方文化史分为三大部分，即古希腊罗马、中世纪和现代时期。这种安排虽然能够将西方文化的发展史非常直观而又清晰地呈现出来，不会使学生产生迷茫感。然而，就时间的纵向绵延来说，中世纪虽然长达一千余年，但因其社会生产力等诸多因素，这个时期的发展相对缓慢。而从文艺复兴开始的现代时期，虽然至今也只有六百多年的历史，却思潮迭起，事件众多，需要介绍与学习的内容极为丰富。因此，本部分共包括六章，即文艺复兴时期、17世纪文化、启蒙时期、浪漫主义、现实主义和现代主义。在这些章节中，涉及各个领域、各种思潮和诸多人物与诸多现象，教师在授课时可根据实际情况进行选择。例如，如果针对的学生是英语专业的学生，由于他们有专门的英国文学与美国文学的课程，那么在授课计划的安排上可以大大缩减文学人物与文学作品的讲解时间。

自文艺复兴以来，西方进入了迅速的发展时期。中世纪神学独大的局面得以扭转。人们在摆脱了神学的严格控制之后，进入了精神上极度兴奋的高昂时期。人类拥有了从未有过的自信与骄傲，对人的高度赞美成就了西方文化的灿烂发展，西方人在自信满满的基础上取得了各方面的卓越成就。然而，这种思潮在历史的长河中却不断地发展和变化，由此形成了西方文化多姿多彩的局面。

文艺复兴是欧洲鲜活而璀璨的一段历史。这个时期的各个领域都表现出对人和人的价值的重新肯定。从文艺复兴最初的文化与文学精神演进上看，对人的本能欲望和人性要求的肯定与讴歌，从个人感情层面上感受到中世纪神学教条的不合理和宗教戒律的反人性因素，进而表现人性的美好和人的世界的幸福快乐，是14世纪前后一百多年间欧洲进步文学的主要内容和价值取向。“文艺复兴开始，文化的觉醒就首先表现在重返古代，对古典和希腊罗马价值观进行深入研究，重新肯定人的价值，表现出前所未有的对人的注意：描写人、歌颂人、把人放在宇宙的中心。”在文艺复兴初期，可以从绘画上看到圣母怀抱耶稣时脸上的微笑，在圣母怀里的耶稣也充满着喜悦与生气，标志着从神性到人性的转变。可以说，文艺复兴正是从圣母抱着圣婴的画中迸发出来的。画中传达的爱的力量再次被确认为各种力量中最伟大的，而母爱又是爱的力量中最伟大的。这样，以圣母的爱为基点，文艺复兴将对人性的确认扩展开来，形成了西方历史上一次尊崇人性、尊崇情感的伟大时期，走出了中世纪将人性压制为神学附庸的干瘪。人文主义的奠基人彼得拉克认为，人的本性、人生的目的和幸福，应该是研究的主题。“人的历史、人的命运、人的形象和人的身体本身成为关注的中心：画家和雕塑家把人的难忘形象刻画下来，哲学家不厌其烦地说：‘人是伟大的奇迹’”。

由于思维模式的根本转变，文艺复兴时代的思想家们开始对神学提出挑战，他们强调人的高贵，强调人生来就有尊严，有个性，有意志，以此反对中世纪把人作为神的奴仆和罪人的角色，以人性来对抗神性。人文主义者同时声称，人生来就有追求现世幸福包括利益和荣誉的欲望，他们把爱情归结为“天性”，不受约束的“自然的力量”，把享乐作为生活的目标，以反对禁欲主义和“来世幸福”的说教。人文主义同时强调人生而平等，主张按知识和能力分贵贱，反对封建等级门第观念，把追求智慧、知识、个人能力的多方面发展作为人的本性之一，以打破神学蒙昧主义。人文主义的兴起，否定了以神为中心的中世纪意识形态，尊重人性、鼓励个人为物质利益而奋斗被确立为新的伦理价值观念，促进了西方民主思想及个体主义思想的成长和发展，同样也为西方文化打上了更鲜明的近代印记。这种印记不只表现在对人性理想的颂扬方面，更表现在其深刻的理性传统的继承上，为17世纪的政治革命和18世纪启蒙运动力图建立一个“理性王国”做了重要铺垫。

17世纪最伟大的词语是“知识就是力量”。加上17世纪末出现的第一次工业革命，使得近代的西方人看到新的思维起点，即从科学出发的思维方式。“17 世纪的西欧是欧洲早期资产阶级革命的时代，是近代科学革命的时代，社会生活的各个方面都发生了翻天覆地的深刻变革。”在英国，17 世纪 40 年代爆发了资产阶级革命，由于社会阶级结构和关系产生剧烈变化，封建旧贵族走向衰落，新的社会阶级——资产阶级开始分化形成，因此，17 世纪的欧洲大陆处在资产阶级和封建贵族继续斗争并在斗争中求平衡的阶段。资本主义萌芽的出现也为欧洲文化复兴和启蒙提供了可能。欧洲资本主义处于萌芽状态，资产阶级正在形成之中，新兴资产阶级为了维护自己的经济和政治利益，要求在意识形态上打破教会的神学观，改变维护封建制度的各种传统观念。

因此，一批先进的思想家适应资本主义经济发展的需要，高举理性大旗，批判封建专制和中世纪宗教神学，主张建立合乎理性的社会和国家。1687 年，牛顿发表论文《自然哲学的数学原理》，对万有引力和三大运动定律进行了描述。自然科学领域的巨大发现进一步印证了科学与智慧的伟大，对理性进行推崇与宣扬的思想不断涌现。17 世纪西班牙思想家、哲学家巴尔塔沙·葛拉西安的《智慧书》便是探讨如何凭借理性的判断与思维去知人观事、评判行动并获得成功的重要作品。“不被激情左右”（to be without passions）便是其崇尚科学与智慧的重要体现。

法国伟大的哲学家、物理学家、数学家、生理学家、解析几何的创始人笛卡尔更是“科学与智慧理性”的重要代表。他反对经院哲学和神学，提出怀疑一切的“系统怀疑的方法”，提出了“我思故我在”的原则。他是方法论的疯狂推崇者，认为不管是学习还是搞研究，甚至是在日常生活中的每一件小事，都需要方法论。从某种意义上讲，方法论是判断人类、人类社会进化发展程度的一个最基本的标准。而方法论应当从研究中来，即从人的智慧中来。作为

“欧洲文艺复兴以来，第一个为人类争取并保证理性权利的人”，笛卡尔将人的科学思辨能力放在人类改善自我、改变自然的最重要位置。由此，以“科学智慧”为核心去认识世界、研究问题成为17世纪的主要思维模式，这种思维模式认为只要凭借人类的思辨能力，提高人类的科学水平，便可以达到理想中的自由王国，实现人类最终的梦想。

18世纪无神论思想的出现，带来了人类文化历史上一种最伟大的思想转型和政治转型。在以前一切的人类历史中，有神论（无论是自然神论还是社会神论，无论是泛神论还是一神论）总是社会文化的基本前提和最重要的基础。以政治和社会领域为例，以往一切最高统治者在谈到自己权力来源的时候，都把自己看成是神的后裔，强调“君权神授”。这样，当无神论出现之后，统治阶级的权力基础就坍塌了，于是形成了以资产阶级革命原则为出发点和逻辑构成的思维方式（或理性）。众所周知，18世纪欧洲的思想是启蒙主义。启蒙主义思想秉承了“科学智慧理性”传统，将理性提高到为一切提供答案的手段的位置上。启蒙主义者普遍认为，发现答案的唯一方法便是正确运用理性。理性的运用已经在物理和化学领域结出硕果，那么当然也应将其应用于政治、伦理、美学、文学等更加复杂的领域，并且在这些领域中找出标准与答案。例如，在美学领域，启蒙主义认为，烂漫飞舞、颜色鲜艳的蝴蝶不是美学，而当这个可怜的东西被大头针固定起来，剩下鲜艳褪尽的亡魂时，才是美学的根本。这种理性思想试图将人类的情感与经验世界导入某些理性的秩序中，毫不理会活力和激情，流动不息的欲望以及人与人观点的差异。在启蒙主义者的思想里，人“即便不是‘经济学意义上的人’，至少也是某种人工的玩具，某种无生命的模型。”根据这种理念，完全可以将美学的复杂思维条分缕析为人人可掌握的公式。自然科学中的进步使他们坚信只要将激发这种进步的方法运用在各个领域，那么就会发生同样的进步，这种进步会推理出使人们获得幸福、自由、道德和正义的方法。这种以理性思辨为内涵的思维方式成为资产阶级蓬勃发展的理论依托与思想支撑，思想家和哲学家将这种理性用诸于社会生活的各个领域。总之，18 世纪是资本主义新制度取代封建主义旧制度的时代，其思维模式是这场资产阶级革命的产物，同时又因袭了其自身产生和发展的内在逻辑，形成了在思想上独尊古典主义、推崇理性思想的局面。因此，这一时期人的情感取向完全以理性为转移。情感在强大而无所不在的理性面前失去了表达自身的基本力量。这一则体现了 17、18 世纪西方文化的特点，二则表明了情感必须摆脱外力的束缚才可以深入人心。

从人的情感出发来思考问题，把情感作为思考问题的出发点和最终的归宿，是一种新的理性思维方式，对这种思维方式的探寻与推崇成为浪漫主义者的终极目标。从传统的观点看，浪漫主义张扬的时期是一个野蛮的无政府主义的时期。在这个时期，社会秩序受到冷落，宗教规则受到抵制，个人情感的张扬也带来了狂妄自大的精神自负。英国浪漫主义运动当属西方浪漫主义的高潮。浪漫主义以崭新的姿态开始了自己的文学历程，它的出现为西方文学注入了新的力量。它把被西方文艺一直以来不能直接面对的情感和想象力提高到了前所未有的高度，同时也表现了对自由的大胆追求和歌颂。浪漫主义体现出来的这种空前的热情与自由精神使人们感到了强烈的震撼。浪漫主义的基本特征是在人性的诸多因素中推崇情感，情感成为构筑浪漫主义理论的基本支点。

表面上浪漫主义思想是对理性的反拨，而从本质却是对理性传统在嬗变中的继承。因此，浪漫主义依然是沿袭了理性传统的情感释放，即情感成为浪漫主义时期特定思维模式的核心，诸位浪漫主义者依然期望通过某种努力而通达理想王国，而这种努力已非希腊时期的欲望满足、中世纪时期的神学途径，也非 17、18 世纪的科学智慧和政治化目标，浪漫主义希望通过情感张扬、情感释放、情感归依达成回归理想世界的目的，因此，浪漫主义的理性形式是“情感理性”，将西方传统的二元对立思维模式的核心嬗变为情感，即现实—情感—理想的思维模式。这种思维模式的内在结构同启蒙时期相比发生了巨大的变化，即情感成为连接现实与理想世界的桥梁，只有通过情感途径，才有可能实现人类的理想。以情感为思维模式之核心的新思想使得人类重新认识了理性思辨之外的身体，感受到来自内心深处的震颤，使情感有史以来第一次堂而皇之地深入到理性之领地，为现代思想最终摈弃理性思维、形成对非理性思想的推崇开辟了道路。

情感理性的内在结构标志着西方理性发展的本质转变，这种以情感为核心的现实——理想结构不但是解读诸浪漫主义诗人思想的核心，也是情感理性不同于其他理性状态的本质所在。这种将情感提升至思维结构核心的方式一反西方理性传统中僵硬与一维的思维方式，因为情感本身是个性的、流动的，甚至是主观的。它与希腊时期的欲望不同，与中世纪时期的神学不同，与文艺复兴时期追求的完美人性不同，与革命时期的政治则更不能同日而语。情感没有绝对标准和终极形式，对情感的确认意味着对个体的尊重、对变化的尊重、对差异的尊重，也就是对每一个生命的尊重。霍克海默说：“欧洲历史有两条线索：一条是明的，一条是暗的。后者包含着被文明压制和扭曲了的人类的本能和激情。”这句话非常准确地说明了理性与情感在西方思想发展史上的地位与关系问题——理性在明，情感在暗，理性为主，情感为辅，理性为根，情感为枝。而浪漫主义时期的“情感理性”对一直处于隐匿地位的情感大力张扬，使西方的理性发展开启了新的一页，西方的理性发展史也因有了情感的加盟而变得灵动而温暖。

西方世界自文艺复兴及资产阶级革命后，就进入了以工业文明为主要标志的资本主义历史阶段。自然科学的旨趣随着资本主义的扩展愿望不断增强，历史上的先进分子们都有一种强烈的内在冲动，这就是征服自然、支配自然。要达到这一目的，首先必须去发现自然界的诸规律。由此，一种实用主义、科学理性主义开始影响人们的思维方式，“工具理性”便成为启蒙以降的西方理性思维模式。工具理性是法兰克福学派批判理论中的一个重要概念，其最直接、最重要的渊源是德国社会学家马克斯·韦伯（Max Weber）所提出的“合理性”（rationality）概念。韦伯将合理性分为两种，即价值（合）理性和工具（合）理性。工具理性是指行动只由追求功利的动机所驱使，行动借助理性达到自己需要的预期目的，行动者纯粹从效果最大化的角度考虑，而漠视人的情感追求和精神价值。

随着资本主义的发展，尤其是到了现代社会，宗教的动力开始丧失，物质和金钱成为人们追求的直接目的，于是工具理性走向了极端化，手段成为了目的，成了套在人们身上的铁的枷锁。随着工具理性的极大膨胀，在追求效率和实施技术的控制中，理性由解放的工具退化为统治自然和人的工具。“工具”成为指导人们思想的核心，即将一切工具化——人性、情感、幸福都成为可利用的工具，在这种思维模式的指导下，获得物质效益和物质成功成为衡量幸福与成功的唯一标准。由于工具理性的泛滥，以至于出现了工具理性霸权，从而使得工具理性变成了支配、控制人的力量。在工具理性的奴役下，一切与灵动的生命相关的事物都被异化，人的情感被丢弃，人的情感追求被完全忽略。然而当工具理性抵制并放逐了人的情感欲求后，却最终使人类灵魂陷入虚无与荒诞。工具理性带来的成功只能征服外在世界，对人的内心却毫无办法。社会的变革、社会的进步、未来的幸福都无法触动个人当下的生活感受，更无法解决个人当下生存中的遇到的问题。可以说，工具理性的泛滥给人类的情感世界还带来了深重的灾难。

威廉·巴雷特在《非理性的人》中说："在理性的尽头，人直面无意义性。"当理性把人的情感生命完全破坏，当情感经过长时间的努力，依然无法与理性抗衡，人就会面对一片情感荒原而不知所措。当代文学艺术破坏了传统的人的形象，人被剥光了一切服饰；不仅如此，还被剥皮，切成碎片，四处抛撒，就像埃及神话中的地狱判官所做的那样。而且，看不出要把这些碎片再聚合起来的迹象，只能无言地等待着。黑色幽默小说家冯尼格特曾借他小说中的人物发问："一个有思想的人能对已经在地球上有过一百万年经验的人类抱什么希望呢?"回答是"什么希望也不抱"，后现代彻底绝望了。

20世纪初代表现代思想的尼采喊出了"上帝死了!"的骇人之语，世人开始惊慌于、恐惧于信仰的消失，世界秩序中的超越意识无力再提供一个价值世界，人与不可见的东西的关系中断了，内在精神的东西不再起作用了。人变得轻浮、疯狂、愚蠢、六亲不认、丧失信念、狂肆情欲，陷入了彻底的孤立无援的状态。丧失了情感、丧失了基本判断之后，人类变得无比恐慌，人类的行为因此变得疯狂，变得无可约束。失去了情感皈依的人们转而在无边的孤独与恐惧中开始对金钱、对酒、对毒品、对色情等不可遏制地攫取，试图从中抓住一些东西来安慰没有方向的灵魂。变态的欲望的最终结果是变态的思想和变态的情感。这种混乱、倒错、美丑不辨、善恶不分的价值取向、审美取向摧毁了人类的最后一丝尊严，使一切都在一种前所未有的错乱中直至最后的毁灭。

这就是历史造成的悖论——通过一系列的革命——地理的（殖民主义）、知识的（文艺复兴、现代科学与启蒙运动）、经济的（资本主义）、政治的（资产阶级革命）、技术的（工业革命）与艺术的（现代主义），人类已经在某种意义上用智慧与能力证明了自己的强力与无所不能，已经成功地从一个征服走向另一个征服，然而在这个辉煌的征服过程中，人却遗失了自己。牛顿与霍金的世界已经从根本上不同于莎士比亚、但丁的世界。内心的、情感的东西逐渐被外在的、统一的、大众的理性约定代替。在如今的世界里，人们被物质挤得没有了思考的空间，或者人越来越主动地放弃思考，成为大众传媒的牺牲品。生命的基本方式是遵守常规，亦步亦趋。技术是理性主义的物质化身，既是理性主义的根源也是理性主义的结果。技术本身与科学同义，它的目的就是对世界、甚至是对社会生活进行理性的控制和整理。人们在科学技术的发展中，在洋洋得意于自己的理性发展与技术进步的同时，忽略了自己的心也被技术与科学异化为机器，没有了感受生活的能力。想一想，我们自己，或是我们身边的人，有谁还会对月感怀，听雨伤情。莎士比亚的价值比不上一支股票，红楼梦中的人物让我们匪夷所思，拜伦和雪莱更是成为千年古董，理性精准、唯利是图的现代人怎么会读它，除非某个手稿有了价值，某幅绘画能拍出高价。所谓的艺术只有在拍卖场中才会让人侧目。

面对西方文化的当代困境，我们希望青年学生能够进行进一步的深入思考，探讨一下中国文化的价值与走向问题。与西方文化不同的是，中国文化强调天人合一，顺天应物，重视伦理本位，贵和尚中。这样的文化传统也许使中国人在征服自然与世界的进程上略逊于西方，但是却在人文关怀与和谐统一的层面上显示出自身的独特魅力。本书并不介绍中国文化，但希望青年学生在学习西方文化的同时，在进行文化对比的基础上，可以更深入地了解我们自己的文化优长。

Chapter 1 Renaissance

1 Defining the Era

1.1 What is Renaissance?

The word "renaissance" originated from Italian, which means "rebirth" or "to be born". The word was first used to characterize the developments in Italian architecture, painting and sculpture. Later writers expanded the meaning of the word to describe a flowering of new knowledge, writings of ancient Greek and Roman authors. And it is used to refer to the attempt by artists and thinkers to recover and apply the ancient learning and standards of Greece and Rome.

The Renaissance was a cultural movement that profoundly affected European intellectual life in the early modern period. It is regarded as the birth of modernity. Beginning in Italy, and spreading to the rest of Europe by the 16th century, its influence was felt in literature, philosophy, art, music, politics, science, religion, and other aspects of intellectual inquiry. Renaissance scholars employed the humanist method in study, and searched for realism and human emotion in art. During the Renaissance, individuals showed an increasing concern for worldly life and self-consciously aspired to shape their destinies, an attitude that is the key to modernity.

1.2 The Background of Renaissance

From the Italian Renaissance of the 14th century through the Age of Enlightenment of the 18th century, the outlook and institutions of the Middle Ages disintegrated and distinctly modern forms emerged. The radical change in European civilization affected every level of society. On the economic level, commerce and industry expanded greatly, and capitalism largely replaced medieval forms of economic organization. On the political level, central government grew stronger at the expense of feudalism. On the religious level, the rise of Protestantism fragmented the unity of Christendom. On the social level, middle-class townspeople, increasing in number and wealth, began to play a more important role in economic and cultural life. On the cultural level, the clergy lost its monopoly over learning, and the otherworldly orientation of the Middle Ages gave way to a secular outlook in literature and the arts. Theology, the queen of knowledge in the Middle Ages, surrendered its crown to science, and reason, which independence. Many of these tendencies manifested themselves dramatically during the Renaissance.

1.3 Timeline of Renaissance

The cultural changes that launched the Renaissance began to take shape around 1350. At about that time, new developments in learning, the arts, politics, and society emerged in Italy. Many Italian intellectuals became interested in humanism with its focus on ancient Greek and Roman culture. By the late 1400s these developments had spread to the rest of Europe, aided by the invention of printing. In northern Europe, other factors, such as new religious ideas, influenced Renaissance thought. No single date marks the end of the Renaissance. Nevertheless, it is generally believed that by the mid-1600s, the artistic and intellectual trends of the period had run their course and new ideas were emerging. Events such as the Thirty Years' War (1618 - 1648) had changed the political map of Europe. By then, humanists had revived the learning of ancient Greece and Rome, and made it part of the curriculum at European schools and universities.

1. 3. 1 The Birth of the Renaissance: Italian Renaissance

The European Renaissance began in Central Italy, and centered in the cities of Florence and Siena. It later spread to Venice, where the remains of ancient Greek culture were brought together, providing humanist scholars with new texts.

The Italian Renaissance is best known for its cultural achievements. Accounts of Renaissance literature usually begin with Petrarch and his contemporary Boccaccio. Besides these two great writers, there were a flourish of writers and poets in Italian states. Italian Renaissance painting also had a dominant influence on European painting for centuries afterwards, with numerous artists. The same is true for architecture, there emerged a large quantity of works include Florence Cathedral, St. Peter's Basilica in Rome, and the Tempio Malatestiano in Rimini among many others.

The Italian Renaissance was the earliest manifestation of the general European Renaissance. Aided by the invention of printing, the Renaissance spread to Germany, France, England, and Spain in the late fifteenth and sixteenth centuries. In its migration northward, Renaissance culture adapted itself to conditions different from those in Italy.

1. 3. 2 The High Renaissance

The High Renaissance actually has been taken to refer to a short period of exceptional artistic production in the Italian states, principally Rome, capital of the Papal States, under Pope Julius II. In art history, High Renaissance is the period of art flourishing. The High Renaissance period is traditionally taken to begin in the 1490s, with Leonardo's fresco of the *Last Supper* in Milan and the death of Lorenzo de' Medici in Florence, and to have ended in 1527 with the sacking of Rome by the troops of Charles V.

During this period, the understanding of the new age was fully expressed in the work of the Great masters, Michelangelo, Raphael, Leonardo etc. The paintings in the Vatican by Michelangelo and Raphael are deemed to represent the High Renaissance style in painting, because of the ambitious scale of these works, coupled with the complexity of their composition, closely observed human figures, can be viewed as emblematic of the High Renaissance.

The Renaissance in Italy laid the foundation for the development of western art. The many iconic works in both painting and sculpture influenced successive generations of artists, an influence that continues to the present day.

1. 3. 3 Renaissance in England

The English Renaissance was a cultural and artistic movement in England dating from the late 15th and early 16th centuries to the early 17th century. It is associated with the pan-European Renaissance. The beginning of the English Renaissance is often taken to be 1485, when the Battle of Bosworth Field ended the Wars of the Roses and inaugurated the Tudor Dynasty. Renaissance style and ideas, however, were slow in penetrating England, and the Elizabethan era in the second half of the 16th century is usually regarded as the height of the English Renaissance.

The English Renaissance is characterized by the works of writers William Shakespeare, Christopher Marlowe, Edmund Spenser, Sir Thomas More, Francis Bacon, Sir Philip Sidney as well as great artists, architects, and composers such as Thomas Tallis, John Taverner, and William Byrd.

1.4 Renaissance Humanism

Humanism is regarded as the most characteristic intellectual movement of the Renaissance, it was a cultural and educational program based on the study of ancient Greek and Roman literature.

In culture, Renaissance humanists valued ancient classics for its clear and graceful style and for its insights into human nature. From the ancient classics, humanists expected to learn much that could not be provided by medieval writings: for instance, how to live well in this world and how to perform one's civic duties. For the humanists, the classics were a guide to the good life, the active life. To achieve self-cultivation, to write well, to speak well, and to live well, it was necessary to know the classics.

In education, humanism was a challenge to medieval scholastic education by emphasizing practical, pre-professional and scientific studies. One of humanists learning approaches was to create and educate a citizenry (frequently including women), so that citizens would be capable of engaging the civic life of their communities and persuading others to virtuous and prudent actions. This was to be accomplished through the study of humanities: grammar, rhetoric, history, poetry and moral philosophy.

Renaissance Humanism was an optimistic philosophy that saw man as a rational and sentient being, with the ability to decide and think for himself, and saw man as inherently good by nature, which was in contrast with the Christian view of man as the original sinner needing redemption. It provoked fresh insight into the nature of reality, questioning beyond God and spirituality, and provided for knowledge about history beyond Christian history.

2 Renaissance Literature

Due to the widespread of humanist studies, the Renaissance was an extremely fruitful period for European literature. Scholars studied these classical texts and used them to form theories about writing, for example, Aristotle's *Poetics* greatly influenced the writing of poetry, drama, and fiction. Being inspired by these ancient texts, people of this period developed new theories about the use of language and the value of poetry. There also emerged a debate on writing languages. The domain of Latin was broken, some authors began to produce works in vernacular languages. Thus, a distinct national literature emerged.

2.1 Italian Literature

Just as in many other fields, Italy started the blossom of Renaissance literature. At the outset of the Renaissance, Italian scholars drew on the work of certain medieval writers, particularly the poet Dante Alighieri of Florence (1265 - 1321). His great poem *The Divine Comedy* became a cornerstone in the evolution of Italian as an established literary language. He is a forerunner of the Renaissance, with its effort to create vernacular literature in competition with earlier classical writers.

2.1.1 Francesco Petrarch

Petrarch (1304 - 1374) was an Italian scholar and poet, and one of the earliest humanists. Petrarch is traditionally called the "Father of Humanism" and considered by many to be the "Father of the Renaissance".

Petrarch promoted the study of Greek and Latin, and praised ancient works as models of clarity and elegance. He worked to create a link between the secular ideas of the ancient world and Christian religious beliefs.

Petrarch also gained fame as a poet. As a poet, Petrarch's sonnets were admired and imitated throughout Europe during the Renaissance and became a model for lyrical poetry. One of the key features of the Renaissance was individualism — an awareness of emphasis on the individual. Petrarch was identified as displaying this characteristic in his sonnets. The poet expressed his personal interests rather than following an established philosophical system. His *Canzoniere* (*songbook*), a collection of love lyrics and other poems written in Italian, influenced poets throughout Europe — especially his description of the emotional ups and downs of love.

2.1.2 Giovanni Boccaccio

Like Petrarch, Boccaccio (1313 – 1375) paid a great deal of attention to Greek and Latin sources. He also introduced new literary forms, such as the pastoral to Italy. Boccaccio's masterpiece, the *Decameron*, written in Italian, wove together 100 stories told by a group of young men and women. Various Renaissance playwrights, including William Shakespeare, borrowed plots from this work.

2.2 French Literature

In France, the Renaissance period both transformed and renewed

French literature. Centuries-old traditions of poetry, fiction, and drama gave way to new forms that lasted into the twenty-first century. The period produced some of the greatest literary works ever written in French, including François Rabelais's mock epics and Michel de Montaigne's *Essays*. Michel de Montaigne was one of the leading French writers of the Renaissance. His influential Essays introduced a new form of writing that contrasted with earlier works in a classical style.

2.3 Spanish Literature

Spain, like other parts of Europe, was influenced by the revival of classical languages and culture during the Renaissance. Some scholars have described the 1500s and 1600s as a golden age of Spanish literature. A variety of new literary forms emerged during this period.

Spanish Renaissance fiction reached its peak with the novel *Don Quixote* by Miguel de Cervantes (1547 – 1616). During the 1500s, many types of fiction appeared in Spain. In the first part of the century, romances in the tradition of chivalry were extremely popular. These works combined tales of skill and courage with scenes of courtly love. They often portrayed knights as models of Christian virtue. Cervantes started the novel in order to parody the many romances of chivalry which were circulating in those times and which the Church was unsuccessfully trying to check.

Part 1 of *Don Quixote*, published in 1605, met with immediate success. Part 2 appeared ten years later, shortly before the author's death. Widely regarded as the world's first modern novel, it tells the story of a minor nobleman who sets out as a wandering knight to right the wrongs of the world.

Alonso Quijano, the protagonist of the novel, is a retired country gentleman nearing fifty years of age, living in an unnamed section of La Mancha with his niece and housekeeper. He is so crazy about reading chivalry novels that he believes in and admires the adventurous knights in books. So he decides to go out as a knight in search of adventure. He dons an old suit of armour, renames himself "Don Quixote de la Mancha", and names his skinny horse "Rocinante" (means a reversal). He designates a neighboring farm girl as his lady love, renaming a lady name, while she knows nothing about this. With a farmer Sancho as his squat, the two went on the journey of seeking adventures. During their adventures, Don Quixote did a lot of crazy things like fighting against windmill or "saving" ladies from "captivity". At the end of each adventure, Don Quixote faced nothing but frustration.

The book is unsurpassed as a masterpiece of droll humor, a witty portrait of 16th century Spanish society. The character of *Don Quixote* is very successful that children may handle him, youths may read him, men may understand him, and old men may celebrate him as some critics say. The complex treatment of character, plot, and themes in *Don Quixote* has had a lasting impact on the development of modern novels.

In poetry, Garcilaso de la Vega (1501 – 1536) was a Spanish poet. He was the most influential poet to introduce Italian Renaissance verse forms, poetic techniques and themes to Spain.

2.4 English Literature

In England, after the nation broke away from the Roman Catholic Church in the 1530s, English became the preferred language for Bibles and writing. During the reign of Elizabeth I (1558 – 1603), English literature blossomed. The Elizabethan age was a rich period for English literature. A variety of genres such as poetry, prose, romance, bawdy and drama became popular, in which drama, no doubt, was the most prosperous one. Together with the medieval author Geoffrey Chaucer, the greatest English dramatist and poet William Shakespeare, poet Edmund Spenser and John Milton was viewed as four authors whose works form the foundation of English literature.

2. 4. 1 Christopher Marlowe

Christopher Marlowe (1564 – 1593) was an English dramatist and poet of the Elizabethan era. Marlowe was the foremost Elizabethan tragedian of his day. He greatly influenced his contemporary William Shakespeare.

The most famous themes of the Elizabethan Drama are: Revenge, Sensationalism, Melodrama and Vengeance. Christopher Marlowe's subject matter focuses more on the moral drama of the Renaissance man than any other thing. Drawing on German lore, he introduced *Dr. Faustus* to England, a scientist and magician who is obsessed by the thirst of knowledge and the desire to push man's technological power to its limits.

2. 4. 2 William Shakespeare

William Shakespeare (1564 – 1616) was an English poet and playwright, known throughout the world as one of the greatest writers who ever lived. His surviving works consist of about 38 plays, 154 sonnets, two long narrative poems, etc. His plays have been translated into every major language and are performed more often than those of any other playwright.

Shakespeare's plays cover a wide range of dramatic forms, including comedy, tragedy, and history. His early plays were mainly comedies and histories. He then wrote mainly tragedies until about 1608, including

Hamlet, *King Lear*, *Othello*, *Macbeth*, *Romeo and Juliet*, *Othello*, *King Lear*, *Macbeth*, *Antony and Cleopatra*, and *The Tempest* considered some of the finest works in the English language.

One of Shakespeare's greatest skills was his ability to portray every possible emotional state. His works deal with the essential elements of human life, such as love, friendship, growing old, and facing the approach of death.

Hamlet is Shakespeare's longest play and among the most powerful and influential tragedies in all of English literature. The play was one of Shakespeare's most popular works during his lifetime and still ranks among his most-performed, topping the Royal Shakespeare Company's performance list since 1879. It has inspired writers from Goethe and Dickens to Joyce and Murdoch, and has been described as one of the world's most filmed stories.

Set in the Kingdom of Denmark, the play *Hamlet* dramatizes the revenge Prince Hamlet exacts on his uncle Claudius since Claudius murdered his father, robbed his throne and married his mother, the former queen. The play vividly portrays both true and feigned madness — from overwhelming grief to seething rage — and explores themes of treachery, revenge, incest, and moral corruption and family.

Othello was believed to have been written in approximately 1603. The work revolves around four central characters: Othello, a Moorish general in the Venetian army; his beautiful wife, Desdemona; his lieutenant, Cassio; and his trusted ensign, Iago. Iago, jealous of Othello and Cassio, planted a plot to make Othello believe that his wife Desdemona and Cassio had an affair. The doubt and hatred of Othello got stronger, which led to a tragic end — Othello murdered his wife, and killed himself after

Desdemona's innocence being proved.

The character of Iago is one of Shakespeare's most sinister villains. Shakespeare contrasts Iago with Othello's nobility and integrity. Iago is a Machiavellian schemer and manipulator, as he is often referred to as "honest Iago", displaying his skill at deceiving other characters so that not only do they not suspect him, but they count on him as the person most likely to be truthful. Because of its varied and current themes of racism, love, jealousy, and betrayal, *Othello* is still often performed in professional and community theatres alike and has been the basis for numerous operatic, film, and literary adaptations.

Romeo and Juliet was among Shakespeare's most popular plays during his lifetime and still is today. Along with *Hamlet*, it is one of his most frequently performed plays. Today, the title characters are regarded as archetypal young lovers.

The story took place in Verona city. There were two huge family groups, the Montague family and the Capulet family. The two families were locked in continuous struggles, however their younger generation fell in love with each other deeply at the first sight. In the garden, with the moonlight, Romeo and Juliet expressed their love. They got married secretly. Unfortunately, Romeo was to be banished because he killed Juliet's cousin in a conflict. The couple was in great sorrow. Misfortunes never come singly. Juliet was forced to marry another one. With the help of Friar Lawrence, Juliet took a sleeping medicine to feign death and asked Friar Lawrence to send a letter to Romeo to rescue her. However Romeo didn't get the massage in time. With grief and madness, he came to the tomb with poison and killed himself there because he thought Juliet had been dead. Just at this moment, Juliet woke up. Seeing her husband's death, Juliet took suicide at once out of grievances. Mourning their loss, the two families were moved by the lovers' sincere love and made reconcile. The play is full of emotions, and Shakespeare glorifies these emotions, which reflects the characteristics of Renaissance humanist.

For centuries Shakespeare's insights and words have influenced other important writers, from the late Renaissance poet John Milton to the modern American author William Faulkner. His works have spread throughout the globe, and his famous phrases have also found their way into the everyday speech of countless generations of readers. As the English playwright George Bernard Shaw once observed: Shakespeare has a word for everything.

2. 4. 3 Elizabethan Poetry

In the later 16th century English poetry was characterized by elaboration of language and extensive allusion to classical myths. Along with his plays, Shakespeare created a great number of poems. He wrote more than 150 sonnets as well as long verses. These short poems deal largely with two major relationships in the poet's life. The first is his friendship with a young man, whose forgetfulness and ungratefulness are a source of pain for the author. The other is a love-hate affair with a mysterious woman known as the Dark Lady, who is as unfaithful to the poet as she is to her own husband. The sonnets also discuss other emotions the author has faced: jealousy of other writers, concerns about aging, the desire for fame, and the fear of losing his skill with words. The other most important poets of this era include Edmund Spenser and Sir Philip Sidney. Elizabeth herself, a product of Renaissance humanism, produced occasional poems.

3 Renaissance Philosophy

3.1 Scholasticism and Humanism

The study of philosophy changed a great deal over the course of the Renaissance. With the rise of humanism, human beings took center stage in philosophy, as they did in most areas of culture and thought. Thus humanism often came into conflict with the traditional studying method Scholasticism.

The two movements took very different approaches to the search for truth. Many humanist thinkers criticized the Scholasticism of the Middle Ages. Humanists sought practical knowledge to guide human life. Scholastics, by contrast, focused on abstract truths.

Renaissance scholars based their study of ethics on the writings of ancient thinkers, especially the ancient Greek philosopher Aristotle. His work *Ethics* became the main university textbook on the subject.

3.2 Neo-Platonism

Renaissance thinkers revived the Neo-Platonist idea, which were developed from Platonism Ancient Greek and formed in Ancient Rome, that all of nature has a soul. In exploring this idea, they tried to find a connection between the human soul and a larger "world-soul". They sought this connection through such different fields as music, number symbolism, and astrology. Philosophers also explored Plato's ideas about love, which they saw as the longing or desire for beauty. The Neo-Platonist's thoughts about love and desire had a great influence on other fields, such as art and literature.

3.3 Religious Reformation

The Protestant Reformation was a religious movement that began in Germany in the 1500s and eventually spread throughout western and central Europe. Before the Reformation, the Roman Catholic Church was the center of Christianity in Europe. By the end of the 1500s, however, various rival churches had formed to challenge its dominance. These changes in religion had profound effects on political, social, economic, and intellectual life. They also contributed to the outbreak of civil wars in Germany, France, the Netherlands, and Scotland.

During this period, people believed the Catholic Church was spiritually declining. Popes of the period was regarded as gold diggers and power fans instead of focusing on religious matters. Many Catholics sought reforms within the church. Some of the most powerful voices for reform belonged to the humanists of the early Renaissance. Among these voices, Lutheran reforms and Calvinism shook the position of the Catholic Church, while in England, the Protestant movement triumphed.

During this century-long reformation, people found a breakthrough from the Catholic Church. Although the reformation led to civil wars around Europe, the Thirty Years' War (1618 – 1648), for example, a new map appeared, which would promote the development of new ideas.

3.4 Machiavellianism

By turning away from the religious orientation of the Middle Ages and discussing the human condition in secular terms, Renaissance humanists opened up new possibilities for thinking about political and moral problems.

Niccolò Machiavelli (1469 – 1527) was a founder of modern political science, and more specifically political ethics. His work *The Prince* was regarded as his masterpiece.

The Prince is very controversial because Machiavelli argues that a prince may use any means to maintain his power. If necessary, a prince should be ruthless, cruel, cunning, and willing to disregard accepted standards of behavior and morality. Since then on, the employment of cunning and duplicity in statecraft or in general conduct was regarded as the essence of Machiavelli's political thought, which was given a term as Machiavellianism.

Machiavelli made politics more secular by separating it from Christian thought and values. He ranks as one of the most influential western political writers. He raised many important issues about the relationship between politics, religion, and morality and revived political debates. All these issues are originated in ancient times and continue today.

4 Renaissance Art

The essential meaning of the Renaissance is conveyed through its art, particularly architecture, sculpture, and painting. All three art forms reflect a style that stressed proportion, balance, and harmony. To a considerable extent, Renaissance art also reflects the values of Renaissance humanism: a return to classical models in architecture, to the rendering of the nude figure, and to a heroic vision of human beings. Renaissance artists shattered the dominance of religion over art by shifting attention from heaven to the natural world and to the human being. They depicted the human qualities of men and women and celebrated the beauty and grace of the human form. The reference was less to the other world and more to this world, and people were treated as creatures who found their spiritual destiny as they fulfilled their human one. Renaissance artists also developed a new conception of visual space, which resulted in a naturalistic, three-dimensional rendering of the real world. Renaissance artists employed reason and mathematics and portrayed the essential form of the object in perspective, as it would appear to the human eye. Thus, at its most distinctive, Renaissance art represents a conscious revolt against the art of the Middle Ages. This revolt produced revolutionary discoveries that served as the foundation of western art up to the twentieth century.

4.1 Renaissance Paintings and Statues

The first major contributor to Renaissance painting was the Florentine painter Giotto (1276 – 1337). Borrowing from Byzantine painting, he created figures delineated by alterations in light and shade. He also developed several techniques of perspective, representing three-dimensional figures and objects on two-dimensional surfaces so that they appear to stand in space. Giotto's figures look remarkably alive. They are drawn and arranged in space to tell a story, and their expressions and the illusion of movement they convey heighten the dramatic effect. Giotto's best works were frescoes, wall paintings painted while the plaster was still wet, or fresh.

The greatest Renaissance artists included Leonardo da Vinci Michelangelo Buonarroti , and Raphael Santi .

4.1.1 Leonardo da Vinci

Leonardo da Vinci (1452 – 1519) was an Italian Renaissance polymath: painter, sculptor, architect, musician, scientist, mathematician, engineer, inventor, anatomist, geologist, cartographer, botanist, and writer. His genius, perhaps more than that of any other figure, epitomized the Renaissance humanist ideal. Leonardo has often been described as the archetype of the Renaissance Man. He is widely considered to be one of the greatest painters of all time and perhaps the most diversely talented person ever to have lived.

Leonardo was and is renowned primarily as a painter. Among his works, the *Mona Lisa* is the most famous and most parodied portrait. It is a small portrait which won the fame as the most famous painting in the world. The woman in the portrait was the young wife of a Florentine merchant. He painted her sitting peacefully with her hands folded in front of her. A gentle smile barely lifts her smooth cheeks. Leonardo spent three years on it, and his rest of life retouching it. Its fame rests, in particular, on the elusive smile on the woman's face, which attracts generations' endless interests and earns various interpretations.

The *Mona Lisa* was a landmark in portraits. Leonardo da Vinci had brought his painting to life like no one else other had ever done. His picture became the model of a true Renaissance portrait. It had captured the spirit of humanism — a philosophy of man for his own sake rather than as an object or a creation of God.

The Last Supper is Leonardo's most famous painting of the 1490s and the most reproduced religious painting of all time. The painting represents the last meal shared by Jesus with his disciples before his capture and death. It shows specifically the moment when Jesus has just said "one of you will betray me". With Leonardo's magic hand, the Last Super was more than a mural, but a moment of an intense drama. On hearing the news, the twelve apostles are angry, in shock, or eager to show loyalty to Jesus, while Judas grabs his purse and shows fear and shock in his face. It took him three years to finish the piece. For centuries, Leonardo da

Vinci's The Last Supper has remained one of his most profound works of art.

Leonardo also fascinated by science. His notebooks cover almost every field. His drawing of the *Vitruvian Man* is also regarded as a cultural icon, being reproduced on items as varied as the Euro, textbooks, and T-shirts. His works, together with his notebooks, which contain drawings, scientific diagrams, and his thoughts on the nature of painting, compose a contribution to later generations of artists, which is rivaled only by that of his contemporary, Michelangelo.

4. 1. 2 Michelangelo

Michelangelo di Lodovico Buonarroti Simoni (1475 – 1564) was an Italian Renaissance sculptor, painter, architect, poet, and engineer who exerted an unparalleled influence on the development of Western art. He is often considered the archetypal Renaissance man, along with fellow Italian Leonardo da Vinci. A number of his works in painting, sculpture, and architecture rank among the most famous in existence.

Michelangelo was a sculptor of the highest genius whose approach to his art was poetic and visionary. Among his greatest sculptures are *David*, *Moses*, and *The Dying Slave*. *David* is a masterpiece of Renaissance sculpture created between in his 20s. The statue represents the Biblical hero David.

Michelangelo's *David* is a Renaissance interpretation of a common ancient Greek theme of the standing heroic male nude. In *David*, the figure stands with one leg holding its full weight and the other leg relaxed. This classic pose causes the figure's hips and shoulders to rest at opposite angles, giving a slight s-curve to the entire torso. In addition, the head turns to the left while the left arm is raised to his left shoulder with his sling flung down behind his back. *David* has become one of the most recognized works of Renaissance sculpture, becoming a symbol of both strength and youthful human beauty.

Despite his low opinion of painting, Michelangelo also created two of the most influential works in fresco in the history of Western art: *The Creation of Adam* on the ceiling and *The Last Judgment* on the altar wall of the Sistine Chapel in Rome.

In Michelangelo's lifetime, he was also often called "the divine one". There were the attempts of subsequent artists to imitate Michelangelo's impassioned and highly personal style that resulted in Mannerism, the next major movement in Western art after the High Renaissance.

4. 1. 3 Raphael Santi

Raphael (1483 - 1520) was an Italian painter and architect of the High Renaissance. His work is admired for its clarity of form and ease of composition and for its visual achievement of the Neoplatonic ideal of human grandeur. Together with Michelangelo and Leonardo da Vinci, he forms the traditional trinity of great masters of that period.

Raphael was enormously productive, running an unusually large workshop. He died at 37, but a large body of his work remains. The best known work is the painting *Madonna of the Meadow* and *The School of Athens* in the Vatican Stanza della Segnatura.

In *Madonna of the Meadow*, the three saint figures in a calm green meadow are linked by looks and touching hands. The Virgin Mary is shown in a contrapposto pose, wearing a gold-bordered blue mantle set against a red dress and with her right leg lying along a diagonal. The blue symbolizes the church and the red Christ's death, with the Madonna the uniting of Mother Church with Christ's sacrifice. With her eyes fixed on Christ, her head is turned to the left and slightly inclined, and in her hands she holds up Christ, as he leans forward unsteadily to touch the miniature cross held by John. The poppy refers to Christ's passion, death and resurrection.

The School of Athens is one of Raphael's most famous frescoes. It was painted in the Apostolic Palace in the Vatican. The picture has long been seen as Raphael's masterpiece and the perfect embodiment of the classical spirit of the High Renaissance.

The *School of Athens* is one of a group of four main frescoes on the walls of the Stanza. The figures on the walls below exemplify Philosophy, Poetry (including Music), Theology, and Law. Early every great Greek philosopher can be found within the painting. In the fresco's semi-circular setting, Raphael had Plato and Aristotle at its center. Although Raphael didn't give any evidence to show the identities of the other figures in it, people still recognized these figure as not only ancient Greek great men but also Raphael's contemporary ones, including Leonardo da Vinci, Michelangelo and even Raphael himself. *The School of Athens* as a "visualization of knowledge", which is the exact spirit of Renaissance.

4. 2 Renaissance Architecture

Like other art forms in the Renaissance, architecture drew increasingly on the traditions of ancient Greece and Rome. Renaissance style places emphasis on symmetry, proportion, geometry and the regularity of parts as they are demonstrated in the architecture of classical antiquity and in particular ancient Roman architecture. Orderly arrangements of columns, pilasters and lintels, as well as the use of semicircular arches, hemispherical domes, niches and aedicules replaced the more complex proportional systems and irregular profiles of medieval buildings.

Michelangelo, as one of the creative giants whose achievements mark the High Renaissance, excelled in architecture too. His architectural fame lies chiefly in two buildings: the interiors of the Laurentian Library and its lobby at the monastery of San Lorenzo in Florence, and St. Peter's Basilica in Rome. The church of St. Peter in Rome combines traditional forms with elements of classical architecture with a large dome and long central hall. St. Peter's was praised as "the greatest creation of the Renaissance", and a great number of architects contributed their skills to it.

5. Renaissance Science

In Renaissance period, scientific studies and discoveries experienced a revolutionary development. Great advances occurred in geography, astronomy, chemistry, physics, mathematics, manufacturing, and engineering. The whole era is included in the so-called Scientific Revolution.

One important development of science during Renaissance period was not any specific discovery, but rather the further development of the process for discovery, the scientific method. It focused on empirical evidence, the importance of mathematics, and discarded Aristotelian science. Early and influential proponents of these ideas included Copernicus and Galileo and Francis Bacon. The new scientific method led to great contributions in the fields of astronomy, physics, biology, and anatomy.

5.1 Anatomy

Leonardo da Vinci, as the most famous Renaissance Man, is also regarded as a scientific and technical genius. His approach to science was an observational one. He drew many studies of the human skeleton and its parts, as well as muscles and sinews. He studied the mechanical functions of the skeleton and the muscular forces that are applied to it in a manner that prefigured the modern science of biomechanics. He drew the heart and vascular system, the sex organs and other internal organs, making one of the first scientific drawings of an infant in a womb. As an artist, Leonardo closely observed and recorded the effects of age and of human emotion on the physiology, studying in particular the effects of rage.

5.2 Astronomy

The astronomy of the late Middle Ages was based on the geocentric model described by Claudius Ptolemy in antiquity. Nicolaus·Copernicus (1473 – 1543) was among the first generation of astronomers to be trained with Renaissance ideas. He spent the rest of his life attempting a mathematical proof of heliocentrism. *De revolutionibus orbium coelestium* was finally published in 1543 on his deathbed.

In astronomy, the Renaissance of science can be said to have ended with the truly novel works of Johannes Kepler and Galileo Galilei.

Johannes Kepler (1571 – 1630) was a German mathematician, astronomer and astrologer. A key figure in the 17th century scientific revolution, he is best known for his eponymous laws of planetary motion. His works also provided one of the foundations for Isaac Newton's theory of universal gravitation.

Galileo Galilei (1564 – 1642) was an Italian physicist, mathematician, astronomer, and philosopher who played a major role in the Scientific Revolution. His achievements include improvements to the telescope and consequent astronomical observations and support for Copernicanism. His contributions to observational astronomy include the telescopic confirmation of the phases of Venus, the discovery of the four largest satellites of Jupiter and the observation and analysis of sunspots.

Galileo's heliocentrism was controversial within his lifetime. He was investigated by the Roman Inquisition in 1615, and they concluded that it could be supported as only a possibility, not an established fact. He was tried by the Inquisition, found guilty, forced to recant, and spent the rest of his life under house arrest.

6 Renaissance Citizen Life

During Renaissance period, with the emergence of a bourgeois class, demand for music as entertainment greatly increased. Many familiar modern instruments, including the violin, the guitar, and keyboard instruments, were born during the Renaissance. Thus secular music gradually broke through the domain of sacred music. By the end of the 16th century, opera arose at this time in Florence.

Although dance has been part of human culture since ancient times, it took on new importance during the Renaissance. Dancing became an important skill for members of both the aristocracy and the middle classes. Many of them employed professional dance masters to teach them dance, music, and martial arts such as fencing. Many types of social occasions involved dancing. It was the main event at balls and played a significant part in weddings as well. During the 1500s, dance began to play a role in grand theatrical events such as the English masque. A masque was a series of poems, songs, and dances loosely tied together by a story line, often performed as part of wedding celebrations. This type of dance is performed by masked actors, or a ball or party at which all guests wear masks or costumes.

The most complex dances of the 1500s were Italian dances such as the balletto, which eventually developed into ballet.

7 Renaissance Women

During the Renaissance, some women found opportunities to get educated and involved in social activities. Some of them can write and read in Latin. As a result, women's views of themselves began to change during this period. Several women of this period governed their countries either as rulers or as regents.

Between 1400s and 1700s several bright and capable woman became rulers of their countries. Elizabeth I of England, Christina of Sweden, and Isbella of Castile all reigned as queens in their own right, while Catherine de Medicis and Anne of Austria acted as regents for their sons. These powerful women served as living proof that a woman could perform and even excel at male activities.

Elizabeth I (1533 – 1603) was the queen of England and Ireland from 1558 until her death. After a series of power struggles, in 1558, Elizabeth became the queen of England. She was never married through her life and was called the Virgin Queen. During her excellent reign, England got rid of the control of Catholic Church and became prosperous in a lot of fields such as economics, literature, drama, and even political expanding. And Elizabeth I herself became one of the most famous and favored queens in the history.

By the end of the Renaissance there were hundreds and perhaps thousands of women writing in Italian, French, and English. Women penned religious poetry, love poetry, stories, novels, and plays. They also wrote diaries, family histories, and advice books for other women on topics such as cooking, fashion, child care, and herbal lore. A few women knew Latin and Greek and translated ancient works from these languages into the vernacular.

8 Geography and the New World

The Renaissance Era is also the "Age of Discovery". The new discoveries revealed shortcomings in classical knowledge; they also opened European imagination to new possibilities.

Christopher Columbus (1451 – 1506) was an explorer and colonizer. Under the auspices of the Spanish queen, he completed four voyages across the Atlantic Ocean, and "discovered" the American continent. These voyages and his efforts to establish permanent settlements on the continent initiated the European colonization of the New World. Beyond that, the "discovery" of the New World challenged the world-view and helped to arouse the willingness to question previously held truths and search for new answers resulted in a period of major scientific advancements.

9 Influence of Renaissance

Scholars have been studying the Renaissance since it ended. They have compared the Renaissance with the periods before and after it; noted the forms it took in various parts of Europe; examined the relationship between the Renaissance and the Protestant Reformation; and traced the influence of the Renaissance on later culture. For centuries, most historians shared the view of the period as a rebirth after the darkness of the Middle Ages. The Renaissance affected every area of human activity and knowledge, from art to zoology. It transformed Europe and, eventually, the rest of the world. In addition, it left a legacy that still shapes many aspects of modern life.

Questions for Discussion

1. What conditions gave rise to the Italian Renaissance?

2. What is the historical significance of Renaissance humanism?

3. How did Machiavelli's political thought mark a break with the medieval outlook?

4. What are the general features of Renaissance art?

5. Why is the Renaissance considered a departure from the Middle Ages and the beginning of modernity?

6. How did the Reformation contribute to the shaping of the modern world?

Chapter 2 Europe of the Seventeenth Century

The 17th century falls into the early modern period of Europe and in that continent was characterized by the Dutch Golden Age, the Baroque cultural movement, the French Grand Siècle dominated by Louis XIV, the Scientific Revolution, and The General Crisis. This last is characterized in Europe most notably by the Thirty Years' War, the Great Turkish War, the end of the Dutch Revolt, the disintegration of the Polish-Lithuanian Commonwealth and the English Civil War.

European politics during the Crisis were dominated by the France of Louis XIV, where royal power was solidified domestically in the civil war of the Fronde, in which the semi-feudal territorial French nobility was weakened and subjugated to the power of an absolute monarchy through the reinvention of the Palace of Versailles from a hunting lodge to a gilded prison in which a greatly expanded royal court could be more easily kept under surveillance. With domestic peace assured, Louis XIV caused the borders of France to be expanded to include, among other regions, Rousillon, Artois, Dunkirk, Franche-Comté, Strasbourg, Alsace and Lorraine.

By the end of the century, Europeans were also aware of logarithms, electricity, the telescope and microscope, calculus, universal gravitation, Newton's Laws of Motion, air pressure and calculating machines due to the work of the first scientists of the Scientific Revolution, including Isaac Newton, Gottfried Leibniz, Galileo Galilei, René Descartes, Pierre Fermat, Robert Hooke, Robert Boyle, Antonie van Leeuwenhoek and William Gilbert among other luminaries.

1 The Dutch Golden Age

The Dutch Golden Age was a period in Dutch history, roughly spanning the 17th century, in which Dutch trade, science, military, and art were among the most acclaimed in the world. The first half is characterized by the Eighty Years' War till 1648. The Golden Age went on in peace time during the Dutch Republic until the end of the century.

1.1 Causes of the Golden Age

In 1568, the Seven Provinces that later signed *the Union of Utrecht* (Dutch: *Unie van Utrecht*) started a rebellion against Philip II of Spain that led to the Eighty Years' War. The United Provinces (roughly today's Netherlands) fought on until the *Twelve Years' Truce*, which did not end the hostilities. *The Peace of Westphalia* in 1648, which ended the Thirty Years' War, brought the Dutch Republic formal recognition and independence from the Spanish crown. Political reunion and economic development made it possible for culture to flourish throughout the Republic.

1.2 Culture in the Golden Age

Culture during this period is mostly expressed on painting, architecture and sculpture, though there is also achievement in literature.

1. 2. 1 Literature

The Golden Age was also an important time for developments in literature. Some of the major figures of this period were Gerbrand Adriaenszoon Bredero, Jacob Cats, Pieter Corneliszoon Hooft and Joost van den Vondel. Gerbrand Adriaensz Bredero (1585 – 1618) was a Dutch poet and playwright in the period known as the Dutch Golden Age. Jacob Cats (1577 – 1660) was a Dutch poet, humorist, jurist and politician. He is most famous for his emblem books. Pieter Corneliszoon Hooft (1581 – 1647) was a Dutch historian, poet and playwright from the period known as the Dutch Golden Age. Hooft was a prolific writer of plays, poems and letters, but he concentrated from 1618 onwards on writing his history of the Netherlands, inspired by Roman historian Tacitus. His focus was primarily on the Eighty Years' War between the Netherlands and Spain. Joost van den Vondel (1587 – 1679) was a Dutch writer and playwright. He is considered the most prominent Dutch poet and playwright of the 17th century. His plays are the ones from that period that are still most frequently performed, and his epic *Joannes de Boetgezant* (1662), on the life of John the Baptist, has been called the greatest Dutch epic.

1. 2. 2 Painting

Dutch Golden Age painting followed many of the tendencies that dominated Baroque art in other parts of Europe, such as Caravaggesque and naturalism, and it was the leader in developing the subjects of still life, landscape, and genre painting. Portraiture was also popular, but History painting — traditionally the most-elevated genre struggled to find buyers. Church art was virtually non-existent, and little sculpture of any kind produced. While art collecting and painting for the open market was also common elsewhere, art historians point to the growing number of wealthy Dutch middle-class and successful mercantile patrons as driving forces in the popularity of certain pictorial subjects.

1. 2. 3 Architecture

The most famous Dutch architects of the 17th century were Jacob van Campen, Pieter Post, Pieter Vingbooms, Lieven de Key, Hendrick de Keyser. The Kaaswaag (Cheese Weigh House) in Gouda, finished in 1667, was designed by architect Pieter Post (1608 – 1669).

Dutch architecture was taken to a new height in the Golden Age. Due to the thriving economy, cities expanded greatly. New town halls, weigh houses and storehouses were built. In the countryside, many new castles and stately homes were built, but most of them have not survived.

Early in the 17th century late Gothic elements still prevailed, combined with Renaissance motives. After a few decades, French classicism gained prominence. In the last decades of the century this trend towards sobriety intensified.

1. 2. 4 Sculpture

Dutch 17th-century achievements in sculpture are less prominent than in painting and architecture, and fewer examples were created than in neighboring countries.

Hendrick de Keyser, who was active at the dawn of the Golden Age, is one of the few prominent home-grown sculptors. In the 1650s and 1660s, the Flemish sculptor Artus I Quellinus, along with his family and followers like Rombout Verhulst, were responsible for the classicizing decorations for the Amsterdam city hall (now the Royal Palace, Amsterdam). This remains the major monument of Dutch Golden Age sculpture.

2 The Baroque Period

The Baroque is a period of artistic style that used exaggerated motion and clear, easily interpreted detail to produce drama, tension, exuberance, and grandeur in sculpture, painting, architecture, literature, dance and music. The style began around 1600 in Rome, Italy and spread to most of Europe.

The popularity and success of the Baroque style were encouraged by the Roman Catholic Church, which had decided at the time of the Council of Trent, in response to the Protestant Reformation, that the arts should communicate religious themes in direct and emotional involvement. The aristocracy also saw the dramatic style of Baroque architecture and art as a means of impressing visitors and expressing triumphant power and control.

According to the Oxford English Dictionary, the word *baroque* is derived from the Portuguese word "barroco", Spanish "barroco", or French "baroque", all of which refer to a "rough or imperfect pearl", though whether it entered those languages via Latin, Arabic, or some other source is uncertain. The 1911 Encyclopedia Britannica 11th edition, thought the term was derived from the Spanish "barrueco", a large, irregularly-shaped pearl, and that it had for a time been confined to the craft of the jeweler. Others derive it from the mnemonic term "Baroco", a supposedly laboured form of syllogism in logical Scholastics. The root can be found in "bis-roca", a Latin word.

The Baroque age centered itself on system, centralization, extension and movement. In many cities, the whole landscape was transformed into a net work of centralized systems. Buildings were organized in correspondence to the lifestyle and the architectural environment of the time. Religion and politics determined many aspects of baroque art. The Roman Catholic Church was highly influential patron, and its Counter Reformation, a movement to battle the spread of Protestantism, utilized emotional, realistic and dramatic art as a means of spreading the faith. The absolute monarchies of France and Spain encouraged the creation of works that reflected in their size and splendor the majesty of their kings.

2. 1 Baroque Paintings

Baroque painting is the painting associated with the Baroque cultural movement. The movement is often identified with Absolutism, the Counter Reformation and Catholic Revival, but the existence of important Baroque art and architecture in non-absolutist and Protestant states throughout Western Europe underscores its widespread popularity.

The most important and major painting during the period beginning around 1600 and continuing throughout the 17th century, and into the early 18th century is identified today as Baroque painting. Baroque art is characterized by great drama, rich and deep color, and intense light and dark shadows. As opposed to the Renaissance art, which usually showed the moment before an event took place, Baroque artists chose the most dramatic point, the moment when the action was occurring.

Among the greatest painters of the Baroque period are Rembrandt, Caravaggio, Rubens, Velázquez, Poussin, and Vermeer, of whom we will focus on the first three.

2. 1. 1 Rembrandt Harmenszoon van Rijn

Rembrandt (15 July 1606 – 4 Oct. 1669) was a Dutch painter and etcher. He is generally considered one of the greatest painters and printmakers in European art history and the most important in Dutch history. His contributions to art came in a period of great wealth and cultural achievement that historians call the Dutch Golden Age when Dutch Golden Age painting, although in many ways antithetical to the Baroque style that dominated Europe, was extremely prolific and innovative.

Rembrandt's greatest creative triumphs are exemplified especially in his portraits of his contemporaries, self-portraits and illustrations of scenes from the Bible. His self-portraits form a unique and intimate biography, in which the artist surveyed himself without vanity and with the utmost sincerity. He was famous for his work popularly known as *The Night Watch*, painted in 1642.

2. 1. 2 Michelangelo Merisi da Caravaggio

Caravaggio (28 Sept. 1571 - 18 July 1610) was an Italian artist active in Rome, Naples, Malta, and Sicily between 1593 and 1610. His paintings, which combine a realistic observation of the human state, both physical and emotional, with a dramatic use of lighting, had a formative influence on the Baroque school of painting.

His first version of *Saint Matthew and the Angel*, featured the saint as a bald peasant with dirty legs attended by a lightly clad over-familiar boy-angel, was rejected and a second version had to be painted as *The Inspiration of Saint Matthew*.

Other works included *Entombment*, *the Madonna di Loreto* (*Madonna of the Pilgrims*), the *Grooms' Madonna*, and the *Death of the Virgin*. The history of these last two paintings illustrates the reception given to some of Caravaggio's art, and the times in which he lived.

2. 1. 3 Peter Paul Rubens

(Sir) Peter Paul Rubens (28 June 1577-30 May 1640), was a Flemish Baroque painter, and a proponent of an extravagant Baroque style that emphasized movement, color, and sensuality. He is well known for his Counter-Reformation altarpieces, portraits, landscapes, and history paintings of mythological and allegorical subjects.

Altarpieces such as *The Raising of the Cross* (1610) and *The Descent from the Cross* (1611 - 1614) for the Cathedral of Our Lady were particularly important in establishing Rubens as Flanders' leading painter.

His fondness of painting full-figured women gave rise to the terms "Rubensian" or "Rubenesque" for plus-sized women.

Rubens was a great admirer of Leonardo da Vinci's work. Using an engraving done 50 years after Leonardo started his project on the Battle of Anghiari, Rubens did a masterly drawing of the Battle which is now in the Louvre in Paris.

2.2 Baroque Architecture and Sculpture

Baroque architecture is the building style of the Baroque era, starting in late 16th century Italy, that took the Roman vocabulary of Renaissance architecture and used it in a new rhetorical and theatrical fashion, often to express the triumph of the Catholic Church and the absolutist state. It was characterized by new explorations of form, light and shadow and dramatic intensity.

Whereas the Renaissance drew on the wealth and power of the Italian courts and was a blend of secular and religious forces, the Baroque was, initially at least, directly linked to the Counter-Reformation, a movement within the Catholic Church to reform itself in response to the Protestant Reformation. Baroque architecture and its embellishments were on the one hand more accessible to the emotions and on the other hand, a visible statement of the wealth and power of the Church.

By the middle of the 17th century, the Baroque style had found its secular expression in the form of grand palaces, first in France — with the Château de Maisons (1642) near Paris and then throughout Europe.

During the 17th century, Baroque architecture spread through Europe and Latin America, where it was particularly promoted by the Jesuits.

2. 2. 1 The Church of St. Peter's in Rome

St. Peter's, the most magnificent church in Christendom and the fruit of many talents, soars triumphantly above the Vatican Hill. For nearly 150 years, a succession of Popes entertained the idea of glorifying the shrine of their patron saint. The present structure of the St. Peter's was built mainly between 1506 and 1626 on the original site of the Vatican cemetery and an early shrine to St. Peter the prince. In terms of its structure, the brick dome 138 feet in diameter rises 452 feet above the street, and 390 feet above the floor, with four iron chains for a compression ring. The dome is supported by the apses, and internally by four massive piers more than 60 feet thick. The Basilica of St. Peter's in Vatican also contains a whole collection of famous monuments, including works by Michelangelo, Bernini, among others.

2. 2. 2 Gian Lorenzo Bernini

Bernini (also spelled Gianlorenzo or Giovanni Lorenzo) (7 Dec. 1598 - 28 Nov. 1680) was an Italian artist and a prominent architect who worked principally in Rome. He was the leading sculptor of his age, credited with creating the Baroque style of sculpture. In addition, he painted, wrote plays, and designed metalwork and stage sets.

By the time he was 22, he had completed a series of sculpture masterpieces: *Aeneas, Anchises, and Ascanius* (1619), *The Rape of Proserpina* (1621 - 1622), *Apollo and Daphne* (1622 - 1625), and

David (1623 – 1624). Later more mature output appeared, including the *Ecstasy of St. Theresa*, and *Santa Maria della Vittoria*. Amongst his most well known works is the *Piazza San Pietro* (1656 – 1667).

2. 2. 3 The Baroque and Colonialism

Though the tendency has been to see Baroque architecture as a European phenomenon, it coincided with, and is integrally enmeshed with, the rise of Europeancolonialism. Colonialism required the development of centralized and powerful governments with Spain and France, the first to move in this direction. Colonialism brought in huge amounts of wealth, not only in the silver that was extracted from the mines in Bolivia, Mexico and elsewhere, but also in the resultant trade in commodities, such as sugar and tobacco. The need to control trade routes, monopolies, and slavery, which lay primarily in the hands of the French during the 17th century, created an almost endless cycle of wars between the colonial powers: the French religious wars, the Thirty Years' War (1618 and 1648), Franco-Spanish War (1653), the Franco-Dutch War (1672 – 1678), and so on. The initial mismanagement of colonial wealth by the Spaniards bankrupted them in the 16th century (1557 and 1560), recovering only slowly in the following century. This explains why the Baroque style, though enthusiastically developed in Spain, was to a large extent, in Spain, architecture of surfaces and façades, unlike in France and Austria where we see the construction of numerous huge palaces and monasteries.

3 France: Absolutism

The political and cultural history of France from 1562 to 1598 saw the realm shaken by eight civil wars — the Wars of Religion — as France fought with the Protestant Reformation, which was both a theological dispute about the proper understanding and practice of Christianity and a political controversy about the legal status of the new Reformation churches. In France, the conflict took on a further political dimension when members of the high nobility attempted to take advantage of the chaos to extort power from the king. The weakened monarchy had to re-conquer Paris (1594), and Henry IV finally reestablished the monarchy's legitimacy when he finally recognized French Protestants and gave them freedom of worship.

Henry IV's conversion to Catholicism in 1594 brought a new era and a new dynasty of French kings, the Bourbons. The French language itself became an object of government and a way of an overall state control over politics and culture. Once the last rebellion of the feudal nobility was suppressed, the framework and mechanism of absolute monarchy were in place, needing only the arrival of Louis XIV to complete the scene.

International recognition of French creativity in the arts, literature and science formed an essential part of Louis XIV's plan to dominate European culture. The need to control supreme in cultural matters also produced the French classicism, the crowning cultural achievement of France's golden age under Louis XIV.

Due to differences in the European countries, literature in the 17th century Europe took on different looks, among which the French and English literature represented the heights of literature achievement of the century. The Thirty Years War gave birth to a serious theme for German literature, which enhanced a national consciousness for Germans.

3.1 French Literature

The 17th-century French literature was written throughout the Grand Siècle of France, spanning the reigns of Henry IV of France, the Regency of Marie de Medici, Louis XIII of France, the Regency of Anne of Austria (and the civil war called the Fronde) and the reign of Louis XIV of France. The literature of this period is often equated with the Classicism of Louis XIV's long reign, during which France led Europe in political and cultural development; its authors expounded the classical ideals of order, clarity, proportion and good taste. In reality, the 17th-century French literature encompasses far more than just the classicist masterpieces of Jean Racine and Madame de La Fayette and its most marvelous achievement lay in the fields of dramas.

3.1.1 Cardinal Richelieu

Cardinal Richelieu (1585 – 1642) was a French clergyman, noble and statesman. He was often known by the title of the King's "Chief Minister" or "First Minister". As a result, he is considered to be the world's first Prime Minister, in the modern sense of the term. He sought to consolidate royal power and crush domestic factions. By restraining the power of the nobility, he transformed France into a strong, centralized state. Richelieu's tenure was a crucial period of reform for France. Earlier, the nation's political structure was largely feudal, with powerful nobles and a wide variety of laws in different regions. This system gave way to centralized power under Richelieu. Local and even religious interests were subordinated to those of the whole nation, and of the embodiment of the nation — the King.

Richelieu was also famous for his patronage of the arts; most notably, he founded the Académie Française, the learned society responsible for matters pertaining to the French language.

The Académie was officially established in 1635 and was suppressed in 1793 during the French Revolution. Later it was restored in 1803 by Napoleon Bonaparte. It is the oldest of the five académies of the Institut de France. It is also a body that asserted state control over cultural activity.

3. 1. 2 Nicolas Boileau-Despréaux

Nicolas Boileau-Despréaux (1636 – 1711) was a French poet and critic, who did much to reform the prevailing form of French poetry. He was greatly influenced by Horace. In 1674 his two masterpieces, *The Poetic Art* and *The Choin*, were published. The first, in imitation of the*The Art of Poetry* of Horace, lays down the code for all future French verse, and may be said to fill in French literature a parallel place to that held by its prototype in Latin. On English literature the maxims of Boileau, through the translation revised by Dryden, and through the magnificent imitation of them in Pope's *Essay on Criticism*, have exercised no slight influence. Boileau does not merely lay down rules for the language of poetry, but analyses carefully the various kinds of verse composition, and enunciates the principles peculiar to each.

3. 1. 3 Pierre Corneille

Pierre Corneille (1606 – 1684) was a French tragedian who was one of the three great seventeenth-century French dramatists, along with Molière and Racine. He has been called "the founder of French tragedy" and produced plays for nearly forty years.

It is unknown exactly when he wrote his first play, but the play, the comedy *Mélite*, surfaced when Corneille brought it to a group of traveling actors in 1629. The play was a success in Paris and Corneille began writing plays on a regular basis. He moved to Paris in the same year and soon became one of the leading playwrights of the French stage. His early comedies, starting with *Mélite*, depart from the French farce tradition by reflecting the elevated language and manners of fashionable Parisian society. Corneille describes his variety of comedy as "une peinture de la conversation des honnêtes gens" ("a painting of the conversation of the gentry"). His first true tragedy is *Médée*, produced in 1635.

3.1.4 Jean Racine

Jean Racine (1639 – 1699), was a French dramatist, one of the three great playwrights of 17th-century France (along with Molière and Corneille), and an important literary figure in the Western tradition. Racine was primarily a tragedian, producing such "examples of neoclassical perfection" as *Phèdre*, *Andromaque*, and *Athalie*, although he did write one comedy, *Les Plaideurs*, and a muted tragedy, *Esther*, for the young.

On 20 June 1664, Racine's tragedy *The Thebans or The Enemy Brothers* (*La Thébaïde ou les frères ennemis*) was produced by Molière's troupe at the Théâtre du Palais-Royal, in Paris. The following year, Molière also put on Racine's second play, *Alexandre le Grand*. However, such good feedback from the public made Racine able to secretly negotiate with a rival play company, the Hôtel de Bourgogne, to perform the play for this company had a better reputation for performing tragedies. Molière could never forgive Racine for this betrayal, and Racine simply widened the rift between him and his former friend by seducing Molière's leading actress, Thérèse du Parc, into becoming his companion both professionally and personally. From this point on the Hôtel de Bourgogne troupe performed all of Racine's secular plays.

Though both *The Thebans* (1664) and its successor, *Alexandre*

(1665), had classical themes, Racine was already entering into controversy and forced to field accusations that he was polluting the minds of his audiences. He broke all ties and proceeded with *Andromaque* (1667), which told the story of Andromache, widow of Hector, and her fate following the Trojan War. *Phèdre* was representative of Racine's psycho-tragedy, which was based on ancient Greek tragedy *Hippolytus* by Euripides, whose writing was based on the myth of Hippolytus, son of Theseus.

Racine's plays displayed his mastery of the dodecasyllabic alexandrine; he is renowned for elegance, purity, speed, and fury. The linguistic effects of Racine's poetry are widely considered to be untranslatable, although many eminent poets have attempted to do so, including Lowell, Ted Hughes, and Derek Mahon into English, and Schiller into German. The latest attempt to translate Racine's plays into English earned a 2011 American Book Award for the poet Geoffrey Argent. Racine's dramaturgy is marked by his psychological insight, the prevailing passion of his characters, and the nakedness of both the plot and stage.

3. 1. 5 Molière

Jean-Baptiste Poquelin, known by his stage name Molière, (Jan. 15, 1622 – Feb. 17, 1673) was a French playwright and actor, who is considered to be one of the greatest masters of comedy in Western literature. Among Molière's best-known works are *The Misanthrope* (*Le Misanthrope*), *The School for Wives* (*L'ecole des femmes*), *Tartuffe or the Imposter*, (*Tartuffe ou L'Imposteur*), *The Miser* (*L'Avare*), *The Imaginary Invalid* (*Le Malade Imaginaire*), and *The Bourgeois Gentleman* (*Le Bourgeois Gentilhomme*).

Tartuffe, or *The Impostor* (*Tartuffe, ou l'Imposteur*) is one of his most famous theatrical comedies, which tells a story of a pious fraud Tartuffe with the Orgon family.

Though *Tartuffe* was received well by the public and even by Louis XIV, it immediately sparked conflict amongst many different groups who were offended by the play. The factions opposed to Molière's work included part of the hierarchy of the French Roman Catholic Church, members of upper-class French society, and the illegal underground organization called the Compagnie du Saint-Sacrement. *Tartuffe*'s popularity was cut short when the Archbishop of Paris issued an edict threatening excommunication for anyone who watched, performed in, or read the play. Although public performances of the play were banned, private performances for the French aristocracy were permitted. Molière attempted to assuage church officials by re-writing his play to seem more secular and less critical of religion, but the church could not be budged. The revised version of the play was called *The Impostor* and had a main character titled Panulphe instead of Tartuffe.

L'Avare

The Miser (*L'Avare*) is a five-act satirical comedy, which is a comedy of manners about a rich moneylender named Harpagon. His feisty children escape from his penny-pinching household and marry their respective lovers. Although the 17th-century French upper classes presumably objected to the play's message, it is less savage and somewhat less realistic than Molière's earlier play, *Tartuffe*, which attracted a storm of criticism on its first performance.

The play's ending is also self-consciously ridiculous, mocking the French idea of comedy to better the comical effect of the play and its parts, while still taking in hand the tragedy of Harpagon and his life.

In 1673, during a production of his final play, *The Imaginary Invalid* (*Le Malade Imaginaire*), Molière, who suffered from pulmonary tuberculosis, was seized by a coughing fit and a haemorrhage while playing the hypochondriac Argan. He finished the performance but collapsed again and died a few hours later.

3.1.6 Jean de La Fontaine

Jean de La Fontaine (July 8, 1621 – Apr. 13, 1695) was the most famous French fabulist and one of the most widely-read French poets of the 17th century. He is known above all for his *Fables*, which provided a model for subsequent fabulists across Europe and numerous alternative versions in France, and in French regional languages.

The Fables of Jean de La Fontaine were issued in several volumes from 1668 to 1694. They are classics of French literature. Divided into 12 books, there are 239 of the *Fables*. The subject of each of the *Fables* is often common property of many ages and races. What gives *La Fontain's Fables* their rare distinction is the freshness in narration, the deftness of touch, the unconstrained suppleness of metrical structure, the unfailing humor of the pointed the consummate art of their apparent artlessness. Keen insight into the foibles of human nature is found throughout, but in the later books ingenuity is employed to make the fable cover, yet convey, social doctrines and sympathies more democratic than the age would have tolerated in unmasked expression. Almost from the start, the *Fables* entered French literary consciousness to a greater degree than any other classic of its literature.

For generations many of these little apologues have been read, committed to memory, recited, and paraphrased, by every French school child. Countless phrases from them are current idioms, and familiarity with them is assumed. According to Flaubert, he was the only French poet to understand and master the texture of the French language before Hugo. A set of postage stamps celebrating La Fontaine and the *Fables* was issued by France in 1995.

3. 1. 7 Madame de La Fayette

Marie-Madeleine Pioche de La Vergne, comtesse de La Fayette (18 Mar. 1634 – 25 May 1693), better known as Madame de La Fayette, was a French writer, the author of *La Princesse de Clèves*, France's first historical novel and one of the earliest novels in literature.

La Fayette's most famous novel was *La Princesse de Clèves*, first published anonymously in March 1678. An immense success, the work is often taken to be the first true French novel and a prototype of the early psychological novel.

The death of her husband in 1683 led La Fayette to lead a less active social life in her later years. Three works were published posthumously: *La Comtesse de Tende* (1718), *Histoire d'Henriette d'Angleterre* (1720), and *Memoires de la Cour de France* (1731).

4 England: The Civil War

4.1 The Civil War

4. 1. 1 Background

In England, the relation that seemed to work well through the second half of the 16th century between Queen Elizabeth and the Parliament became somewhat worse in the last years of her reign. With the accession of James I in 1603, the conflict grew because the king held firm belief in the divine right of kings and led a corrupt and luxurious life. The Parliament refused to pass the king's bills for new taxes, and the king repeatedly dissolved parliament. When Charles I succeeded to the throne in 1625, the situation grew worse. Like his father, Charles I believed in absolute political power for the crown, and after his dissolution of the House of Commons in 1629, he ran the country without any parliament for 11 years. In 1640, serious troubles, financial or otherwise, forced the king to summon a new parliament which he dismissed within a month. Then in November, another parliament had to be called which remained in session until 1653. A peaceful settlement between the angry parliament and the king became impossible, and the king soon had to abandon London and went to the north of England to prepare for armed struggle with the parliament. The Civil War or the English Bourgeois Revolution broke out in 1642.

4. 1. 2 Brief Introduction to the Civil War

The English Civil War (1642 – 1651) was a series of armed conflicts and political machinations between Parliamentarians (Roundheads) and Royalists (Cavaliers). The first (1642 – 1646) and second (1648 – 1649) civil wars pitted the supporters of King Charles I against the supporters of the Long Parliament, while the third war (1649 – 1651) saw fighting between supporters of King Charles II and supporters of the Rump Parliament. The Civil War ended with the Parliamentary victory at the Battle of Worcester on 3 September 1651.

The English Civil War led to the trial and execution of Charles I, the exile of his son, Charles II, and replacement of English monarchy with, first, the Commonwealth of England (1649 – 1653), and then with a Protectorate (1653 – 1659), under Oliver Cromwell's personal rule. The monopoly of the Church of England on Christian worship in England ended with the victors consolidating the established Protestant Ascendancy in

Ireland. Constitutionally, the wars established the precedent that an English monarch cannot govern without Parliament's consent, although this concept was legally established only with the Glorious Revolution later in the century.

Cromwell died in 1658, and his son Richard succeeded as Lord Protector who was actually too weak to deal with the internal troubles. The bourgeoisie and the aristocracy were afraid of the common people who were suffering from greater miseries, and felt the need of a stronger authority to keep the people from revolt. So in 1660, the son of the beheaded king, then in exile in France, was welcomed back as King Charles II, and this has been known as the Restoration. Before holding power, Charles II had promised to recognize religious freedom, not to make any revenge and to break the interests of those who during the revolution had acquired land confiscated from the church and from the royalists. But he failed to do that. The Anglican Church was restored to its former authority, and the king took inclination toward Catholic Church. Then after James II succeeded to the throne in 1685, Catholicism was again proclaimed the official religion in England. Charles II and then James II also took force to suppress all dissatisfaction among the common people. In parliament, two rival political parties, the Tories and the Whigs, were formed, with the former supporting the king and the latter opposed him. Finally, in 1688 the so-called "glorious revolution" took place as James II fled to France and his daughter Mary and her husband William Duke of Orange, both Protestants, were welcomed to England to become joint ruler of the country. The feudal rule of an absolute monarch in England now definitely came to an end and the bourgeoisie was successful in its appeal for state power.

4. 2 English Literature

English literature during the 17th century bore a clear mark of the social and political changes of the time, which was reflected in two respects. On the one hand, the content is mostly about the struggle between the new and old powers in politics and theology, on the other hand it was also influenced by the literary tide on the European continent.

4. 2. 1 The Metaphysical Poets

The metaphysical poets is a term coined by the poet and critic Samuel Johnson to describe a loose group of British lyric poets of the 17th century, whose works were characterized by the inventive use of conceits, and by speculation about topics such as love or religion. These poets were not formally affiliated; most of them did not even know or read each other.

John Donne (between 24 Jan. and 19 June 1572 – 31 Mar. 1631) was an English poet, satirist, lawyer and a cleric in the Church of England. He is considered the pre-eminent representative of the metaphysical poets.

His works are noted for their strong, sensual style and include sonnets, love poetry, religious poems, Latin translations, epigrams, elegies, songs, satires and sermons. His poetry is noted for its vibrancy of language and inventiveness of metaphor, especially compared to that of his contemporaries. Donne's style is characterized by abrupt openings and various paradoxes, ironies and dislocations. These features, along with his frequent dramatic or everyday speech rhythms, his tense syntax and his tough eloquence, were both a reaction against the smoothness of conventional Elizabethan poetry and an adaptation into English of European baroque and mannerist techniques. He is particularly famous for his mastery of metaphysical conceits.

4. 2. 2 John Milton

John Milton (1608 – 1674) was an English poet, polemicist, a scholarly man of letters, and a civil servant for the Commonwealth of England under Oliver Cromwell. He stands alongside playwright William Shakespeare as one of the most celebrated English poets of all time. Milton wrote of his desire to use all his skills to enrich the English language. He also promoted political and religious reforms and sought to advance the cause of liberty. Milton's poetry and prose reflect deep personal convictions, a passion for freedom and self-determination. He is best known for his epic poem *Paradise Lost*, which was written at a time of religious flux and political upheaval. His other famous works include *Paradise Regained and* Samson *Agonistes*. His celebrated *Areopagitica* (written in condemnation of pre-publication censorship), is among history's most influential and impassioned defenses of free speech and freedom of the press.

Milton's use of blank verse, in addition to his stylistic innovations (such as grandiloquence of voice and vision, peculiar diction and phraseology) influenced later poets. At the time poetic blank verse was considered distinct from its use in verse drama, and *Paradise Lost* was taken as a unique exemplar. "Miltonic verse" might be synonymous for a century with blank verse as poetry, a new poetic terrain independent from both the drama and the heroic couplet.

Paradise Lost

Paradise Lost was originally published in 1667 in ten books, with a total of over ten thousand individual lines of verse. A second edition followed in 1674, changed into twelve books (in the manner of the division of Virgil's *Aeneid*) with minor revisions throughout and a note on the versification.

The poem concerns the Biblical story of the Fall of Man: the temptation of Adam and Eve by the fallen angel Satan and their expulsion from the Garden of Eden. The story of Adam and Eve's temptation and fall is a fundamentally different, new kind of epic: a domestic one. Adam and Eve are presented for the first time in Christian literature as having a full relationship while still being without sin. They have passions and distinct personalities. Satan, disguised in the form of a serpent, successfully tempts Eve to eat from the Tree through cheating. Adam, learning that Eve has sinned, knowingly commits the same sin. He declares to Eve that since she was made from his flesh, they are bound to one another so that if she dies, he must also die. In this manner, Milton portrays Adam as a heroic figure, but also as a greater sinner than Eve, as he is aware that what he is doing is wrong.

After eating the fruit, Adam and Eve have lustful sex, and at first, Adam is convinced that Eve was right in thinking that eating the fruit would be beneficial. However, they soon fall asleep and have terrible nightmares, and after they awake, they experience guilt and shame for the first time.

Eve encourages Adam and Eve both to approach God, to "bow and sue for grace with suppliant knee", and to receive grace from God. Adam is shown a vision by the angel Michael, in which Adam witnesses everything that will happen to mankind until the Great Flood. Adam is very upset by this vision of humankind's future, and so Michael also tells him about humankind's potential redemption from original sin through Jesus Christ.

Adam and Eve are cast out of Eden, and Michael says that Adam may find "a paradise within thee, happier far". Adam and Eve also now have a more distant relationship with God, who is omnipresent but invisible

Milton's purpose, stated in Book I, is to "justify the ways of God to men". *Paradise Lost* is widely considered one of the greatest literary works in the English language.

Samson Agonistes

Samson Agonistes is a tragic closet drama that appeared with the publication of Milton's *Paradise Regained* in 1671, as the title page of that volume states: "Paradise Regained / A Poem / In IV Books / To Which Is Added / Samson Agonistes".

Samson Agonistes draws on the story of Samson from the Old Testament. Samson has been captured by the Philistines, had his hair, the container of his strength, cut off and his eyes cut out. Samson is "Blind among enemies, O worse than chains" (line 66). Finally, he pulled down the pillars and died with his enemies.

Samson Agonistes combines Greek Tragedy with Hebrew Scripture, which alters both forms. Milton believed that the Bible was better in classical forms than those written by the Greeks and Romans. In his introduction, Milton discusses Aristotle's definition of tragedy and sets out his own paraphrase of it to connect it to *Samson Agonistes*.

4. 2. 3 John Bunyan

John Bunyan (1628 - 1688) was an English Christian writer and preacher, who was well known for his book *The Pilgrim's Progress*. He is remembered in the Church of England with a Lesser Festival on August 30, and on the liturgical calendar of the Episcopal Church (US) on August 29. Some other Churches of the Anglican Communion, such as the Anglican Church of Australia, honor him on the day of his death (August

31).

Bunyan wrote *The Pilgrim's Progress* in two parts, the first of which was published in London in 1678 and the second in 1684. He began the work in his first era of imprisonment, and probably finished it during the second. The earliest edition in which the two parts combined in one volume came in 1728. Its full title is *The Pilgrim's Progress from This World to That Which Is to Come.*

The Pilgrim's Progress is arguably one of the most widely known allegories ever written, and has been extensively translated. Protestant missionaries commonly translated it as the first thing after the Bible.

Two other successful works of Bunyan's are less well-known: *The Life and Death of Mr. Badman* (1680), an imaginary biography, and *The Holy War* (1682), an allegory. A third book which reveals Bunyan's inner life and his preparation for his appointed work is *Grace Abounding to the Chief of Sinners* (1666). It is a classic example of a spiritual autobiography, and thus is focused on his own spiritual journey; his motive in writing it was plainly to exalt the Christian concept of grace and to comfort those passing through experiences like his own.

4. 2. 4 John Dryden

John Dryden (1631 – 1700) was an influential English poet, literary critic, translator, and playwright who dominated the literary life of Restoration England to such a point that the period came to be known in literary circles as the Age of Dryden. Walter Scott called him "Glorious John". He was made Poet Laureate in 1668.

During the Protectorate, Dryden published his first important poem, *Heroique Stanzas* (1658), a eulogy on Cromwell's death. He quickly established himself as the leading poet and literary critic of his day and he transferred his allegiances to the new government. Along with Astraea Redux, Dryden welcomed the new regime with two more panegyrics: *To His Sacred Majesty: A Panegyric on his Coronation* (1662), and *To My Lord Chancellor* (1662).

Dryden was the dominant literary figure and influence of his age. He established the heroic couplet as a standard form of English poetry by writing successful satires, religious pieces, fables, epigrams, compliments, prologues, and plays with it; he also introduced the alexandrine and triplet into the form. Dryden's heroic couplet became the dominant poetic form of the 18th century. Alexander Pope was heavily influenced by Dryden, and often borrowed from him; other writers were equally influenced by Dryden and Pope. One of the first attacks on Dryden's reputation was by Wordsworth, who complained that Dryden's descriptions of natural objects in his translations from Virgil were much inferior to the originals. However, several of Wordsworth's contemporaries, such as George Crabbe, Lord Byron, and Walter Scott (who edited Dryden's works), were still keen admirers of Dryden.

4. 2. 5 The Comedy of Manners

The comedy of manners is a genre of play which satirizes the manners and affectations of asocial class or of multiple classes, often represented by stereotypical stock characters, such as the boastful soldier in ancient times, the fop and the rake during the Restoration, or an old person pretending to be young. Restoration comedy is used as a synonym of Comedy of manners. The plot of the comedy, often concerned with scandal, is generally less important than its witty dialogue.

The comedy of manners was first developed in the new comedy of the Ancient Greek playwright Menander. His style, elaborate plots, and stock characters were imitated by the Roman playwrights Plautus and Terence, whose comedies were widely known and copied during the Renaissance.

In England, William Shakespeare's *Much Ado about Nothing* might be considered the first comedy of manners, but the genre really flourished during the Restoration period. Restoration comedy, which was influenced by Ben Jonson's comedy of humours, made fun of affected wit and acquired follies of the time. The masterpieces of the genre were the plays of William Wycherley (*The Country Wife*, 1675) and William Congreve (*The Way of the World*, 1700).

5 Philosophy

5.1 Brief Introduction

17th-century philosophy in the Western world is generally regarded as being the start of modern philosophy, and a departure from the medieval approach, especially Scholasticism. Early 17th-century philosophy is often called the Age of Reason or Age of Rationalism and is considered to succeed the Renaissance philosophy era and precede the Age of Enlightenment. During this time, there appeared in history a great many philosophers such as John Lock, Thomas Hobbes, René Descartes, Baruch Spinoza, Gottfried Leibniz, Galileo Galilei, and Isaac Newton, of whom some are also great figures in science.

5.2 John Locke

John Locke (1632 - 1704), widely known as the Father of Classical Liberalism, was an English philosopher and physician, regarded as one of the most influential thinkers. His work had a great impact upon the development of epistemology and political philosophy. His writings influenced Voltaire and Rousseau, many Scottish Enlightenment thinkers, as well as the American revolutionaries. His contributions to classical republicanism and liberal theory are reflected in the United States *Declaration of Independence*.

Considered as one of the first of the British empiricists, following the tradition of Francis Bacon, he is equally important to Social Contract Theory, on which his political theory was founded. Locke believed that human nature allowed men to be selfish. This is apparent with the introduction of currency. In a natural state all people were equal and independent, and everyone had a natural right to defend his "Life, health, liberty, or possessions". Most scholars trace the phrase, "life, liberty, and the pursuit of happiness," in the American *Declaration of Independence* to Locke's theory of rights, though other origins have been suggested. Locke also advocated governmental separation of powers and believed that revolution is not only a right but an obligation in some circumstances. These ideas would come to have profound influence on the *Declaration of Independence* and the *Constitution of the United States*.

Like Hobbes, Locke assumed that the sole right to defend in the state of nature was not enough, so people established a civil society to resolve conflicts in a civil way with help from government in a state of society.

The *Two Treatises of Government* is a work of political philosophy published anonymously in 1689 by John Locke. The *First Treatise* attacks patriarchalism in the form of sentence-by-sentence refutation of Robert Filmer's *Patriarcha* and the *Second Treatise* outlines his ideas for a more civilized society based on natural rights and contract theory.

5.3 Thomas Hobbes

Thomas Hobbes (1588 – 1679) was an English philosopher, best known today for his work on political philosophy.

Hobbes was a champion of absolutism for the sovereign, but he also developed some of the fundamentals of European liberal thought: the right of the individual; the natural equality of all men; the artificial character of the political order (which led to the later distinction between civil society and the state); the view that all legitimate political power must be "representative" and based on the consent of the people; and a liberal interpretation of law which leaves people free to do whatever the law does not explicitly forbid.

He was one of the founders of modern political philosophy. His 1651 book *Leviathan* established the foundation for most of Western political philosophy from the perspective of social contract theory. In *Leviathan*, Hobbes set out his doctrine of the foundation of states and legitimate governments-originating social contract theory. *Leviathan* was written during the English Civil War; much of the book is occupied with demonstrating the necessity of a strong central authority to avoid the evil of discord and civil war.

In addition to political philosophy, Hobbes also contributed to a diverse array of other fields, including history, geometry, the physics of gases, theology, ethics, and general philosophy.

5.4 René Descartes

René Descartes (31 Mar. 1596 – 11 Feb. 1650) was a French philosopher, mathematician, and writer who spent most of his adult life in the Dutch Republic. He has been dubbed the "Father of Modern

Philosophy", and much subsequent Western philosophy is a response to his writings, which are studied closely to this day. In particular, his *Meditations on First Philosophy* continues to be a standard text at most university philosophy departments.

In his natural philosophy, he differs from the schools on two major points: First, he rejects the analysis of corporeal substance into matter and form; second, he rejects any appeal to ends — divine or natural — in explaining natural phenomena. In his theology, he insists on the absolute freedom of God's act of creation.

Descartes was a major figure in 17th-century continentalrationalism, later advocated by Baruch Spinoza and Gottfried Leibniz, and opposed by the empiricist school of thought consisting of Hobbes, Locke, Jean-Jacques Rousseau, and Hume.

He is perhaps best known for the philosophical statement "Cogito ergo sum" (French: Je pense, donc je suis; English: I think, therefore I am), found in part IV of *Discourse on the Method* (1637) and part I of *Principles of Philosophy* (1644).

5.5 Baruch Spinoza

Baruch Spinoza (1632-1677) was a Jewish-Dutch philosopher. Revealing considerable scientific aptitude, the breadth and importance of Spinoza's work was not fully realized until years after his death. He came to be considered one of the great rationalists of 17th-century philosophy. His magnum opus, the posthumous *Ethics*, in which he opposed Descartes's mind-body dualism, has earned him recognition as one of Western philosophy's most important contributors.

In *Ethics*, Spinoza wrote the last indisputable Latin masterpiece, and one in which the refined conceptions of medieval philosophy are finally turned against themselves and destroyed entirely. Philosopher Georg Wilhelm Friedrich Hegel said of all contemporary philosophers, "You are either a Spinozist or not a philosopher at all."

5.6 Gottfried Wilhelm von Leibniz

Gottfried Leibniz was born on July 1, 1646 in Leipzig, Saxony at the end of the Thirty Years' War. He occupies a prominent place in the history of mathematics and the history of philosophy.

In philosophy, Leibniz is mostly noted for his optimism, e. g., his conclusion that our Universe is, in a restricted sense, the best possible one that God could have created. Leibniz, along with René Descartes and Baruch Spinoza, was one of the three great 17th century advocates of rationalism. The work of Leibniz anticipated modern logic and analytic philosophy, but his philosophy also looks back to the scholastic tradition, in which conclusions are produced by applying reason to first principles or prior definitions rather than to empirical evidence.

6 Scientific Revolution

The scientific revolution was the dawning of modern science during the early modern period, when developments in mathematics, physics, astronomy, biology, medicine and chemistry transformed views of society and nature. According to traditional accounts, the scientific revolution began in Europe towards the end of the Renaissance era and continued through the late 18th century, influencing the intellectual social movement known as the Enlightenment. While its dates are disputed, the publication in 1543 of Nicolaus Copernicus' *On the Revolutions of the Heavenly Spheres*

(*De revolutionibus orbium coelestium*) and Andreas Vesalius' *On the Fabric of the Human body* (*De humani corporis fabrica*) is often cited as marking the beginning of the scientific revolution. By the end of the 18th century the scientific revolution had given way to the "Age of Reflection".

6.1 Sir Isaac Newton

Sir Isaac Newton (1642 – 1726) was an English physicist, mathematician, astronomer, natural philosopher, alchemist and theologian who has been considered by many to be the greatest and most influential scientist who ever lived. His monograph *Philosophie Naturalis Principia Mathematica*, published in 1687, laid the foundations for most of classical mechanics. In this work, Newton described universal gravitation and the three laws of motion, which dominated the scientific view of the physical universe for the next three centuries.

Leibniz, Spinoza and Descartes were all well versed in mathematics as well as philosophy, and Descartes and Leibniz contributed greatly to science as well.

6.2 René Descartes

Descartes' influence in mathematics is equally apparent; the Cartesian coordinate system — allowing reference to a point in space as a set of numbers, and allowing algebraic equations to be expressed as geometric shapes in a two-dimensional coordinate system (and conversely, shapes to be described as equations) — was named after him. He is credited as the father of analytical geometry, the bridge between algebra and geometry, crucial to the discovery of infinitesimal calculus and analysis. Descartes was also one of the key figures in the scientific revolution and has been described as an example of genius.

6.3 Gottfried Wilhelm von Leibniz

Leibniz (1646 - 1716) was a German mathematician and philosopher. He occupied a prominent place in the history of mathematics and the history of philosophy.

Leibniz developed the infinitesimal calculus independently of Isaac Newton, and Leibniz's mathematical notation has been widely used ever since it was published. His visionary Law of Continuity and Transcendental Law of Homogeneity only found mathematical implementation in the 20th century. He became one of the most prolific inventors in the field of mechanical calculators, who was the first to describe a pinwheel calculator in 1685 and invented the Leibniz wheel, used in the arithmometer, the first mass-produced mechanical calculator. He also refined the binary number system, which is at the foundation of virtually all digital computers.

Leibniz made major contributions to physics and technology, and anticipated notions that surfaced much later in philosophy, probability theory, biology, medicine, geology, psychology, linguistics, and information science. He wrote in several languages, but primarily in Latin, French, and German. As of 2013, there is no complete gathering of the writings of Leibniz

Questions for Discussion

1. What is the influence of the 17th century in the history of European culture?

2. What is the realistic significance of John Milton's *Paradise Lost*?

3. Why are there no representative Baroque style arts in Spain despite the fact that the Baroque arts originated there?

4. How did France during the 17th century become the leading power in Europe both politically and culturally?

5. What is the historic significance of the English Glorious Revolution?

6. Did the 17th century philosophy in Europe bear its marks on the American colonies?

Chapter 3 The Age of Enlightenment

1 The Background

The scientific discoveries and philosophic ideas in the 17th century bore in the 18th century, an era often referred to as the Age of Reason. The Age of Reason was marked by four different trends. The first was the growing concentration of political power in the great states, each of which was controlled by a ruling dynasty — a development that had begun during the Baroque era. France was the most powerful of these states, followed by Great Britain, Prussia, Austria, Russia and the Netherlands. The second was the return of the aristocracy to importance after a century or more of decline. The third trend was the achievement of political and cultural distinction by the middle class after a centuries-long rise from their origins in medieval times. The middle class supported those progressive thinkers who advocated social justice, and a thorough revolution of society. The intellectual and cultural movement encouraged by these thinkers is called the Enlightenment, and it constitutes the fourth and most important trend that helped to reshape Western life in the 1700s.

The Enlightenment was a progressive intellectual movement, which began in the 17th century and peaked in the 18th century throughout Western Europe, in the American colonies and in Russia in the 19th

century. It was an expression of the bourgeoisie against feudalism with a goal of "liberty, fraternity and equality". Its purpose was to reform society using reason (rather than tradition, faith and revelation) and advance knowledge through science. It promoted science and intellectual interchange and opposed superstition, intolerance and some abuses by church and state. It resulted in a wide variety of new ideas and advances in the fields of philosophy, science and medicine. Many historians marked the French Revolution as the crowning event of the Enlightenment era.

The Enlightenment Movement can be considered as the second significant intellectual movement since the Renaissance. It advocated freedom of politics and learning and "enlightenment" or "education" is considered to be the chief means for the betterment of society. Meanwhile, it also believed in the power of reason, which was considered as a yardstick for the measurement of all human activities and social relations.

According to scholarly opinion, the Enlightenment was preceded by the Age of Reason (if thought of as a short era) or by the Renaissance and the Reformation (if thought of as a long era). It was followed by Romanticism.

2 Literature during the Enlightenment Era

Literary works during this era bear clear marks of political tendency and democracy, depicting ordinary folks' life and criticizing the nobility. It also shows a respect for order and reason with emphasis on clarity of thought and orderly structure.

2.1 English Literature

2.1.1 Daniel Defoe

Daniel Defoe (1659 – 1731) was an English trader, writer, journalist, pamphleteer and spy, who gained fame for his novel *Robinson Crusoe*. Defoe is notable for being one of the earliest proponents of the novel, as he helped to popularize the literary form in Britain, and, along with others such as Richardson, is among the founders of the English realistic novel. A prolific and versatile writer, he wrote more than 500 books, pamphlets and journals on various topics including politics, crime, religion, marriage, psychology and the supernatural.

Defoe's novel *Robinson Crusoe* (1719) tells of a man's shipwreck on a deserted island and his subsequent adventures. The author based part of his narrative on the story of the Scottish castaway Alexander Selkirk, who spent four years stranded on the island of Juan Fernandez. He may have also been inspired by the Latin or English translation of a book by the Andalusian-Arab Muslim polymath Ibn Tufail, who was known as "Abubacer" in Europe. The Latin edition of the book was entitled *Philosophus Autodidactus* and it was an earlier novel that is also set on a deserted island.

Defoe's next novel was *Captain Singleton* (1720), a bipartite adventure story whose first half covers a traversal of Africa and whose second half taps into the contemporary fascination with piracy. It has been commended for its sensitive depiction of the close relationship between the eponymous hero and his religious mentor, the Quaker William Walters.

2.1.2 Jonathan Swift

Jonathan Swift (1667 – 1745) was an Anglo-Irish satirist, essayist, political pamphleteer (first for the Whigs, then for the Tories), poet and cleric who became Dean of St Patrick's Cathedral, Dublin.

He is remembered for works such as *Gulliver's Travels*, *A Modest Proposal*, *A Journal to Stella*, *Drapier's Letters*, *The Battle of the Books*, *An Argument Against Abolishing Christianity*, and *A Tale of a Tub*. Swift is probably the foremost prose satirist in the English language, and is less well known for his poetry. Swift originally published all of his works under pseudonyms — such as Lemuel Gulliver, Isaac Bickerstaff, MB Drapier — or anonymously. He is also known for being a master of two styles of satire: the Horatian and Juvenalian styles.

Gulliver's Travels was published in 1726, which is regarded as his masterpiece. As with his other writings, the *Travels* was published under a pseudonym, the fictional Lemuel Gulliver. Though it has often been mistakenly thought of and published in bowdlerized form as a children's book, it is a great and sophisticated satire of human nature based on Swift's experience of his times. *Gulliver's Travels* is an anatomy of human nature, a sardonic looking-glass, often criticized for its apparent misanthropy. Critics hail the work as a satiric reflection on the shortcomings of Enlightenment thought.

Drapier's Letters (1724) was a series of pamphlets against the monopoly granted by the English government to William Wood to provide the Irish with copper coinage. It was widely believed that Wood would need to flood Ireland with debased coinage in order to make a profit. In these "letters" Swift posed as a shop-keeper — a draper — in order to criticize the plan.

Swift's first major prose work, *A Tale of a Tub*, demonstrates many of the themes and stylistic techniques he would employ in his later work. It is at once wildly playful and funny while being pointed and harshly critical of its targets. In its main thread, the *Tale* recounts the exploits of three sons, representing the main threads of Christianity, who receive a bequest from their father of a coat each, with the added instructions to make no alterations whatsoever. However, the sons soon find that their coats have fallen out of current fashion, and begin to look for loopholes in their father's will that will let them make the needed alterations. As each finds his own means of getting around their father's admonition, they struggle with each other for power and dominance.

2. 1. 3 Alexander Pope

Alexander Pope (1688 – 1744) was an 18th-century English poet, best known for his satirical verse and for his translation of Homer. Famous for his use of the heroic couplet, he is the third-most frequently quoted writer in *The Oxford Dictionary of Quotations*, after Shakespeare and Tennyson. He made enormous literary achievements.

An Essay on Criticism was first published anonymously on 15 May 1711. Pope began writing the poem early in his career and took about three years to finish it. At the time the poem was published, the heroic couplet style in which it was written was a moderately new genre of poetry, and it was Pope's most ambitious work. *An Essay on Criticism* was an attempt to identify and refine his own positions as a poet and critic. The poem was said to be a response to an ongoing debate on the question of whether poetry should be natural, or written according to predetermined artificial rules inherited from the classical past.

Pope's most famous poem is*The Rape of the Lock*, first published in 1712, with a revised version published in 1714. A mock-epic, it satirizes a high-society quarrel between Arabella Fermor (the "Belinda" of the poem) and Lord Petre, who had snipped a lock of hair from her head without her permission. The satirical style is tempered, however, by a genuine and almost voyeuristic interest in the "beau-monde" (fashionable world) of 18th-century English society.

The *Essay on Man* is a philosophical poem, written in heroic couplets and published between 1732 and 1734. Pope intended this poem to be the centerpiece of a proposed system of ethics that was to be put forth in poetic form. It was a piece of work that Pope intended to make into a larger work; however, he did not live to complete it.

Translation of the *Iliad*

Pope had been fascinated by Homer since childhood. In 1713, he announced his plans to publish a translation of the *Iliad*. The work would be available by subscription, with one volume appearing every year over the course of six years.

His translation of the *Iliad* appeared between 1715 and 1720. Encouraged by the success of the *Iliad*, Pope translated the *Odyssey* and the translation appeared in 1726.

Edition of Shakespeare's Works

In this period, Pope was also employed by the publisher Jacob Tonson to produce an opulent new edition of Shakespeare. Pope also demoted about 1560 lines of Shakespearean material to footnotes, arguing that they were so "excessively bad" that Shakespeare could never have written them.

By the mid-18th-century new fashions in poetry emerged. A decade after Pope's death, Joseph Warton claimed that Pope's style of poetry was not the most excellent form of the art. The Romantic Movement that rose to prominence in early 19th – century England was more ambivalent towards his work. In the 20th century Pope's reputation was revived. The postwar period stressed the power of Pope's poetry, recognizing that Pope's immersion in Christian and Biblical culture lent depth to his poetry. Modern criticism of Pope focuses on the man, his circumstances and motivations, prompted by theoretical perspectives such as Marxism, feminism and other forms of post-structuralism.

2. 1. 4 Samuel Richardson

Samuel Richardson (1689 – 1761) was an 18th-century English writer and printer. He is best known for his three epistolary novels: *Pamela: Or, Virtue Rewarded* (1740), *Clarissa: Or the History of a Young Lady* (1748) and T*he History of Sir Charles Grandison* (1753). Richardson was an established printer and publisher for most of his life and printed almost 500 different works, with journals and magazines.

Richardson lost his first wife along with their five sons, and eventually remarried. Although with his second wife he had four daughters who lived to become adults, they had no male heir to continue running the printing business. While his print shop slowly ran down, at the age of 51 he wrote his first novel and immediately became one of the most popular and admired writers of his time. Richardson made the transition from master printer to novelist on 6 November 1740 with the publication of *Pamela: or, Virtue Rewarded*. *Pamela* was sometimes regarded as "the first English novel".

He knew leading figures in 18th-century England, including Samuel Johnson and Sarah Fielding. In the London literary world, he was a rival of Henry Fielding, and the two responded to each other's literary styles in their own novels. And his name was on the Index Librorum Prohibitorum, a list established by the Pope containing the names of books that Catholics were not allowed to read.

2. 1. 5 Henry Fielding

Henry Fielding (1707 – 1754) was an English novelist and dramatist known for his rich earthy humor and satirical prowess, and as the author of the novel *Tom Jones*. *The History of Tom Jones, a Foundling*, often known simply as *Tom Jones*, is a comic novel, which is both a Bildungsroman and Picaresque novel. First published on 28 February 1749, *Tom Jones* is among the earliest English prose works describable as a novel. The novel, totaling 346,747 words, is divided into 18 smaller books, each preceded by a discursive chapter, often on topics totally unrelated to the book itself. It is dedicated to George Lyttleton.

Aside from his literary achievements, he has a significant place in the history of law-enforcement, having founded (with his half-brother John) what some have called London's first police force, the Bow Street Runners, using his authority as a magistrate. His younger sister, Sarah, also became a successful writer. Fielding's ardent commitment to the cause of justice as a great humanitarian in the 1750s (for instance, his support of Elizabeth Canning) coincided with a rapid deterioration in his health. This continued to such an extent that he went abroad to Portugal in 1754 in search of a cure. He died in Lisbon two months later. His tomb is located inside the city's English Cemetery

2.2 French Literature

The great thinkers active in the philosophical arena during the French enlightenment were also important figures in literature.

2. 2. 1 Voltaire

Voltaire, the pseudonym of François-Marie Arouet (1694 – 1778), was a French Enlightenment writer.

Voltaire was considered to be a versatile writer, producing works in almost every literary form, including plays, poems, novels, essays, and historical and scientific works. He wrote more than 20,000 letters and more than 2,000 books and pamphlets. His most enduring works *Candide* is a French satire first published in 1759, in which he cast his sharpest criticism against nobility, philosophy, the church and cruelty. It begins with a young man, Candide, who is living a sheltered life in an Edenic paradise and being indoctrinated with Leibnizian optimism (or simply Optimism) by his mentor, Pangloss. The work describes the abrupt cessation of this lifestyle, followed by Candide's slow, painful disillusionment as he witnesses and experiences great hardships in the world.

Candide is characterized by its sarcastic tone, as well as by its erratic, fantastical and fast-moving plot. As expected by Voltaire, *Candide* has enjoyed both great success and great scandal. Immediately after its secretive publication, the book was widely banned because it contained religious blasphemy, political sedition and intellectual hostility hidden under a thin veil of naïveté. However, with its sharp wit and insightful portrayal of the human condition, the novel has since inspired many later authors and artists to mimic and adapt it.

Today, *Candide* is recognized as Voltaire's magnum opus and is often listed as part of the Western canon; it is arguably taught more than any other work of French literature. Though often considered as a representative text of the Enlightenment, the novel actually savagely criticized a number of Enlightenment philosophies and demonstrated that the Enlightenment was far from a massive movement.

2. 2. 2 Montesquieu

Charles-Louis de Secondat, baron de La Brède et de Montesquieu (1689 - 1755), generally referred to as simply Montesquieu, was a French social commentator and political thinker who lived during the Enlightenment.

He achieved literary success with his *Lettres Persanes* (*Persian Letters*) (1721), a literary work recounting the experiences of two Persian noblemen, Usbek and Rica, who are traveling through France. In the book, the king, the absolute monarchy, the Parliament, the Academy, University, were all very clearly ridiculed.

2. 2. 3 Jean-Jacques Rousseau

Jean-Jacques Rousseau (1712 - 1778), was a French philosopher, writer, and composer who was born in Geneva.

Emile (*On Education*) (1762) was Rousseau's works in which he presented the ideal citizen and the means of training the child for the State in accordance with nature, even to a sense of God. The most admirable part in this was that Rousseau showed a true, natural susceptibility to religion and to God.

Confessions, which is Rousseau's autobiographical writings, initiated the modern autobiography.

2. 2. 4 Denis Diderot

Denis Diderot (1713 - 1784) was a French philosopher, art critic, and writer. He was a prominent person during the Enlightenment and is best known for serving as co-founder and chief editor of and contributor to the *Encyclopédie* along with Jean le Rond d'Alembert.

Although the *Encyclopédie* (*Encyclopedia*) was Diderot's monumental piece, he was the author of many other works that sowed nearly every field of intellectual interest with new and creative ideas. He wrote sentimental plays, *Le Fils Naturel* (*The Natural Son*) (1757) and *Le Père de Famille* (*The Father of the Family*) (1758), accompanying them with essays on theatrical theory and practice, including "*Les Entretiens sur Le Fils Naturel*" (*Conversations on The Natural Son*), in which he announced the principles of a new drama: the "serious genre", a realistic midpoint between comedy and tragedy that stood in opposition to the stilted conventions of the classical French stage. His art criticism was also highly influential. Diderot's *Essais sur la Peinture* (*Essay on Paint*) was described by Johann Wolfgang von Goethe, as "a magnificent work, which speaks even more helpfully to the poet than to the painter, though to the painter too it is as a blazing torch".

2. 3 German Literature

By the mid-18th century the German Enlightenment in music, philosophy, science and literature emerged as an intellectual force. Frederick the Great (1712 – 1786), the King of Prussia (1740 – 1786), saw himself as a leader of the Enlightenment and patronized philosophers and scientists at his court in Berlin.

2. 3. 1 Gotthold Ephraim Lessing

Lessing (1729 – 1781) was aGerman writer, philosopher, dramatist, publicist and art critic, and one of the most outstanding representatives of the Enlightenment era. His plays and theoretical writings substantially influenced the development of German literature. He is widely considered by theatre historians to be the first dramaturg.

Lessing is important as a literary critic for his work *Laocoon: An Essay on the Limits of Painting and Poetry*. In this work, he argues against the tendency to take Horace's "ut pictura poesis" (as painting, so poetry) as prescriptive for literature. In other words, he objected to trying to write poetry using the same devices as one would in painting. Instead, poetry and painting each has its character (the former is extended in time; the latter is extended in space). This is related to Lessing's turn from French classicism to Aristotelian mimesis.

2. 3. 2 Wolfgang von Goethe

Wolfgang von Goethe (1749 – 1832) was a German writer, artist, and politician. His body of work includes epic and lyric poetry written in a variety of metres and styles: prose and verse dramas; memoirs; an autobiography; literary and aesthetic criticism; treatises on botany, anatomy, and colour; and four novels.

Among all his literary works, *Faust* is considered as his masterpiece and to be one of the greatest works of German literature, which is a tragic play in two parts: *Faust: Der Tragödie erster Teil* (*Faust: The First Part of the Tragedy*) and *Faust: Der Tragödie zweiter Teil* (*Faust: The Second Part of the Tragedy*). Although rarely staged in its entirety, it is the play with the largest audience numbers on German-language stages.

The short epistolary novel, *Die Leiden des jungen Werthers* (*The Sorrows of Young Werther*) published in 1774, recounts an unhappy romantic infatuation that ends in suicide. The novel remains in print in dozens of languages and its influence is undeniable; its central hero, an obsessive figure driven to despair and destruction by his unrequited love for the young Lotte, has become a pervasive literary archetype.

2. 3. 3 Johann Christoph Friedrich von Schiller

Johann Christoph Friedrich von Schiller (1759 – 1805) was a German poet, philosopher, historian, and playwright. During the last seventeen years of his life (1788 – 1805), Schiller struck up productive, if complicated, friendship with already famous and influential Johann Wolfgang von Goethe. They frequently discussed issues concerning aesthetics, and Schiller encouraged Goethe to finish works he left as sketches. This relationship and these discussions led to a period now referred to as Weimar Classicism. They also worked together on *Xenien*, a collection of short satirical poems in which both Schiller and Goethe challenge opponents to their philosophical vision.

A pivotal work by Schiller was *On the Aesthetic Education of Man in a Series of Letters*, first published in 1794, which was inspired by the great disenchantment Schiller felt about the French Revolution, its degeneration into violence and the failure of successive governments to put its ideals into practice.

Intrigue and Love was considered to be Schiller's masterpiece, which was his third play that shows how cabals and their intrigue destroy the love between Ferdinand von Walter, a nobleman's son, and Luise Miller, daughter of a middle-class musician.

3 Philosophy during the Enlightenment Era

The primary feature of Enlightenment philosophy was a profound faith in the power of reason and rational thought, which was regarded as the decisive source of all knowledge. The Age of Enlightenment had its beginnings in the Netherlands and in England where philosophers and teachers of constitutional law like Thomas Hobbes and John Locke developed a concept of an innate natural law, a natural religion, a social contract and human rights. Meanwhile, many philosophers during this era were also great literary figures, such as Voltaire, Rousseau, Montesquieu, etc.

3.1 French Enlightenment

Though John Locke was considered as the most influential Enlightenment thinkers, Enlightenment's greatest intellectual, social and political impact was felt in France. Among its strongest advocates were Voltaire, Montesquieu, Rousseau, and Diderot.

3.1.1 Voltaire

Voltaire, a French Enlightenment writer, historian and philosopher, was famous for his wit and for his advocacy of civil liberties, including freedom of religion, freedom of expression, free trade and separation of church and state and he was one of several Enlightenment figures whose works and ideas influenced important thinkers of both the American and French Revolutions.

3.1.1.1 Religion and Religious Tolerance

Voltaire did not believe that any single religious text or tradition of revelation was needed to believe in God. Voltaire's focus was rather on the idea of universal laws, demonstrable, and in the main, still waiting to be discovered in the physical world as well as those of the moral world, underlying every religious system, along with respect for nature reflecting the contemporary pantheism.

Like other key thinkers during the European Enlightenment, Voltaire considered himself a deist, expressing the idea: "What is faith? Is it to believe that which is evident? No. It is perfectly evident to my mind that there exists a necessary, eternal, supreme, and intelligent being. This is no matter of faith, but of reason."

3.1.1.2 Race and Slavery

Voltaire rejected the Christian Adam and Eve story and was a polygenist who speculated that each race had separate origins.

His most famous remark on slavery is found in "*Candide*", where the hero is horrified to learn "at what price we eat sugar in Europe". Elsewhere, he wrote caustically about "whites and Christians [who] proceed to purchase negroes cheaply, in order to sell them dear in America"

3. 1. 2 Montesquieu

Montesquieu, as a French social commentator and political thinker living during the Enlightenment, achieved not only literary success with his *Lettres Persanes* (*Persian Letters*) (1721), but also philosophical success in political theory.

Lettres Persanes prepared Montesquieu to his later and greatest work, *L'Esprit des lois* (*The Spirit of Law*, 1748), which made him famous for his articulation of the theory of separation of powers and which is taken for granted in modern discussions of government and implemented in many constitutions throughout the world.

Montesquieu's "*The Spirit of Law*" is the first consistent attempt to survey the varieties of human society, to classify and compare them and, within society, to study the inter-functioning of institutions. In this most influential work he divided French society into three classes (or trias politica, a term he coined): the monarchy, the aristocracy, and the commons. Montesquieu saw two types of governmental power existing: the sovereign and the administrative. The administrative powers were the executive, the legislative, and the judicial. These should be separate from and dependent upon each other so that the influence of any one power would not be able to exceed that of the other two, either singly or in combination. This was a radical idea because it completely eliminated the three Estates structure of the French Monarchy: the clergy, the aristocracy, and the people at large represented by the Estates-General, thereby erasing the last vestige of a feudalistic structure.

Montesquieu was somewhat ahead of his time in advocating major reform of slavery in *The Spirit of Law*. As part of his advocacy he presented a satirical hypothetical list of arguments for slavery, which has been open to contextomy. However, like many of his generation, Montesquieu also held a number of views that might today be judged controversial. He firmly accepted the role of a hereditary aristocracy and the value of primogeniture, and while he endorsed the idea that a woman could head a state, he held that she could not be effective as the head of a family.

3.1.3 Jean-Jacques Rousseau

Besides his achievements in literature, Rousseau's political philosophy influenced the French Revolution as well as the overall development of modern political, sociological and educational thought.

3.1.3.1 Theory of Natural Human

Rousseau criticized Hobbes for asserting that since man in the "state of nature … has no idea of goodness he must be naturally wicked; that he is vicious because he does not know virtue". On the contrary, Rousseau holds that "uncorrupted morals" prevail in the "state of nature" and he especially praised the admirable moderation of the Caribbeans in expressing the sexual urge despite the fact that they live in a hot climate, which "always seems to inflame the passions".

Rousseau asserted that the stage of human development associated with what he called "savages" was the best and most optimal in human development, between the less-than optimal extreme of brute animals on the one hand and the extreme of decadent civilization on the other.

3. 1. 3. 2 *The Social Contract*

Perhaps Rousseau's most important work is *The Social Contract*, which outlines the basis for a legitimate political order within a framework of classical republicanism. Published in 1762, it became one of the most influential works of political philosophy in the Western tradition. The treatise begins with the dramatic opening lines, "Man is born free, and everywhere he is in chains. Those who think themselves the masters of others are indeed greater slaves than they."

According to Rousseau, by joining together into civil society through the social contract and abandoning their claims of natural right, individuals can both preserve themselves and remain free. This is because submission to the authority of the general will of the people as a whole guarantees individuals against being subordinated to the wills of others and also ensures that they obey themselves because they are, collectively, the authors of the law.

The Social Contract, together with his another discourse *The Origin of Inequality* are cornerstones in modern political and social thought. During the era of the French Revolution, Rousseau was the most popular of the philosophers among members of the Jacobin Club. Rousseau was interred as a national hero in the Panthéon in Paris, in 1794, 16 years after his death.

3. 2 English Enlightenment

Figures such as John Locke and Thomas Hobbes sometimes are said to be Enlightenment figures, but in this book we would like to think them as great thinkers of the 17th century, even though their ideas and works had great influence on the Enlightenment.

Other 18th-century influential thinkers, such as Francis Hutcheson, Adam Smith and David Hume, paved the way for the modernization of Scotland and the entire Atlantic world.

3.2.1 Francis Hutcheson

Francis Hutcheson (1694 – 1746) was a philosopher born in Ireland to a family of Scottish Presbyterians who became one of the founding fathers of the Scottish Enlightenment. He championed political liberty and the right of popular rebellion against tyranny.

Hutcheson was an important influence on the works of several significant Enlightenment thinkers, including David Hume and Adam Smith.

3.2.2 Adam Smith

Adam Smith (1723 – 1790) was a Scottish moral philosopher and a pioneer of political economy. One of the key figures of the Scottish Enlightenment, Adam Smith is best known for two classic works: *The Theory of Moral Sentiments* (1759), and *An Inquiry into the Nature and Causes of the Wealth of Nations* (1776). The latter, usually abbreviated as *The Wealth of Nations*, is considered his magnum opus and the first modern work of economics. Smith is cited as the father of modern economics and is still among the most influential thinkers in the field of economics today. In 2009, Smith was named among the "Greatest Scots" of all time, in a vote run by Scottish television channel STV.

3.2.3 David Hume

David Hume (1711 – 1776) was a Scottish philosopher, historian, economist, and essayist, known especially for his philosophical empiricism and skepticism. He was one of the most important figures in the history of Western philosophy and the Scottish Enlightenment. Hume is often grouped with John Locke, George Berkeley, and a handful of others as a British Empiricist.

3.3 German Philosophy

In the Enlightenment era, philosophy was not just felt in France; it was also felt in Germany, where Immanuel Kant was considered as a representative figure.

Immanuel Kant (1724 - 1804) was a German philosopher who researched, lectured and wrote on philosophy and anthropology during the Enlightenment at the end of the 18th century.

Kant's major work, *the Critique of Pure Reason* aimed to unite reason with experience to move beyond what he took to be failures of traditional philosophy and metaphysics.

His ideas influenced many thinkers in Germany during his lifetime. He settled and moved philosophy beyond the debate between the rationalists and empiricists. The philosophers Fichte, Schelling, Hegel and Schopenhauer amended and developed the Kantian system, thus bringing about various forms of German idealism. Kantian philosophy, particularly as developed by the Hegel, was the basis on which the structure of Marxism was built; the dialectical method, used by both Hegel and Karl Marx, was a product of the method of reasoning used by Kant. Therefore, he is seen as a major figure in the history and development of philosophy. German and European thinking progressed after his time, and his influence still inspires philosophical work today.

4 Arts in the Enlightenment Era

4.1 Rococo Style

Rococo, less commonly roccoco, also referred to as "Late Baroque", is an 18th-century artistic movement and style, which affected several aspects of the arts including painting, sculpture, architecture, interior design, decoration, literature, music and theatre. The Rococo developed in the early part of the 18th century in Paris, France as a reaction against the grandeur, symmetry and strict regulations of the Baroque, especially that of the Palace of Versailles. In such a way, Rococo artists opted for a more jocular, florid and graceful approach to Baroque art and architecture. Rococo art and architecture in such a way was ornate and made strong usage of creamy, pastel-like colors, asymmetrical designs, curves and gold. Unlike the more politically focused Baroque, the Rococo had more playful and often witty artistic themes.

In a broad sense, rococo style applies to decoration, paintings, sculpture, furniture and architecture, etc. In terms of the interior decoration, rococo means, firstly, the forms are almost flat instead of being, as in baroque schemes, in high relief; second, architectural and sculptural features are eliminated so that the designer is confronted with a smooth surface, interrupted only by the window recesses and the chimneypiece. In Rococo painting, the powerful rhythms, dark colors, and heroic subjects characteristic of baroque painting gave way to quick, delicate movements, pale colors, and subjects illustrating the varieties of love: romantic love, as in the Antoine Watteau *Pilgrimage to Cythera* (1717); bodily love, as in the Francois Boucher *Cupid a Captive* (1754). Sculpture was equally lively, but its most typical expression was portrait busts. During the second quarter of the 18th century, the rococo style spread from France to other countries, and above all to Germany, where the rococo took a more fanciful and original turn with greater emphasis on forms derived from nature, and evolved out of, rather than in reaction against the baroque style.

The rococo style began to decline in the 1760s, and within 20 years it was replaced, together with the baroque, by neoclassicism.

Critics who condemned it criticized it as tasteless, playful, and symbolic of a corrupt society. Owing to Rococo love of shell-like curves and focus on decorative arts, some critics used the term to derogatively imply that the style was frivolous or merely modish. When the term was first used in English in about 1836, it was a colloquialism meaning "old-fashioned", especially when compared to neoclassicism; despite this, it has been praised for its aesthetic qualities, and since the mid-19th century, the term has been accepted by art historians. While there is still some debate about the historical significance of the style to art in general, Rococo is now widely recognized as a major period in the development of European art.

4.2 Music

Ever since the 17th century onwards, the 400 hundred years in Europe experienced four stages, namely, the Baroque Music, the Classical Music, the Romantic Music and the Modern Music. During this period, there appeared various types of music such as serenade, sonata, symphony, concerto, fantasy, romance, minuet, and ballade. Among the great composers in this period, two must be mentioned. Their achievements had paved the way for the development and achievement of music during the Enlightenment Era.

4. 2. 1 J. S. Bach

J. S. Bach (1685 - 1750) was a German composer, organist, harpsichordist, violist, and violinist of the Baroque period. He enriched many established German styles through his skill in counterpoint, harmonic and motivic organization, and the adaptation of rhythms, forms, and textures from abroad, particularly from Italy and France. Many of Bach's works are still known today, such as the *Brandenburg Concertos*, the *Mass in B minor*, Matthauspassion, the *Well-Tempered Clavier*, his cantatas, chorales, partitas, passions, and organ works. His music is revered for its intellectual depth, technical command, and artistic beauty.

4. 2. 2 George F. Handel

George F. Handel (1685 - 1759) was a German-born British Baroque composer, famous for his operas, oratorios, anthems and organ concertos. Handel was born in a family indifferent to music. He received critical musical training in Halle, Hamburg and Italy before settling in London (1712) and becoming a naturalized British subject in 1727. By then he was strongly influenced by the great composers of the Italian Baroque and the middle-German polyphonic choral tradition.

Handel is regarded as one of the greatest composers of all time, with works such as *Water Music*, *Music for the Royal Fireworks* and *Messiah* remaining popular. Handel composed more than forty operas in over thirty years, and since the late 1960s, with the revival of baroque music and original instrumentation, interest in Handel's operas has grown. His operas contain remarkable human characterization — especially for a composer not known for his love affairs.

4. 2. 3 Franz Joseph Haydn

Franz Joseph Haydn (1732 – 1809), known as Joseph Haydn, was an Austrian composer, one of the most prolific and prominent composers of the Classical period. He is often called the "Father of the Symphony" and "Father of the String Quartet" because of his important contributions to these forms. He was also instrumental in the development of the piano trio and in the evolution of sonata form. Haydn's work was central to the development of what came to be called sonata form. His practice, however, differed in some ways from that of Mozart and Beethoven, his younger contemporaries who likewise excelled in this form of composition.

A lifelong resident of Austria, Haydn spent much of his career as a court musician for the wealthy Esterházy family on their remote estate. Isolated from other composers and trends in music until the later part of his long life, he was, as he put it, "forced to become original". At the time of his death, he was one of the most celebrated composers in Europe. *London* and *Surprise* are among his most famous works.

4. 2. 4 Wolfgang Amadeus Mozart

Mozart (1756 – 1791) was a prolific and influential composer of the Classical era. Mozart showed prodigious ability from his earliest childhood. Already competent on keyboard and violin, he composed from the age of five and performed before European royalty. At 17, he was engaged as a court musician in Salzburg, but grew restless and traveled in search of a better position, always composing abundantly. While visiting Vienna in 1781, he was dismissed from his Salzburg position. He chose to stay in the capital, where he achieved fame but little financial security. During his final years in Vienna, he composed many of his best-known symphonies, concertos, and operas, and portions of the *Requiem*, which was largely unfinished at the time of his death. The circumstances of his early death have been much mythologized. He was survived by his wife Constanze and two sons.

Among his works, *the Marriage of Figaro*, *Don Juan* and *the Magic Flute* were considered as representative of his works.

4. 2. 5 Ludwig van Beethoven

Ludwig van Beethoven (1770 – 1827) was a German composer and pianist. A crucial figure in the transition between the Classical and Romantic eras in Western art music, he remains one of the most famous and influential of all composers. His best known compositions include 9 symphonies, 5 concertos for piano, 32 piano sonatas, and 16 string quartets. He also composed other chamber music, choral works (including the celebrated *Missa Solemnis*), and songs.

Third Symphony was completed in 1804, which was considered by Beethoven as his most favorite symphony. It was originally dedicated to Napoleon. But when he learned Napoleon proclaimed to be an emperor, he tore the cover of the score on which was written the dedication to Napoleon.

Questions for Discussions

1. What is the influence of Enlightenment on the French Revolution?

2. Compare the New Culture Movement in China and the Enlightenment Movement.

3. In terms of anti-superstition, the Enlightenment far surpassed the Renaissance. How to understand this?

4. What are the main reasons for the rise of the Enlightenment?

5. Compare and contrast the Renaissance and the Enlightenment Movement.

6. Why did Montesquieu put up the "separation of powers"?

7. What are the main ideas put forward by Rousseau in his *Social Contract*?

Chapter 4 Romanticism

1 Introduction

Romanticism (or the Romantic Era/Period) was an artistic, literary, and intellectual movement that originated in Western Europe, and gained strength during the Industrial Revolution. Romanticism began in 1798, the year of the first edition of *Lyrical Ballads* by Wordsworth and Coleridge and of the composition of *Hymns to the Night* by Novalis, and ended in 1832, the year which marked the deaths of both Sir Walter Scott and Goethe. It was partly a revolt against aristocratic social and political norms of the Age of Enlightenment and a reaction against the scientific rationalization of nature. It was embodied most strongly in the visual arts, music, and literature, but had a major impact on historiography, education and the natural sciences. Its effect on politics was considerable and complex; while for much of the peak Romantic period it was associated with liberalism and radicalism, in the long term its effect on the growth of nationalism was probably more significant.

Resulting in part from the libertarian and egalitarian ideals of the French Revolution, the romantic movements had in common only a revolt against the prescribed rules of classicism. The basic aims of romanticism were various: a return to nature and to belief in the goodness of humanity;

the rediscovery of the artist as a supremely individual creator; the development of nationalistic pride; and the exaltation of the senses and emotions over reason and intellect. In addition, romanticism was a philosophical revolt against rationalism.

Although the movement was rooted in the German *Sturm und Drang* movement, which prized intuition and emotion over Enlightenment rationalism, the ideologies and events of the French Revolution laid the background from which both Romanticism and the Counter-Enlightenment emerged. The confines of the Industrial Revolution also had their influence on Romanticism, which was in part an escape from modern realities; indeed, in the second half of the 19th century, Realism was offered as a polarized opposite to Romanticism. Romanticism elevated the achievements of what it perceived as heroic individualists and artists, whose pioneering examples would elevate society. It also legitimized the individual imagination as a critical authority, which permitted freedom from classical notions of form in art.

2 Historical Background

2.1 Industrial Revolution

Britain's Industrial Revolution began during the mid-18th century and lasted until the turn of the 20th century. The Industrial Revolution in England was characterized by the replacement of manual labor by machines, the emergence of large-scale manufacturing, the modernization of cities, and the social impact of these changes. The Industrial Revolution changed the look of cities across Britain.

The Industrial Revolution was a positive era to have occurred in Britain. In the beginning, however, the Industrial Revolution appeared to bring no benefits at all to the country. Living conditions in cities became unsanitary, as well as cramped and impoverished. Factories subjected men, women, and even children workers to low wages, harsh punishments, and unprotected work around dangerous machinery. The tremendous use of coal in industrial production polluted the atmosphere, as well as people's lungs, and workers' conditions in the coal mines were not much better than in factories. Food was expensive for poor factory workers, and thus they could afford only to eat rancid meats, fatty fried foods, and stale bread, which contributed to the extreme malnutrition and sickness in the cities.

There were many artistic movements during the period of Britain's industrialization, each of which was a reaction to the feelings of the time, as well as to the movement which had preceded it. By the time that the Industrial Revolution really took hold, some artists were at differences with the ideals which it espoused, such as those of discipline, temperance, structure, and views of the Enlightenment. These feelings translated into the Romantic Movement, which encouraged individualism, freedom, and emotion. Romanticism was probably the most important artistic movement to flourish during the Industrial Revolution. It had the most widespread effects on the general population, and its artistic achievements are still admired today.

The Industrial Revolution changed the landscape. Small towns grew into huge cities. In the countryside, bridges, viaducts, railroad lines, and canals were built to improve transportation. The destruction of the natural beauty of the landscape triggered a nostalgic reaction in art and literature. The literature of the Industrial Revolution includes essays, fiction, and poetry that respond to the enormous growth of technology. Romanticism in

British literature developed in a different form slightly later, mostly associated with the poets William Wordsworth and Samuel Taylor Coleridge. Both poets were also involved in utopian social thought in the wake of the French Revolution. The poet and painter William Blake is the most extreme example of the Romantic sensibility in Britain, epitomized by his claim "I must create a system or be enslaved by another man's". Romanticism also refers specifically to late-18th-and early-19th-century European culture, as contrasted with 18th-century classicism. Inspired by the ideas of Jean Jacques Rousseau and by contemporary social change and revolution, Romanticism emerged as a reaction to 18th-century values, asserting emotion and intuition over rationalism, the importance of the individual over social conformity, and the exploration of natural and psychic wildernesses over classical restraint.

2.2 French Revolution

The French Revolution (1789 – 1799), was a period of radical social and political upheaval in France that had a lasting impact on French history and more broadly throughout the world. French society underwent an epic transformation, as feudal, aristocratic and religious privileges evaporated under a sustained assault from radical left-wing political groups, masses on the streets, and peasants in the countryside. Old ideas about tradition and hierarchy — of monarchy, aristocracy, and religious authority — were abruptly overthrown by new Enlightenment principles of equality, citizenship and inalienable rights.

The French Revolution played a huge role in influencing Romantic writers. As the Revolution began to play out, the absolute monarchy that had ruled France for centuries collapsed in only three years. This resulted in a complete transformation of society. A majority of the population was greatly in favor of this as the working class had been suffering oppression for many years. According to Albert Hancock, in his book *The French Revolution and the English Poets: a study in historical criticism*, "The French Revolution came, bringing with it the promise of a brighter day, the promise of regenerated man and regenerated earth. It was hailed with joy and acclamation by the oppressed, by the ardent lovers of humanity, by the poets, whose task it is to voice the human spirit."

A common theme among some of the most widely known romantic poets is their acceptance and approval of the French Revolution. William Wordsworth, Samuel Taylor Coleridge, Lord Byron, and Percy Shelley all shared the same view of the French Revolution as it being the beginning of a change in the current ways of society and helping to better the lives of the oppressed. As the French Revolution changed the lives of virtually everyone in the nation and even continent because of its drastic and immediate shift in social reformation, it greatly influenced many writers at the time. Hancock writes, "There is no need to recount here in detail how the French Revolution, at the close of the last century, was the great stimulus to the intellectual and emotional life of the civilized world, how it began by inspiring all liberty-loving men with hope and joy."

Prior to the French Revolution, poems and literature were typically written about and to aristocrats and clergy, and rarely for or about the working man. However, when the roles of society began to shift resulting from the French Revolution, and with the emergence of Romantic writers, this changed. Romantic poets such as Wordsworth, Coleridge, Byron, and Shelley started to write works for and about the working man; pieces that the common man could relate to.

Literature began to take a new turn when the spirit of the revolution caught the entire nation and turned things in a whole new direction. The newly acquired freedom of the common people did not only bring about just laws and living but ordinary people also had the freedom to think for themselves, and in turn the freedom to express themselves. Triggered by the revolutionary spirit, the writers of the time were full of creative ideas and were waiting for a chance to unleash them. Under the new laws writers and artists were given a considerable amount of freedom to express themselves which did well to pave the way to set a high standard for literature.

3 Origins and Inspiration

By the late 18th century in France and Germany, literary taste began to turn from classical and neoclassical conventions. Inspiration for the romantic approach initially came from two great shapers of thought, French philosopher Jean Jacques Rousseau and German writer Johann Wolfgang von Goethe.

3.1 The Romantic Spirit

Rousseau established the cult of the individual and championed the freedom of the human spirit; his famous announcement was "I felt before I thought". Goethe and his compatriots, philosopher and critic Johann Gottfried von Herder and historian Justus Möser, provided more formal precepts and collaborated on a group of essays entitled *Von deutscher Art und Kunst* (*Of German Style and Art*, 1773). In this work the authors extolled the romantic spirit as manifested in German folk songs, Gothic architecture, and the plays of English playwright William Shakespeare.

Goethe sought to imitate Shakespeare's free and untrammeled style in his *Götz von Berlichingen* (1773; translated 1799), a historical drama about a 16th-century robber knight. The play, which justifies revolt against political authority, inaugurated the Sturm und Drang (storm and stress) movement, a forerunner of German romanticism. Goethe's novel *The Sorrows of Young Werther* (1774; translated 1779) was also in this tradition. One of the great influential documents of romanticism, this work exalts sentiment, even to the point of justifying committing suicide because of unrequited love. The book set a tone and mood much copied by the romantics in their works and in their personal lives: a fashionable tendency to frenzy, melancholy, world-weariness, and even self-destruction.

3.2 The Romantic Style

The preface to the second edition of *Lyrical Ballads* (1800), by English poets William Wordsworth and Samuel Taylor Coleridge was also of prime importance as a manifesto of literary romanticism. Here, the two poets affirmed the importance of feeling and imagination to poetic creation and disclaimed conventional literary forms and subjects. Thus, as romantic literature everywhere developed, imagination was praised over reason, emotions over logic, and intuition over science — making way for a vast body of literature of great sensibility and passion. This literature emphasized a new flexibility of form adapted to varying content, encouraged the development of complex and fast-moving plots, and allowed mixed genres (tragicomedy and the mingling of the grotesque and the sublime) and freer style.

No longer tolerated, for example, were the fixed classical conventions, such as the famous three unities (time, place, and action) of tragedy. An increasing demand for spontaneity and lyricism — qualities that the adherents of romanticism found in folk poetry and in medieval romance — led to a rejection of regular meters, strict forms, and other conventions of the classical tradition. In English poetry, for example, blank verse largely superseded the rhymed couplet that dominated 18th-century poetry. The opening lines of the swashbuckling melodrama *Hernani* (1830; translated 1830), by the great French romantic writer Victor Hugo, are a departure from the conventional 18th-century rules of French versification; and in the preface to his drama *Cromwell* (1827; translated 1896), a famous critical document in its own right, Hugo not only defended his break from traditional dramatic structure but also justified the introduction of the grotesque into art. In their choice of heroes, the romantic writers replaced the static universal types of classical 18th-century literature with more complex, idiosyncratic characters; and a great deal of drama, fiction, and poetry was devoted to a celebration of Rousseau's "common man".

4 The Great Romantic Themes

As the Romantic Movement spread from France and Germany to England and then to the rest of Europe and across to the western hemisphere, certain themes and moods, often intertwined, became the concern of almost all 19th-century writers.

4.1 Libertarianism

Many of the libertarian and abolitionist movements of the late 18th and early 19th centuries were engendered by the romantic philosophy — the desire to be free of convention and tyranny, and the new emphasis on the rights and dignity of the individual. Just as the insistence on rational, formal, and conventional subject matter that had typified neoclassicism was reversed, the authoritarian regimes that had encouraged and sustained neoclassicism in the arts were inevitably subjected to popular revolutions. Political and social causes became dominant themes in romantic poetry and prose throughout the Western world, producing many vital human documents that are still pertinent. The year 1848, in which Europe was wracked by political upheaval, marked the flood tide of romanticism in Italy, Austria, Germany, and France.

In *William Tell* (1804; translated 1825), by German dramatist Friedrich von Schiller, an obscure medieval mountaineer becomes an immortal symbol of opposition to tyranny and foreign rule. In the novel *The Betrothed* (1825 – 1827; translated 1834), by Italian writer Alessandro Manzoni, a peasant couple become instruments in the final crushing of feudalism in northern Italy. Lord Byron and Percy Bysshe Shelley, who for some most typify the romantic poet (in their personal lives as well as in their work), wrote resoundingly in protest against social and political wrongs and in defense of the struggles for liberty in Italy and Greece. Russian poet Aleksandr Sergeyevich Pushkin, whose admiration for the work of Byron is clearly manifested, attracted notoriety for his *Ode to Liberty* (1820); like many other romanticists, he was persecuted for political subversion.

The general romantic dissatisfaction with the organization of society was often channeled into specific criticism of urban society. *La maison du berger* (*The Shepherd's Hut*, 1844), by French poet Alfred Victor de Vigny, expresses the view that such an abode has more nobility than a palace. Earlier, Rousseau had written that people were born free but that everywhere civilization put them in chains. This feeling of oppression was frequently expressed in poetry — for example, in the works of English visionary William Blake, writing in the poem "Milton" (about 1804 – 1808) of the "dark Satanic mills" that were beginning to deface the English countryside; or in Wordsworth's long poem *The Prelude* (1850), which speaks of "... the close and overcrowded haunts/Of cities, where the human heart is sick".

4.2 Nature

Basic to such sentiments was an interest central to the Romantic Movement: the concern with nature and natural surroundings. Delight in unspoiled scenery and in the (presumably) innocent life of rural dwellers is perhaps first recognizable as a literary theme in such a work as *The Seasons* (1726 – 1730), by Scottish poet James Thomson. The work is commonly cited as a formative influence on later English romantic poetry and on the nature tradition represented in English literature, most notably by Wordsworth. Often combined with this feeling for rural life is a generalized romantic melancholy, a sense that change is imminent and that a way of life is being threatened. Such intimations were early evinced in *Ode to Evening* (1747) by William Collins, *Elegy Written in a Country Churchyard* (1751) by Thomas Gray, and *The Borough* (1810) by George Crabbe. The melancholic strain later developed as a separate theme, as in *Ode on Melancholy* (1820) by John Keats, or — in a different time and place — in the works of American writers: the novels and tales of Nathaniel Hawthorne, which probe the depths of human nature in puritanical New England, or the macabre tales and melancholy poetry of Edgar Allan Poe.

In another vein in American literature, the romantic interest in untrammeled nature is found in such writers as Washington Irving, whose *The Sketch Book of Geoffrey Crayon, Gent.* (1819 – 1820), a collection of descriptive stories about the Hudson River valley, reflects the author's knowledge of European folktales as well as contemporary romantic poetry and the Gothic novel. The *Leather-Stocking Tales* by James Fenimore Cooper celebrates the beauty of the American wilderness and the simple frontier life; in romantic fashion they also idealize the Native American as (in Rousseau's phrase) the "noble savage". By the middle of the 19th century the nature tradition was absorbed by American literary transcendentalism, chiefly expressed in the essays of Ralph Waldo Emerson and Henry David Thoreau.

4.3 The Lure of the Exotic

In the spirit of their new freedom, romantic writers in all cultures expanded their imaginary horizons spatially and chronologically. They turned back to the Middle Ages (5th century to 15th century) for themes and settings and chose locales ranging from the awesome Hebrides of the Ossianic tradition, as in the work of Scottish poet James MacPherson, to the Asian setting of Xanadu evoked by Coleridge in his unfinished lyric "Kubla Khan". The compilation of old English and Scottish ballads by English poet Thomas Percy was a seminal work; his *Reliques of Ancient English Poetry* (1765) exerted a significant influence on the form and content of later romantic poetry. The nostalgia for the Gothic past mingled with the tendency to the melancholic and produced a fondness for ruins, graveyards, and the supernatural as themes. In English literature, representative works include Keats' *The Eve of St. Agnes*, the Gothic novels of Matthew Gregory Lewis, and *The Castle of Otranto* (1764) by Horace Walpole. *The Lay of the Last Minstrel* (1805), by Scottish writer Sir Walter Scott, and his historical novels, the Waverley series (1814 – 1825) combine these concerns: love of the picturesque, preoccupation with the heroic past, and delight in mystery and superstition.

4.4 The Supernatural

The trend toward the irrational and the supernatural was an important component of English and German romantic literature. It was reinforced on the one hand by disillusion with 18th-century rationalism and on the other by the rediscovery of a body of older literature — folktales and ballads — collected by Percy and by German scholars Jacob and Wilhelm Karl Grimm and Danish writer Hans Christian Andersen. From such material comes, for example, the motif of the doppelgänger (German for "double"). Many romantic writers, especially in Germany, were fascinated with this concept, perhaps because of the general romantic concern with self-identity. Poet Heinrich Heine wrote a lyric apocryphally titled *Der Doppelgänger* (1827; translated 1846); *The Devil's Elixir* (1815 – 1816; translated 1824), a short novel by E. T. A. Hoffmann, is about a double; and *Peter Schlemihl's Remarkable Story* (1814; translated 1927), by Adelbert von Chamisso, the tale of a man who sells his shadow to the devil, can be considered a variation on the theme. Later, Russian master Fyodor Mikhaylovich Dostoyevsky wrote his famous novel *The Double* (1846), an analysis of paranoia in a humble clerk.

5 Romanticism in Different Countries

5.1 Germany

At the outset, the German romanticism was definitely a *movement*. It was organized, self-conscious, and critical. Indeed, it was in criticism and not in creative literature that its highest successes were won. The German romanticists constituted a compact group with coherent aims. They were intimate friends and associates; travelled, lived, and worked together; edited each other's books and married each other's sisters. They had a theory of art, a programme, and a propaganda; were aggressive and polemical, attacking their adversaries in reviews, and in satirical tales, poems, and plays. Their headquarters were at Jena. Their organ was the *Athenoeum*, established by Friedrich Schlegel at Berlin in 1798, the date of Wordsworth's and Coleridge's "Lyrical Ballads", and the climacteric year of English and German romanticism.

A second respect of German romanticism was its thoroughgoing character. It is the disposition of the German mind to synthesize thought and life, to carry out theory into practice. It seeks to interpret all human activities from a central principle; to apply its highest abstractions to literature, government, religion, the fine arts, and society. "Tragedies and romances," wrote Mme. De Stael, "have more importance in Germany than in any other country. They take them seriously there; and to read such and such a book, or see such and such a play, has an influence on the destiny and the life. What they admire as art, they wish to introduce into real life; and poetry, philosophy, the ideal, in short, have often an even greater empire over the Germans than nature and the passions." In proof of this, she adduces the number of young Germans who committed suicide in consequence of reading "Werther"; or took to highway robbery in emulation of "Die Rauber".

The German romantic school, in the limited and precise sense of the term, consisted of the brothers August Wilhelm and Friedrich Schlegel,

Ludwig Tieck, Friedrich von Hardenberg (Novalis), Johann Dietrich Gries, Tieck's friend Wackenroder, and — at a distance — Zacharias Werner, the dramatist; besides a few others, their associates or disciples. These were, as has been said, personal friends, they began to be heard of about 1795; and their quarters were at Jena and Berlin. A later or younger group (*Spaetromantiker*) gathered in 1808 about the *Zeitung fuer Einsiedler*, published at Heidelberg. These were Clemens Brentano, Achim von Arnim, Ludwig Uhland, Joseph Goerres, and the brothers Jacob and Wilhelm Grimm. Arnim, Brentano, and Goerres were residing at the time at Heidelberg; the others contributed from a distance. Arnim edited the *Einsiedler*; Goerres was teaching in the university. There were, of course, many other adherents of the school, working individually at different times and places, scattered indeed all over Germany, and of various degrees of importance or unimportance.

The most popular of the German romanticists was Friedrich Baron de la Motte Fouque, the descendant of a family exiled from France by the Revocation of the *Edict of Nantes*, and himself an officer in the Prussian army in the war of liberation. Fouque's numerous romances, in all of which he upholds the ideal of Christian knighthood, have been, many of them, translated into English. *Aslauga's Knight* appeared in Carlyle's *Specimens of German Romance* (1827); *Sintram*, *Undine*, and *Der Zauberring* had been translated even earlier. *Thiodolf the Icelander* and others have also been current in English circulating libraries.

5.2 France

In France, as in Germany, there was a romantic school, whose members were united by common literary principles and by personal association. There were sharply defined and hostile factions of classics and romantics, with party cries, watchwords, and shibboleths; a propaganda carried on and a polemic waged in pamphlets, prefaces, and critical journals. Above all there was a leader — Victor Hugo.

One point in which the French movement differed from the German was in the suddenness and violence of the outbreak. It was not so much a gradual development as a revolution, an explosion. The reason of this is to be found in the firmer hold which academic tradition had in France, the fountainhead of 18th century classicism. Romanticism had a special work to do in the land of literary convention in asserting the freedom of art and the unity of art and life. Everything that is in life, said Hugo, is, or has a right to be in art. The French, in political and social matters the most revolutionary people of Europe, were the most conservative in matters of taste. The Revolution even intensified the reigning classicism by giving it a republican turn. The Jacobin orators appealed constantly to the examples of the Greek and Roman democracies. The Goddess of Reason was enthroned in place of God, Sunday was abolished, and the names of the months and of the days of the week were changed. Dress under the Directory was patterned on antique modes — the liberty cap was Phrygian — and children born under the Republic were named after Roman patriots, Brutus, Cassius, etc. The great painter of the Revolution was David, who painted his subjects in togas, with backgrounds of Greek temples. Voltaire's classicism was monarchical and held to the Louis XIV. tradition; David's was republican. And yet the recognised formulae of taste and criticism were the same in 1800 as in 1775, or in 1675.

A second feature of the French romanticism was its local concentration at Paris. The centripetal forces have always been greater in France than in

England and Germany. The earlier group of German *Romantiker* was, indeed, united for a time at Jena and Berlin; and the *Spaetromantiker* at Heidelberg. But this was dispersion itself as compared with the intense focusing of intellectual rays from every quarter of France upon the capital.

The French movement kept itself almost entirely within the domain of art, and did not carry out its principles with German thoroughness and consistency into politics and religion. It made no efforts towards a practical restoration of the Middle Ages. Chateaubriand in his *Genie du Christianisme* attempted a sort of aesthetic revival of Catholic Christianity, which had suffered so heavily by the deistic teachings of the last century and the atheism of the Revolution. Victor Hugo began in his *Odes et Ballades* (1822) as an enthusiastic adherent of monarchy and the church. But he advanced quite rapidly towards liberalism both in politics and religion. And of the young men who surrounded him, like Gautier, Labrunie, Sainte-Beuve, Musset, De Vigny, and others, it can only be affirmed that they were legitimist or republican, Catholic or agnostic, just as it happened and without affecting their fidelity to the literary canons of the new school.

The romantic school in France had not only its poets, dramatists, and critics, but its painters, architects, sculptors, musical composers, and actors. Romanticism in France was, in a special sense, an effort for freedom, passion, and originality, as against rule, authority, and convention. "Romanticism," says Victor Hugo, "so many times poorly defined, is nothing else than liberalism in literature…Literary liberty is the child of political liberty."

Another special feature of French romanticism was the important part taken by the theatre in the history of the movement. The stage was the citadel of classical prejudice, and it was about it that the fiercest battles were fought. The climacteric year was 1830, in which year Victor Hugo's tragedy, *Hernani, or Castilian Honour*, was put on at the Theatre Francais on February 25th, and ran for thirty nights. The representation was a fight between the classics and the romantics, and there was almost a mob in the theatre. The dramatic censorship under Charles X, though strict, was used in the interest of political rather than aesthetic orthodoxy.

5.3 Other Countries

Early Russian Romanticism is associated with the writers Konstantin Batyushkov (*A Vision on the Shores of the Lethe*, 1809), Vasily Zhukovsky (*The Bard*, 1811; *Svetlana*, 1813) and Nikolay Karamzin (*Poor Liza*, 1792; *Julia*, 1796; *Martha the Mayoress*, 1802; *The Sensitive and the Cold*, 1803). However, the principal exponent of Romanticism in Russia is Alexander Pushkin (*The Prisoner of the Caucasus*, 1820 - 1821; *The Robber Brothers*, 1822; *Ruslan and Ludmila*, 1820; *Eugene Onegin*, 1825 - 1832). Pushkin's work influenced many writers in the 19th century and led to his eventual recognition as Russia's greatest poet. Other Russian poets include Mikhail Lermontov (*A Hero of Our Time*, 1839), Fyodor Tyutchev (*Silentium!*, 1830), Yevgeny Baratynsky's (*Eda*, 1826), Anton Delvig, and Wilhelm Küchelbecker.

Influenced heavily by Lord Byron, Lermontov sought to explore the Romantic emphasis on metaphysical discontent with society and self, while Tyutchev's poems often described scenes of nature or passions of love. Tyutchev commonly operated with such categories as night and day, north and south, dream and reality, cosmos and chaos, and the still world of winter and spring teeming with life. Baratynsky's style was fairly classical in nature, dwelling on the models of the previous century.

In predominantly Roman Catholic countries Romanticism was less pronounced than in Germany and Britain, and developed later, after the rise of Napoleon; it is often taken to begin with the publication of Adam Mickiewicz's first poems in 1822, and end with the crushing of the January Uprising of 1863 against the Russians. A very strong aspect of Romanticism in Poland was its relation to and inspiration from Polish history. Polish Romanticism revived the old "Sarmatism" traditions of Polish nobility (the szlachta). This close connection between Polish Romanticism and Polish history became one of the defining qualities of the literature of Polish Romanticism period, differentiating it from that of other countries. They had not suffered the loss of national statehood as was the case with Poland.

Romanticism in Spanish literature developed a well-known literature with a huge variety of poets and playwrights. The most important Spanish poet during this movement was José de Espronceda. After him there were other poets like Gustavo Adolfo Bécquer, Mariano José de Larra and the dramatist José Zorrilla, author of *Don Juan Tenorio*.

Spanish Romanticism also influenced regional literatures. For example, in Catalonia and in Galicia there was a national boom of writers in the local languages, like the Catalan Jacint Verdaguer and the Galician Rosalía de Castro, the main figures of the national revivalist movements Renaixença and Rexurdimento, respectively.

Modern Portuguese poetry develops its character from the work of its Romantic epitome, Almeida Garrett, a very prolific writer who helped shape the genre with the masterpiece *Folhas Caídas* (1853). This late arrival of a truly personal Romantic style would linger on to the beginning of the 20th century, notably through the works of poets such as Cesário Verde and António Nobre. However, an early Portuguese expression of Romanticism is found already in Manuel Maria Barbosa du Bocage, especially in his sonnets dated at the end of the 18th century.

In the United States, romantic Gothic literature made an early appearance with Washington Irving's *The Legend of Sleepy Hollow* (1820) and *Rip Van Winkle* (1819), followed from 1823 onwards by the *Leatherstocking Tales* of James Fenimore Cooper, with their emphasis on heroic simplicity and their fervent landscape descriptions of an already-exotic mythicized frontier peopled by "noble savages", similar to the philosophical theory of Rousseau, exemplified by Uncas, from *The Last of the Mohicans*. There are picturesque "local color" elements in Washington Irving's essays and especially his travel books. Edgar Allan Poe's tales of the macabre and his balladic poetry were more influential in France than at home, but the romantic American novel developed fully with the atmosphere and melodrama of Nathaniel Hawthorne's *The Scarlet Letter* (1850). Later Transcendentalist writers such as Henry David Thoreau and Ralph Waldo Emerson still show elements of its influence and imagination, as does the romantic realism of Walt Whitman. The poetry of Emily Dickinson — nearly unread in her own time — and Herman Melville's novel *Moby-Dick* can be taken as epitomes of American Romantic literature. By the 1880s, however, psychological and social realism was competing with romanticism in the novel.

6 Romanticism in Literature

6.1 English Literature

In literature, Romanticism found recurrent themes in the evocation or criticism of the past, the cult of "sensibility" with its emphasis on women and children, the heroic isolation of the artist or narrator, and respect for a new, wilder, untrammeled and "pure" nature.

Furthermore, several romantic authors, such as Edgar Allan Poe and Nathaniel Hawthorne, based their writings on the supernatural/occult and human psychology. Romanticism tended to regard satire as something unworthy of serious attention, a prejudice still influential today.

The precursors of Romanticism in English poetry go back to the first half of the 18th century, with figures such as Joseph Warton and his brother Thomas Warton, professor of Poetry at Oxford University. Joseph maintained that invention and imagination were the chief qualities of a poet. Thomas Chatterton is generally considered to be the first Romantic poet in English. The Gothic novel, beginning with Horace Walpole's *The Castle of Otranto* (1764), was an important precursor of one strain of Romanticism, with a delight in horror and threat, and exotic picturesque settings, matched in Walpole's case by his role in the early revival of Gothic architecture. Tristram Shandy, a novel by Laurence Sterne (1759 – 1767) introduced a whimsical version of the anti-rational sentimental novel to the English literary public.

In English literature, the group of poets now considered the key figures of the Romantic movement includes William Wordsworth, Samuel Taylor Coleridge, John Keats, Mary Wollstonecraft Shelley, Percy Bysshe Shelley, and the much older William Blake, followed later by the isolated figure of John Clare. The publication in 1798 of *Lyrical Ballads*, with many of the finest poems by Wordsworth and Coleridge, is often held to mark the start of the movement. The majority of the poems were by Wordsworth, and many dealt with the lives of the poor in his native Lake

District, or the poet's feelings about nature, which were to be more fully developed in his long poem *The Prelude*, never published in his lifetime. The longest poem in the volume was Coleridge's *The Rime of the Ancient Mariner* which showed the Gothic side of English Romanticism and the exotic settings that many works featured. In the period when they were writing the Lake Poets were widely regarded as a marginal group of radicals, though they were supported by the critic and writer William Hazlitt and others.

In contrast Lord Byron and Walter Scott achieved enormous fame and influence throughout Europe with works exploiting the violence and drama of their exotic and historical settings; Byron was "undoubtedly the greatest genius of our century", according to no less a figure than Goethe. Scott achieved immediate success with his long narrative poem *The Lay of the Last Minstrel* in 1805, followed by the full epic poem *Marmion* in 1808. Both were set in the distant Scottish past. Byron had equal success with the first part of *Childe Harold's Pilgrimage* in 1812, followed by four "Turkish tales", all in the form of long poems, starting with *The Giaour* in 1813, drawing from his Grand Tour which had reached Ottoman Europe, and orientalizing the themes of the Gothic novel in verse. These featured different variations of the "Byronic hero", and his own life contributed a further version. Scott meanwhile was effectively inventing the historical novel, beginning in 1814 with *Waverley*, set in the 1745 Jacobite Rising, which was an enormous and highly profitable success, followed by over 20 further Waverley Novels over the next 17 years, with settings going back to the Crusades that he had researched to a degree that was new in literature.

In contrast to Germany, Romanticism in English literature had little connection with nationalism, and the Romantics were often regarded with suspicion for the sympathy many felt for the ideals of the French Revolution, whose collapse and replacement with the dictatorship of Napoleon was, as elsewhere in Europe, a shock to the movement. Though his novels celebrated Scottish identity and history, Scott was politically a firm Unionist. Several spent much time abroad, and a famous stay on Lake Geneva with Byron and Shelley in 1816 produced the hugely influential novel *Frankenstein* by Shelley's wife-to-be Mary Shelley and the novella *The Vampyre* by Byron's doctor John William Polidori. The lyrics of Robert Burns in Scotland and Thomas Moore, from Ireland but based in London or elsewhere reflected in different ways their countries and the Romantic interest in folk literature, but neither had a fully Romantic approach to life or their work.

Though they have modern critical champions such as Georg Lukács, Scott's novels are today more likely to be experienced in the form of the many operas that continued to be based on them over the following decades, such as Donizetti's *Lucia di Lammermoor* and Vincenzo Bellini's *I puritani* (both 1835). Byron is now most highly regarded for his short lyrics and his generally unromantic prose writings, especially his letters, and his unfinished satire *Don Juan*. Unlike many Romantics, Byron's widely-publicised personal life appeared to match his work, and his death at 36 in 1824 from disease when helping the Greek War of Independence appeared from a distance to be a suitably Romantic end, entrenching his legend. Keats in 1821 and Shelley in 1822 both died in Italy, Blake (at almost 70) in 1827, and Coleridge largely ceased to write in the 1820s. Wordsworth was by 1820 respectable and highly-regarded, holding a government sinecure, but wrote relatively little. In the discussion of English literature, the Romantic period is often regarded as finishing around the 1820s, or sometimes even earlier, although many authors of the succeeding decades were no less committed to Romantic values.

The most significant novelist in English during the peak Romantic period, other than Walter Scott, was Jane Austen, whose essentially conservative world-view had little in common with her Romantic contemporaries, retaining a strong belief in decorum and social rules, though critics have detected tremors under the surface of some works, especially *Mansfield Park* (1814) and *Persuasion* (1817). But around the mid-century the undoubtedly Romantic novels of the Brontë family appeared, in particular Charlotte's *Jane Eyre* and Emily's *Wuthering Heights*, which were both published in 1847.

6.2 German Literature

In Germany the Sturm und Drang school, with its obsessive interest in medievalism, prepared the way for romanticism. Friedrich Schlegel first used the term *romantic* to designate a school of literature opposed to classicism, and he also applied the philosophical ideas of Immanuel Kant and J. G. Fichte to the "romantic ideal". Major German writers associated with romanticism include G. E. Lessing, J. G. Herder, Friedrich Hölderlin, Schiller, and particularly Goethe, who had a mystic feeling for nature and for Germany's medieval past.

6.3 Literature in France and Other European Countries

The credo of French romanticism was set forth by Victor Hugo in the preface to his drama *Cromwell* (1828) and in his play *Hernani* (1830). Hugo proclaimed the freedom of the artist in both choice and treatment of a subject. The French romantics included Chateaubriand, Alexandre Dumas père, Alphonse de Lamartine, Alfred de Vigny, Alfred de Musset, and George Sand. Other leading romantic figures were Giacomo Leopardi and Alessandro Manzoni in Italy, and Aleksandr Pushkin and Mikhail Lermontov in Russia.

6.4 American Literature

In the United States romanticism had philosophic expression in transcendentalism, notably in the works of Emerson and Thoreau. Poets such as Poe, Whittier, and Longfellow all produced works in the romantic vein. Walt Whitman in particular expressed pride in his individual self and the democratic spirit. The works of James Fenimore Cooper reflected the romantic interest in the historical past, whereas the symbolic novels of Hawthorne and Melville emphasized the movement's concern with transcendent reality.

Although greatly influenced by their English counterparts, the American romantic writers revealed unique characteristics of their own in their works and they grew on the native lands. The American national experience of "pioneering into the west" proved to be a rich source of material for American writers to draw upon. They celebrated America's landscape with its virgin forests, meadows, groves, endless prairies, streams, and vast oceans. The wilderness came to function almost as a dramatic character that symbolized moral law. The desire for an escape from society and a return to nature became a permanent convention of American literature. Such a desire is particularly evident in Cooper's *Leather Stocking Tales*, in Thoreau's *Walden* and, later, in Mark Twain's *Adventures of Huckleberry Finn*. With the growth of American national consciousness, American character types speaking local dialects appeared in poetry and fiction with increasing frequency. Then the American Puritanism as a cultural heritage exerted great influences over American moral values and American Romanticism. One of the manifestations is the fact that American romantic writers tended more to moralize than their English and European counterparts. Besides, a preoccupation with the Calvinistic view of original sin and the mystery of evil marked the works of Hawthorne, Melville and a host of lesser writers.

6.5 Features of Romantic Writing

(1) The Romanticists' own aspiration and ideals are in sharp contrast to the common sordid daily life under capitalism. Their writings are filled with strong-willed heroes or even titanic images, formidable events and tragic situations, powerful conflicting passions and exotic pictures. Sometimes they resorted to symbolic methods, with the *active romanticists*, symbolic pictures represent a vague ideal of some future society; while with the *passive romanticists*, these pictures often take on a mystic colour.

(2) The romanticists paid great attention to the spiritual and emotional life of man. Personified nature plays an important role in the pages of their works. Terror, passion, and the Sublime (an idea associated with religious awe, vastness, natural magnificence, and strong emotion which fascinated 18th-century literary critics and aestheticians) are essential concepts in early Romanticism; as is the sense of primitive mystery rediscovered in the Celtic bardic verse of Macpherson's *Ossian*, the folk ballads collected by Percy, and the medieval poetry forged by Chatterton (whom Southey edited).

(3) The tone of Romanticism was shaped by the naked emotionalism

of Rousseau's *Julie*, *ou la nouvelle Heloise* (1761), and the exotic legends and mythology found in Oriental and Homeric literatures and 17th-century travel writers. The stylistic keynote of Romanticism is intensity, and its watchword is "Imagination". Remembered childhood, unrequited love, and the exiled hero were constant themes.

(4) Romanticism expressed an unending revolt against classical form, conservative morality, authoritarian government, personal insincerity, and human moderation. The Romantics saw and felt things brilliantly afresh. They virtually invented certain landscapes — the Lakes, the Alps, and the bays of Italy. They were strenuous walkers, hill-climbers, sea-bathers, or river-lovers. They had a new intuition for the primal power of the wild landscape, the spiritual correspondence between Man and Nature, and the aesthetic principle of "organic" form (seen at their noblest in Wordsworth's *Prelude or* J. M. W. Turner's paintings). In their critical writings and lectures they described poetry and drama with new psychological appreciation (the character of Hamlet, for example); they discussed dreams, dramatic illusion, and romantic sensibility, the process of creativity, the limits of Classicism and Reason, and the dynamic nature of the Imagination.

(5) The second generation of Romanticists absorbed these tumultuous influences, wrote swiftly, and travelled widely (Greece, Switzerland, and Italy), and died prematurely: their life-stories and letters became almost as important for Romanticism as their poetry. They in turn inspired autobiographical prose-writers such as Hazlitt, De Quincey, and Lamb; while the historical imagination found a champion in Sir W. Scott.

7 Romanticism in Visual Arts

In the visual arts, Romanticism first showed itself in landscape painting, where from as early as the 1760s British artists began to turn to wilder landscapes and storms, and Gothic architecture, even if they had to make do with Wales as a setting. 19th-century romanticism was characterized by the avoidance of classical forms and rules, emphasis on the emotional and spiritual, representation of the unattainable ideal, nostalgia for the grace of past ages, and a predilection for exotic themes.

Romantic artists developed precise techniques in order to produce specific associations in the mind of the viewer. To convey verbal concepts they would, for example, endow inanimate objects with human values (e. g. the wild trees and shimmery moonlight used in the paintings of Caspar David Friedrich to suggest an infinity of human longing). The result was often sentimental or ludicrous. In the case of Delacroix, however, his painterly style and color sense exalted the romantic attitude in a singularly effective fashion.

In England landscape gardening was used to express the romantic aesthetic by means of deliberate imitation of the picturesque in nature. In architecture Wyatt's preposterous, mock medieval Fonthill Abbey displayed the romantic building style in extreme form. The host of lesser artists of the romantic tradition included the French Géricault, the Swiss-English Henry Fuseli, the Swiss Arnold Böcklin, the English Pre-Raphaelites, the German Nazarenes, and the American artists of the Hudson River school.

8 Romanticism in Music

Romanticism was later taken up by musicians, to describe the changes in musical style. Unlike Classical composers, Romantic composers aimed for a store powerful expression of emotion, often revealing their innermost thoughts and feelings. Romantic music is not just about the emotion of love, it can also be about hate or death (positive or negative feelings). Many Romantic composers took an interest in art and literature:

- Far off lands
- The distant past
- Dreams
- Night and moonlight
- Rivers, lakes and forests
- Nature and the seasons
- The joy and pain of love
- Fairy tales
- The supernatural
- Magic

Romanticism in music attained its fullest development in the works of German composers. About 1820, Beethoven began to write passionate compositions which often threatened to burst asunder the classical forms in which he worked. His 1824 *Symphony No.* 9 is notable not only for its length and complexity, but for the fact that he introduced vocal soloists and a chorus into the final movement, as if the purely instrumental form of the classical symphony could not express all that he felt. After this radical departure from tradition, many composers felt free to experiment. Although elements of romanticism are present in the music of Beethoven, Weber, and Schubert, it reached its zenith in the works of Berlioz, Mendelssohn, Schumann, Chopin, Liszt, and Wagner. Less totally romantic composers usually placed in the middle period of romanticism are Brahms, Tchaikovsky, Dvorák, and Grieg; those grouped in the last phase include Elgar, Puccini, Mahler, Richard Strauss, and Sibelius.

8.1 The Orchestra

As Romantic composers widened the range of their musical materials, we find richer harmonies, more passionate melodies, and greater use of chromaticism (Chroma is Greek for colour). There was an enormous increase in the size of the orchestra. The tuba was added to the brass section, valves were invented, giving the brass more flexibility. Composers wrote for woodwind instruments in threes of even fours.

A larger string section was formed, to accommodate the extra sound. More varied percussion (e. g. bongos) was added. A larger range of pitch and volume was now possible. New combinations of instruments were brought about. A rich variety of compositions resulted, ranging from piano pieces and songs to large spectacular works. The majority of large works were by Wagner, Berlioz, Mahler and Richard Strauss.

8.2 The German Lied

Songs began to develop in the Romantic period for solo voice and piano. There were two types:

(1) Strophic — same music for every verse

(2) Through-composed — different music for each verse. The voice and words fit very closely together (reflect each other).

The piano was more than just an accompaniment in these

compositions; it was a partner to the voice. Schubert was perhaps the greatest composer of German Lied, who wrote over 600, including *The Earl King*, *The Trout*, and *To Sylvia*. Other composers of this style were Schumann, Brahms, Wolf and Richard Strauss. Sometimes a composer might set a whole group of poems linked to the same idea, perhaps even sketching a story, for example, Schubert's *Winter Journey*.

8.3 Music for Piano

Several improvements were made to the piano in the 19th Century. The piano gained a richer sound, and gradually, a wider range of notes. The sustaining pedal began to be used to a much wider extent. The most famous piano composers of the time were Schubert, Mendelssohn, Chopin, Schumann, Liszt and Brahms. They wrote sonatas (for one instrument, or a soloist with one accompanying instrument), and many short pieces.

Many pieces shared contrasting moods, and were in Ternary form. Another piece of the time was the etude (study). It was meant to improve the playing technique of the player. This period saw the rise of the virtuoso, a person with extraordinary musical skill, such as Paganini, and Liszt.

8.4 Wagner

Wagner wrote many operas, especially German operas. People said Wagner was the most powerful force since Beethoven. His operas are called music dramas. Some examples of his works are *Rhinegold*, *The Master Singers* and *Valkyrie*. Wagner was a master of orchestration. He had a huge orchestra. The operas were on a large scale, and sometimes took four or five hours to perform. Woven into the texture are many short themes called Leitmotiv. Each one represents a character, emotion, object or place.

9 Romanticism outside the Arts

The Romantic Movement affected most aspects of intellectual life, and Romanticism and science had a powerful connection, especially during the period 1800 – 1840. Many scientists were influenced by versions of the *Naturphilosophie* of Johann Gottlieb Fichte, Friedrich Wilhelm Joseph von Schelling and Georg Wilhelm Friedrich Hegel and others, and without abandoning empiricism, sought in their work to uncover what they tended to believe was a unified and organic Nature. The English scientist Sir Humphry Davy, a prominent Romantic thinker, said that understanding nature required "an attitude of admiration, love and worship…a personal response." He believed that knowledge was only attainable by those who truly appreciated and respected nature. Self-understanding was an important aspect of Romanticism. It had less to do with proving that man was capable of understanding nature (through his budding intellect) and therefore controlling it, and more to do with the emotional appeal of connecting himself with nature and understanding it through a harmonious co-existence.

History was very strongly, and many would say harmfully, influenced by Romanticism. In English Thomas Carlyle was a highly influential essayist who turned to historian, and both invented and exemplified the phrase "hero-worship", lavishing largely uncritical praise on strong leaders such as Oliver Cromwell, Frederick the Great and Napoleon. Romantic nationalism had a largely negative effect on the writing of history in the 19th century, as each nation tended to produce its own version of history, and the critical attitude, even cynicism, of earlier historians was often replaced by a tendency to create romantic stories with clearly distinguished heroes and villains. Nationalist ideology of the period placed great emphasis on racial coherence, and the antiquity of peoples, and tended to vastly over-emphasize the continuity between past periods and the present, leading to national mysticism. Much historical effort in the 20th century was devoted to combating the historical myths created in the 19th century.

To insulate theology from reductionism in science, 19th-century post-Enlightenment German theologians moved in a new direction, led by Friedrich Schleiermacher and Albrecht Ritschl. They took the Romantic approach of rooting religion in the inner world of the human spirit, so that it is a person's feeling or sensibility about spiritual matters that comprises religion.

Questions for Discussion

1. Discuss the major ideas of Romanticism and show why they were related to the social, artistic, and literary forces of the age.

2. What gave a push for Romanticism?

3. What are the characteristics of the Romantic literature? Please discuss the question in relation to one or two examples.

4. *Living in England was impossible for him. "I felt," he wrote, "that, if what was whispered, and muttered, and murmured, was true, I was unfit for England; if false, England was unfit for me." On April* 25th, 1816, *he set sail for Europe, never to return. He first went to Switzerland. In* 1823 *he went to Greece and plunged into the struggle for the national independence of that country. In* 1824 *he died there. His death was*

mourned by the Greek people and by all progressive people throughout the world.

Questions:

(1) Who is mentioned in the above words?

(2) What is his masterpiece? In his works appear a kind of heroes, how much do you know about them?

5. *He appealed directly to individual sensations, i. e. pleasure, excitement and enjoyment, as the foundation in the creation and appreciation of poetry. Poetry "takes its origin from emotion recollected in tranquility." A poet's emotion extends from human affairs to nature, but emotion immediately expressed is as raw as wine newly bottled. Tranquil contemplation of an emotional experience matures the feeling and sensation, and makes possible the creation of good poetry like the refining of old wine.*

Questions:

(1) Who does "he" refer to in the above description?

(2) From which work are these quotations taken? What function does this work serve for the English Romantic Movement?

6. *O WILD West Wind, thou breath of Autumn's being—*
Thou, from whose unseen presence the leaves dead
Are driven, like ghosts from an enchanter fleeing,

Yellow, and black, and pale, and hectic red,
Pestilence-stricken multitudes! — O thou
Who chariotest to their dark wintry bed

The winged seeds, where they lie cold and low,
Each like a corpse within its grave, until

Thine azure sister of the Spring shall blow

Her clarion o'er the dreaming earth, and fill
(Driving sweet buds like flocks to feed in air)
With living hues and odours plain and hill —

Wild Spirit, which art moving everywhere —
Destroyer and Preserver — hear O hear!

Questions:

(1) What is the title of the poem? Who is the poet?

(2) Can you find the rhyme scheme of the poem?

(3) What is the symbolic meaning of "the west wind"?

(4) Explain the theme of the poem.

Chapter 5 Realism

1 Background of Realism

The 19th century is the century of greatest change in the history of Western Civilization. In 1830, the French revolution broke. In 1832, the English parliament passed the election rules. In 1838 to 1848, Charted Movement broke out in England. In 1831and 1834, the workers in Russia rose up.

In France, the French Revolution was a period of radical social and political upheaval that had a lasting impact on French history and more broadly throughout the world. The modern era has unfolded in the shadow of the French Revolution. In America, the Civil War affected both the social and the value systems of the country. America had transformed itself into an industrial ized and commercialized society. The industrialization and the urbanization were accompanied by the incalculable sufferings of the laboring people. Therefore, polarization of the wellbeing between the poor and the rich started to show up.

As far as the ideology was concerned, people became dubious about the human nature and the benevolence of God. What Mark Twain referred to as "the Gilded Age" replaced the frontier and the spirit of the frontiersman, which was the spirit of freedom and human connection.

Culturally, the literary scene after the Civil War proved to be quite different a picture. The harsh realities of life as well as the disillusion of heroism resulting from the dark memories of the Civil War had set the nation against the romance. The Americans began to be tired of the sentimental feelings of Romanticism.

In England, since the industrial revolution in the 18th century, the class structure has undergone radical changes; the industrial capitalists began to play a more important role. England became a typical capitalist country. In 1843 there was the passage of the Poor Law. The inhuman workhouses were established, in which poor people had to do heavy tasks and live no better than jails. The great misery of the workers led to an upsurge of labor movements and the organization of the worker into unions, and the working class movement known as Chartism arose in 1836. The crying social contradiction was reflected in the poetry and prose of the time.

2 The Connotation of Realism

2.1 What is Realism?

Realism is an artistic movement begun in 19th century France. Artists and writers strove for detailed realistic and factual description. They tried to represent events and social conditions as they actually are, without idealization.

This form of literature believes in fidelity to actuality in its representation. Realism is about recreating life in literature, which focused on the truthful treatment of the common, average, everyday life, as opposed to kings, queens, and gods as main characters. Realism focuses on the immediate, the here and now, the specific actions and their verifiable consequences and seeks a one-to-one relationship between representation and the subject. Realism aims to interpret the actualities of any aspect of life, free from subjective prejudice, idealism, or romantic color. It is in direct opposition to concerns of the unusual, the basis of Romanticism. It stresses the real over the fantastic, seeks to treat the commonplace truthfully and uses characters from everyday life. In reaction to Romanticism, realistic writers set down their observations impartially and objectively.

2.2 Characteristics of Realism

The basic characteristics of realism include:

Accuracy: Realism strives for absolute accuracy in the depiction of its subjects, devoid of any unnecessary dramatics or artistic affectation. Realistic works refrain from undue embellishment, aiming for a natural (as opposed to an artificial) tone.

Honesty: Realism seeks the depiction of honesty, rather than hiding things behind distortions or opinions. Unpleasant facts or images are presented as they are, as are plain or unassuming details about the subject.

Independence: Philosophical realism stresses the independence of objects from their observer. They have a life and an existence separate from anything else, which will continue regardless of anyone's thoughts on the matter.

Ordinariness: The subjects of realistic works are defined not by their exceptional nature, but by how ordinary they are.

Difficulties: Realistic protagonists are often beset by great forces beyond their control — the natural world, for instance, or the indifference of a larger society — and in many cases they do not triumph in their struggle. Unhappy endings aren't universal in realistic stories, but they are fairly common, while happy endings often entail compromise and pyrrhic victories.

3 Realism in Literature

Literary realism is the trend, beginning with mid-19th century French literature and extending to late nineteenth and early 20th century authors, towards depictions of contemporary life and society as it was, or is. In the spirit of general "realism", realist authors opted for depictions of everyday and banal activities and experiences, instead of a romanticized or similarly stylized presentation. Broadly defined as "the faithful representation of reality", was based on "objective reality", and was focused on showing everyday quotidian activities and life, primarily among the middle or lower class society, without romantic idealization or dramatization. While the preceding romantic era was also a reaction against the values of the Industrial Revolution, realism was in its turn a reaction to romanticism, and for this reason it is also commonly derogatorily referred as "traditional" "bourgeois realism".

3.1 British Realistic Literature

Some writers of Victorian literature produced works of realism. The Victorian era (1837 – 1901) of British history was a long period of peace, prosperity, refined sensibilities and national self-confidence for Britain. Culturally there was a transition away from the rationalism toward romanticism and mysticism with regard to religion, social values, literature and the arts. The era is popularly associated with the values of social and sexual restraint.

Charles Dickens (1812 – 1870), an English Victorian era author wrote numerous highly acclaimed novels including his most autobiographical *David Copperfield* (1848 – 1850). Other famous works such as *Oliver Twist* (1837 –1839), *A Tale of Two Cities* (1859), *Great Expectations* (1860 – 1861) and so on. As a prolific 19th century author of short stories, plays, novellas, novels, and fiction. During his lifetime Dickens became world famous for his remarkable characters, his mastery of prose in the telling of their lives, and his depictions of the social classes and the mores and values of his times. Some considered him the spokesman for the poor, for he definitely brought much awareness to their plight, the downtrodden and the have-nots. He had his share of critics like Virginia Woolf and Henry James, but also many admirers, even into the 21st Century.

David Copperfield

The story deals with the life of David Copperfield from childhood to maturity. David Copperfield was born in England, and six month later his father died, which destined his miserable life. When he was young, he had to fight against his stepfather abuse. After he grown up, he needed to fight for a living. Through these portrayals, the theme of exploitation was exhibited. In the whole story, the author portrays the growth of David and depicts other characters. In the book, the author showed the spirit of persevering against adversity. Perseverance with humor and hope enables David Copperfield to overcome formidable obstacles.

This novel is written in first-person point of view, which portrays the David Copperfield grown-up course. The novel implied the author's unusual life experience. Meanwhile, David Copperfield's destiny symbolized the middle-class intelligentsia questing for roads development in the 19th century British society.

Thomas Hardy (1840 – 1928) is last important novelist and poet of the 19th century. Living at the turn of the century, he is often regarded as a transitional writer. In him we see the influence from both the past and the modern. His literary genius is apparent in his poems and novels. Current scholars believe Hardy to be one of the greatest tragic novelists of English literature. Hardy died at the age of 87 on January 10, 1928. His body was buried in the Westminster Abbey, whereas his heart was buried in Stinsford Churchyard.

He himself grouped his novels into three series: romances and fantasies, novels of ingenuity, and novels of character and environment. His famous novels include *The Return of the Native*, *The Mayor of Casterbridge*, *Tess of the D'urbervilles*, *Jude the Obscure*, *Under the Greenwood Tree*, *Far From the Madding Crowd* and so on.

Tess of the D'urbervilles

The heroine of Hardy's novel is Tess Durbeyfield, a young, beautiful woman. In the course of the novel, Tess met two men who were possible suitors. Hardy characterized Alec as an unsuitable mate while Angel was representative of the ideal.

Tess's tragedy figures that Tess was destroyed by the system of the capitalism. Therefore the meaning of Tess's tragedy is not only a personal fight but rises to the level that all the workers should ask for human right and complaint the whole capitalism system. It is the capitalist invasion into the countryside and destruction of the English peasantry at the end of the 19th century. Naturalistic tendency is strong in the novel.

Thackeray (1811 – 1863) an English novelist, illustrator, moralist, and poet, was ranked second only to Charles Dickens during the Victorian era. Thackeray is one of the greatest critical realists of the 19th century. In his opinion, the existing society was corrupted as well as corrupting. He took it as his duty to expose the vices of his age, especially those in the upper-middle class. And he also regarded snobbery and the money-grabbing as the chief vice in the society. He criticizes the social moral that makes up the society. He always speaks in an ironical, sarcastic and cynical tone of an on-looker. He used his pen to disclose the darkness of society.

Thackeray's Literary Works are *Vanity Fair*, *The History of Henry Esmond*, *The Newcomers*, *The Virginians*, *The luck of Barry Lyndon* and *The Book of Snobs*

Vanity Fair

The novel describes the life of two girls, Becky Sharp and Amelia Sedley. They met at Miss Pinkerton's School for young ladies and then graduated from this school. Amelia Sedley was a sheltered daughter of a rich merchant. On the contrary, Becky was a pretty clever and well-behaved girl. She tasted the taste of poverty, and was determined to control their own destiny, out of trouble.

Her first plan is attempting to marry Joseph Sedley, Amelia's brother, but was foiled by George Osborne, an admirer of Amelia. Then Rebecca (= Becky) took a position as governess at Queen's Crawley, and married, Rawdon Crawley, second son of Sir Pitt Crawley. This made her loss the chance to marry with Pitt Crawley. Rawdon was an ignorant and self-indulgent man who didn't know Becky's well, then Becky became the mistress of Lord Steyne, which was found by her husband finally. This is the plot about Becky.

For Amelia, she married with Osborne, who was flower-hearted and later died in a war. Ten years later, when the two women met again, Becky let Amelia know George's attempt of elopement and finally Amelia married William Dobbin who loved her all the time.

Evans (1819 - 1880), better known by her pen name George Eliot, was an English novelist, journalist and translator, and one of the leading writers of the Victorian era. She is the author of seven novels, including *Adam Bede* (1859), *The Mill on the Floss* (1860), *Silas Marner* (1861), most of which set in provincial England and known for their realism and psychological insight.

She used a male pen name, she said, to ensure her works would be taken seriously. Female authors were published under their own names during Eliot's life, but she wanted to escape the stereotype of women only writing lighthearted romances. Her 1872 work, *Middlemarch*, has been described as the greatest novel in the English language by Martin Amis and by Julian Barnes.

The Mill on the Floss

The novel spans a period of 10 to 15 years, from Tom's and Maggie's childhood up until their deaths in a flood on the Floss. The book is a fictional autobiography in part, reflecting the disgrace that George Eliot (Mary Ann Evans) herself had while in a lengthy relationship with a married man, George Henry Lewes.

The major Themes of the book: like other novels by George Elliot, *The Mill on the Floss* articulates the tension between circumstances and the spiritual energies of individual characters struggling against those circumstances. A certain determinism is at play throughout the novel, from Mr Tulliver's grossly imprudent inability to keep himself from "going to law", and thereby losing his patrimony and bankrupting his family, to the series of events which sets Maggie and Stephen down the river and past the point of no return. People such as Mr Tulliver are presented as unable to determine their own course rationally, and forces, be it the drift of the river or the force of a flood, are presented as determining the courses of people for them. On the other hand, Maggie's ultimate choice not to marry Stephen but to suffer both the privation of his love and the ignominy of their botched elopement demonstrated a final triumph of free will.

Critics assert that Maggie's need for love and acceptance is her underlying motivation throughout *The Mill on the Floss*, and the conflicts that arise in the novel often stem from her frustrated attempts at gaining this acceptance.

3.2 French Realistic Literature

Marie-Henri Beyle (1783 – 1842), better known by his pen name Stendhal, was a 19th-century French writer. Known for his acute analysis of his characters' psychology, he is considered one of the earliest and foremost practitioners of realism in his two novels *Le Rouge et le Noir* (*The Red and the Black*, 1830) and *La Chartreuse de Parme* (*The Charterhouse of Parma*, 1839).

Contemporary readers did not fully appreciate Stendha's realistic style during the Romantic period in which he lived; he was not fully appreciated until the beginning of the 20th century. He dedicated his writing to "the Happy Few". This is often interpreted as a dedication to the few who could understand his writing, or as a sardonic reference to the happy few who are born into prosperity, or as a reference to those who lived without fear or hatred. He did have influence as a literary critic. The German philosopher Friedrich Nietzsche acknowledged his personal debt to the French writer in *the Twilight of the Idols*, stating that "the most beautiful accident of my life, more so than even my discovery of Stendhal". Today, Stendhal's works attract attention for their irony and psychological and historical dimensions.

Le Rouge et le Noir (*The Red and the Black*)

Its title refers to the military and the clergy, the two career paths open to young men of intelligence and ambition but no social standing. Stendhal's hero, Julien Sorel, was such a young man. A seminary student, he was nevertheless an admirer of Napoleon, and dreams of military glory. When he was hired to tutor the mayor's children, he quickly seduced the mayor's wife, then moved on to Paris where he conquered a nobleman's daughter. Sorel came to believe that the secret of success was to outperform the hypocrites and vicious opportunists who surrounded him and he was right. But when the rich and powerful he so admired aligned against him, his downfall became unavoidable. A master of characterization, Stendhal painted a fascinating, multi-layered portrait of Julien Sorel, who endured as one of literature's most complex and surprisingly sympathetic a would-be manipulator out of his depth in a sea of sharks.

Honoré de Balzac (1799 – 1850) was a French novelist and playwright. His magnum opus was a sequence of short stories and novels collectively entitled *La Comédie Humaine* (*The Human Comedy*), which presents a panorama of French life in the years after the 1815 fall of Napoleon.

Due to his keen observation of detail and unfiltered representation of society, Balzac is regarded as one of the founders of realism in European literature. He is renowned for his multifaceted characters, which are complex, morally ambiguous and fully human. His writing influenced many subsequent novelists such as Marcel Proust, Émile Zola, Charles Dickens, etc. Many of Balzac's works have been made into or have inspired films, and they are a continuing source of inspiration for writers, filmmakers and critics.

La Comédie Humaine

After much editing and revision, *La Comédie Humaine* now forms a cohesive overview of French Parisian and Provincial society during the Restoration and July Monarchy. "The country is provincial; it becomes ridiculous when it tries to ape Paris." Critically writing of the Napoleonic empire and French Revolution, the new bourgeois monarch Louis Philippe frames the context for his major works, he explored themes of man and his place in society and the influences of his environment, politics, love, and wealth. He also discussed art, literature, and metaphysics.

Gustave Flaubert (1821 – 1880) was a French writer who is counted among the greatest novelists in Western literature. He is known especially for his first published novel, *Madame Bovary* (1857), and for his scrupulous devotion to his art and style. In September 1849, Flaubert completed the first version of a novel, *The Temptation of Saint Anthony*. He read the novel aloud to his friends over the course of four days, not allowing them to interrupt or give any opinions. At the end of the reading, his friends told him to throw the manuscript in the fire, suggesting instead that he focus on day-to-day life rather than fantastic subjects.

In 1850, Flaubert began to work on *Madame Bovary*. The novel, which took five years to write, was serialized in the Revue de Paris in 1856. Flaubert next wrote *Löducation sentimentale* (*Sentimental*

Education), an effort that took seven years. This was his last complete novel, published in the year 1869.

Madame Bovary

Madame Bovary (1856) is Gustave Flaubert's first published novel and is considered by many critics to be a masterpiece. The story focuses on a doctor's wife, Emma Bovary, who has adulterous affairs and lives beyond her means in order to escape the banalities and emptiness of provincial life. Though the basic plot is rather simple, even archetypal, the novel's true art lies in its details and hidden patterns. Flaubert was a notorious perfectionist and claimed always to be searching for le mot juste ("the right word").

When it was first serialized in *La Revue de Paris* between 1 October 1856 and 15 December 1856, the novel was attacked for obscenity by public prosecutors. The resulting trial, held in January 1857, made the story notorious. After Flaubert's acquittal on 7 February 1857, *Madame Bovary* became a bestseller when it was published as a single volume in April 1857. Flaubert's masterpiece is now considered a seminal work of Realism and one of the most influential novels ever written. In fact, the notable British-American critic James Wood writes in *How Fiction Works*: "Flaubert established for good or ill, what most readers think of as modern realist narration and his influence is almost too familiar to be visible".

Henri René Albert Guy de Maupassant (1850 – 1893) was a popular 19th century French writer, considered one of the fathers of the modern short story and one of the form's finest exponents.

A follower of Flaubert, Maupassant's stories are characterized by their economy of style and efficient, effortless ends. Many of the stories were set during the Franco-Prussian War of the 1870s and several described the futility of war and the innocent civilians who, caught in the conflict, emerge changed. He authored some 300 short stories, six novels, three travel books, and one volume of verse. The story *Boule de Suif* (*Ball of Fat*, 1880) is often accounted his masterpiece. The decade from 1880 to 1891 was the most fertile period of Maupassant's life. Made famous by his first short story, he worked methodically and produced two or sometimes four volumes annually. He combined talent and practical business sense, which made him wealthy.

In 1881 he published his first volume of short stories under the title of *La Maison Tellier*, which reached its twelfth edition within two years. In 1883 he finished his first novel, *Une Vie* (translated into English as *A Woman's Life*), 25,000 copies of which were sold in less than a year. In his novels, he concentrated all his observations scattered in his short stories. His second novel *Bel-Ami*, which came out in 1885, had thirty-seven printings in four months.

Boule de Suif (*Ball of Fat*)

The story happened in Franco-Prussian War. Several French including Suet ball tried to flee from enemy-occupied area by cottage. The other people looked down upon Suet ball though she gave out her food and drink to them. Unfortunately, they were detained by a Prussia officer. The officer didn't let them leave unless Suet ball agreed to sleep with him for a night. At first, she refused. However, in order to leave that area, other French, the so-called nobles, flattered her and persuaded her to do it. Suet ball was so kind that she made a sacrifice for them. Next morning, when she got into the cottage, the nobles stayed away from her and even disdained talking with her because she wasn't useful any more.

When General military drove straight to France, people rose up to defend the homeland. The head of "government of national defense" kept shouting "never surrender", "never give up on the French fortress a stone", but secretly they consorted with the enemy and signed the humiliating peace treaty. Characters in the novel represented all sectors of French society.

3. 3 American Realistic Literature

There has always been a strong tradition of realism in American literature. Far away from the cultural centers on Continent Europe and separated by the Atlantic, the American brands of realism flourished and dominated the art scene for the 300 years. This included works of many genres, some of which we will list here.

Harriet Beecher Stowe (1811 – 1896) was an American abolitionist and author. She wrote more than 20 books, including novel, three travel memoirs, and collections of articles and letters. She was influential both for her writings and her public stands on social issues of the day.

Hernovel *Uncle Tom's Cabin* (1852) was a depiction of life for African-Americans under slavery; it reached millions as a novel and play, and became influential in the United States and United Kingdom. *Uncle Tom's Cabin*; or, *Life Among the Lowly* is an anti-slavery novel. Published in 1852, the novel had a profound effect on attitudes toward African Americans and slavery in the United States, so much in the latter case that the novel intensified the sectional conflict leading to the American Civil War.

After the start of the Civil War, Stowe traveled to Washington, D. C. and there met President Abraham Lincoln on November 25, 1862. Legend had it that, upon meeting her, he greeted her by saying, "so you are the little woman who wrote the book that started this great war?"

Uncle Tom's Cabin

The book focused the novel on the character of Uncle Tom, a long-suffering black slave around whom the stories of other characters — both fellow slaves and slave owners — revolved. The sentimental novel depicts the reality of slavery while also asserting that Christian love can overcome something as destructive as enslavement of fellow human beings.

Uncle Tom's Cabin is dominated by a single theme: the evil and immorality of slavery. Another major theme of *Uncle Tom's Cabin* is the moral power and sanctity of women. Stowe's novel "reaffirmed the importance of women's influence" and helped pave the way for the women's rights movement in the following decades.

Stowe's puritanical religious beliefs showed up in the novel's final, over-arching theme, which was the exploration of the nature of Christianity and how she felt Christian theology was fundamentally incompatible with slavery.

Walter Whitman (1819 – 1892), often called "the father of free verse", was an American poet, essayist and journalist. A humanist, he was a part of the transition between transcendentalism and realism, incorporating both views in his works. His work was very controversial in its time, particularly his poetry collection *Leaves of Grass*. Whitman's work broke the boundaries of poetic form and was generally prose-like. He also used unusual images and symbols in his poetry, including rotting leaves, tufts of straw, and debris.

Whitman wrote in the preface to the 1855 edition of *Leaves of Grass*, "The proof of a poet is that his country absorbs him as affectionately as he has absorbed it." He believed there was a vital and symbiotic relationship between the poet and society. *Leaves of Grass* also responded to the impact that recent urbanization in the United States had on the masses.

Leaves of Grass

Leaves of Grass is a poetry collection. Among the poems in the collection are "Song of Myself", "I Sing the Body Electric", "Out of the Cradle Endlessly Rocking". This book is notable for its delight in and praise of the senses during a time when such candid displays were considered immoral. The symbols he used were governed by the objects he observed. For example, he associated the star with the thought of death; the lilac was a token of life.

The major themes are: Extol transcendent power of love, brotherhood, and comradeship; express the ideals of democracy and equality. His poems revealed a world of equality without rank and hierarchy, attacked the slavery system and racial discrimination; advocated the realization of the individual value. He celebrated the dignity and the self-reliant spirit; the pursuit of love and happiness. He celebrated the joy of common man; sexual love, a rather taboo topic of the time, was displayed frankly as something adorable in his poems; enthusiastic response to the expansion of America. In his poems, we can see the spirit of an emerging America at its most aggressive and daring.

Samuel Langhorne Clemens (1835 – 1910), better known by his pen name Mark Twain, was an American author and humorist. He is most noted for his novel *The Adventures of Tom Sawyer* (1876) and its sequel, *Adventures of Huckleberry Finn* (1885), the latter often called "the Great American Novel". Twain enjoyed immense public popularity. His keen wit and incisive satire earned him praise from both critics and peers. William Faulkner called Twain "the father of American literature".

Adventures of Huckleberry Finn

The book is noted for its colorful description of people and places along the Mississippi River. By satirizing a Southern antebellum society that was already anachronistic at the time, the book is an often scathing look at entrenched attitudes, particularly racism. The drifting journey of Huck and his friend Jim, a runaway slave, down the Mississippi River on their raft may be one of the most enduring images of escape and freedom in all of American literature.

The book has been popular with young readers since its publication and is taken as a sequel to *The Adventures of Tom Sawyer*. It has also been the continued object of study by serious literary critics. The book was criticized upon release because of its coarse language, and became even more controversial in the 20th century because of its perceived use of racial stereotypes and because of its frequent use of the racial slur, "nigger."

Henry James (1843 – 1916), noted American-born English essayist, critic, and a productive author of the realism movement wrote *The Ambassadors* (1903), *The Turn of the Screw* (1898), and *The Portrait of a Lady* (1881). James's works, many of which were first serialized in the magazine *The Atlantic Monthly* include narrative romances with highly developed characters set amongst illuminating social commentary on politics, class, and status, as well as explorations of the themes of personal freedom, feminism, and morality. In his short stories and novels he employed techniques of interior monologue and point of view to expand the readers' enjoyment of character perception and insight.

The Portrait of a Lady

The Portrait of a Lady is a novel first published as a serial in *The Atlantic Monthly* and *Macmillan's Magazine* in 1880 – 1881 and then as a book in 1881. It is one of James' most popular long novels, and is regarded by critics as one of his finest.

The Portrait of a Lady is the story of a spirited young American woman, Isabel Archer, who "affronts her destiny" and found it overwhelming. She inherited a large amount of money and subsequently became the victim of Machiavellian scheming by two American expatriates. Like many of James' novels, it was set mostly in Europe, notably in England and Italy. Generally regarded as the masterpiece of his early phase of writing, this novel reflected James' continuing interest in the differences between the New World and the Old. It also treated in a profound way the themes of personal freedom, responsibility, betrayal, and sexuality.

3.4 The Realistic Literature of Northern Europe

Realism was evident in the works of many writers throughout Europe. Realism existed in many places during the period. The major writers in Northern Europe are as follows:

Johan August Strindberg (1849 – 1912) was a Swedish playwright, novelist, poet, essayist and painter. A prolific writer who often drew directly on his personal experience, Strindberg's career spanned four decades, during which time he wrote over 60 plays and more than 30 works of fiction, autobiography, history, cultural analysis, and politics. A bold experimenter and iconoclast throughout, he explored a wide range of dramatic methods and purposes, from naturalistic tragedy, monodrama, and history plays, to his anticipations of expressionist and surrealist dramatic techniques.

From his earliest work, Strindberg developed forms of dramatic action, language, and visual composition so innovative that many were to become technically possible to stage only with the advent of film. He is considered the "father" of modern Swedish literature and his *The Red Room* (1879) has frequently been described as the first modern Swedish novel. In Sweden, Strindberg is both known as a novelist and a playwright, but in most other countries he is almost only known as a playwright.

Henrik Johan Ibsen (1828 - 1906) was a major 19th-century Norwegian playwright, theatre director, and poet. He is often referred to as "the father of realism" and is one of the founders of Modernism in the theatre. His major works include *A Doll's House*, *Brand*, *Peer Gynt*, *An Enemy of the People*, etc. Several of his plays were considered scandalous to many of his era, when European theatre was required to model strict morals of family life and propriety. Ibsen's work examined the realities that lay behind many façades, revealing much that was disquieting to many contemporaries. It utilized a critical eye and free inquiry into the conditions of life and issues of morality. The poetic and cinematic play Peer Gynt, however, has strong surreal elements. Ibsen is often ranked as one of the truly great playwrights in the European tradition.

4 Realism in Arts

From the West, realistic painting has a long history and profound tradition. The brilliance produced many art masters in the history of great monuments. Before the 20th century, the whole western art history is a realistic painting history, which has never been doubted.

4.1 Realistic Painting in France

The turn of the 20th century ushered in dynamic and fundamental changes for the world of art. It is generally agreed that the Modern era of art began in the Realist movement in France during the 1840's, especially its realistic painting, which plays an essential role in the movement of realism.

Jean Courbet (1819 – 1877) was a French painter who led the Realist movement in 19th century French painting. His works, along with the works of Honoré Daumier and Jean-François Millet, became known as representation of Realism. Courbet occupies an important place in 19th century French painting as an innovator and as an artist willing to make bold social commentary in his works.

Among his paintings of the early 1840s are several self-portraits, romantic in conception, in which the artist portrayed himself in various roles. By 1848, he had gained supporters among the younger critics, the Neo-romantics and Realists.

The *Burial*, one of Courbet's most important works, records the funeral of his grand uncle which he attended in September 1848. People who attended the funeral were the models for the painting. Previously, models had been used as actors in historical narratives, but in *Burial* Courbet said he "painted the very people who had been present at the interment, all the townspeople". The result is a realistic presentation of them, and of life in Ornans.

Courbet achieved greater recognition after the success of his painting *After Dinner at Ornans* at the Salon of 1849. The work earned Courbet a gold medal and was purchased by the state. The gold medal meant that his works would no longer require jury approval for exhibition at the Salon —

an exemption Courbet enjoyed until 1857 when the rule changed.

Courbet was a productive painter, one of his major exhibitions, "The Born Rebel Artist", opened in 2007 at the Grand Palais, and traveled to the Musée Fabre (Montpellier, France) and the Metropolitan Museum of Art (New York City) during 2008.

Honoré Daumier (1808 – 1879) was a French printmaker, caricaturist, painter, and sculptor, whose many works offer commentary on social and political life in France in the 19th century.

Jean-François Millet (1814-1875) was a French painter and one of the founders of the Barbizon school in rural France. Millet is noted for his scenes of peasant farmers, and he can be categorized as part of the naturalism and realism movements. In 1850, Millet exhibited *Haymakers* and *The Sower*, his first major masterpieces and the earliest of the iconic trio of paintings that would include *The Gleaners* and *The Angelus*.

From 1850 to 1853, Millet worked on *Harvesters Resting*, a painting he would consider his most important, and on which he worked the longest. It was also the painting that marked his transition from the depiction of symbolic imagery of peasant life to that of contemporary social conditions. It was the only painting he ever dated, and was the first work to garner him official recognition.

Jean-Baptiste-Camille Corot (1796-1875) was a French landscape painter and printmaker in etching. Corot was the leading painter of the Barbizon school of France in the mid-19th century. He is a pivotal figure in landscape painting. Corot summed up his approach to art around 1860, "I interpret with my art as much as with my eye." The works of Corot are housed in museums in France and the Netherlands, Britain and America.

His famous works include: *Le concert champêtre* (1857), *Orpheus*

Leading Eurydice from the Underworld (1861), *Souvenir de Mortefontaine* (1864), *Femme Lisant* (1869), *L'Albanese* (1872)

4. 2 Realistic Painting in America

During the late 19th century and into the 20th century artists contributed to the idea of realism in the American setting. Each, though slightly different in concept or subject, was defining what was going on in front of his or her eyes, without imagining a past or a future. Writers and musicians were concerned with recording the grit and the true reality of the early 20th century in America.

The Ashcan School was a group of New York City artists who sought to capture the feel of turn-of-the-20th century New York City, through realistic portraits of everyday life. They became known as the revolutionary black gang and apostles of ugliness.

Robert Henri (1865 - 1929) was an important American Realist and a member of The Ashcan School. Henri was interested in the spectacle of common life. He focused on individuals and strangers, quickly passing in the streets in towns and cities. He had a sympathetic portrayal rather than a comic portrayal of people, often using a dark background to add to the warmth of the person portrayed.

In 1910 he organized the first "Exhibition of Independent Artists," between 1911 and 1919 he arranged jury-free exhibitions at the MacDowell Club, and in 1913 he helped the Association of American Painters and Sculptors organize the Armory Show. He taught at the Art Students League from 1915 until 1927. Although Henri was an important portraitist and figure painter, he is best remembered as a progressive and influential teacher. His ideas on art were collected by former pupil Margery Ryerson and published as *The Art Spirit* (Philadelphia, 1923). He died in 1929 at the age of sixty-four.

George B. Luks (1866 – 1933) was an Ashcan School artist who lived on the Lower East Side of Manhattan. In Luks' painting, *Hester Street* (1905), he shows children being entertained by a man with a toy while a woman and shopkeeper have a conversation in the background. The viewer is among the crowd rather than above it. Luks puts a positive spin on the Lower East Side by showing two young girls dancing in *The Spielers*, which is a type of dance that working-class immigrants would engage in; despite the poverty, children dance on the street. He looks for the joy and beauty in the life of the poor rather than the tragedy.

4.3 Sculpture

François-Auguste-René Rodin (1840 – 1917), known as Auguste Rodin, was a French sculptor. Although Rodin is generally considered the progenitor of modern sculpture, he did not set out to rebel against the past. Sculpturally, Rodin possessed a unique ability to model a complex, turbulent, deeply pocketed surface in clay. Many of his most notable sculptures were roundly criticized during his lifetime. They clashed with the predominant figure sculpture tradition, in which works were decorative, formulaic, or highly thematic.

A commission to create a portal for Paris' planned Museum of Decorative Arts was awarded to Rodin in 1880. Although the museum was never built, Rodin worked throughout his life on *The Gates of Hell*, a monumental sculptural group depicting scenes from *Dante's Inferno* in high relief. Often lacking a clear conception of his major works, Rodin compensated with hard work and a striving for perfection.

The Gates of Hell comprised 186 figures in its final form. Many of Rodin's best-known sculptures started as designs of figures for this composition, such as *The Thinker*, *The Three Shades*, and *The Kiss*, and were only later presented as separate and independent works. Other well-known works derived from *The Gates* are *Ugolino*, *Fugit Amor*, *The Falling Man*, and *The Prodigal Son*.

The Thinker (originally titled The Poet, after Dante) was to become one of the most well-known sculptures in the world. The original was a 27.5-inch (700 mm) -high bronze piece created between 1879 and 1889, designed for the Gates' lintel, from which the figure would gaze down upon Hell. While *The Thinker* most obviously characterizes Dante, aspects of the Biblical Adam, the mythological Prometheus, and Rodin himself have been ascribed to him. Other observers de-emphasize the apparent intellectual theme of *The Thinker*, stressing the figure's rough physicality and the emotional tension emanating from it.

Questions for Discussion

1. How do you understand the statement that an industrialized and commercialized society has certain influence on the emergence of the thought of realism?

2. Comment on the basic characteristics of realism and analyze why realism has such characteristics.

3. What is the influence of Jean Désiré Gustave Courbet on the history of realistic painting in the world?

4. Upon meeting Harriet Beecher Stowe, President Abraham Lincoln greeted her by saying, "so you are the little woman who wrote the book that started this Great War." Why President Abraham Lincoln made such comment about her?

5. Comment on the realistic literature in America and analyze how it reflects the social values and problems of that time.

Chapter 6 Modernism

1 Background

The term of modernism refers to the radical shift in aesthetic and cultural sensibilities evident in the art and literature of the post-World War One period. The ordered, stable and inherently meaningful world view of the nineteenth century could not, wrote T. S. Eliot, accord with "the immense panorama of futility and anarchy which is contemporary history". Modernism thus marks a distinctive break with Victorian bourgeois morality; rejecting nineteenth-century optimism, they presented a profoundly pessimistic picture of a culture in disarray. This despair often results in an apparent apathy and moral relativism.

1.1 Social Events

During the first half of the 20th century, rampant industrialization matured into international industrial capitalism, which fueled the rise of consumer economics. These developments presented society with great promise and significant problems. The twentieth century began with a strong sense of social breakdown. A series of wars fought on the international scene during the first part of the century were to affect the life of westerners and their artistic creativeness. Among them the two World

Wars, especially the First World War (1914 – 1918), became the emblem of all wars in the twentieth century, which means violence, devastation, blood and death. Meanwhile, the following Great Depression, and the great development in technology have touched almost everyone's life.

1. 1. 1 World War I

The development of advanced European and American societies led to expansion. This expansion has been called imperialism. This imperialism was capitalist and expansionist establishing colonies as raw material resources, manufacturing markets, and territories. This also brought on the great missionary thrusts into Africa and other places. The goal was to bring the "light" of Christianity and civilization to "backward peoples" and educating "inferior races". Darwin's influence was evident in the thinking that imperialism was also survival of the fittest.

The development of nation states did not lead to peace and harmony. Nationalism and the imperialistic spirit led to competition instead. Countries negotiated treaties and alliances to protect their interests. These alliances led to World War I, which lasted from 1914 – 1918. WWI destroyed any romantic illusions about war. Nine million people were killed in battle. The introduction of poison gas added to the horror of the inhumanity. The devastation of WWI brought widespread misery, social disruption, and economic collapse.

The First World War wiped out a generation of young men in Europe, catapulted Russia into a catastrophic revolution, and sowed the seeds for even worse conflagrations in the decades to follow. By the war's end in 1918, the centuries-old European domination of the world had ended and the "American Century" had begun. For artists and many others in

Europe, it was a time of profound disillusion with the values on which a whole civilization had been founded. But it was also a time when the avant-garde experiments that had preceded the war would, like the technological wonders of the airplane and the atom, inexorably establish a new era, which we call modernism.

1. 1. 2 Technological Revolution

The technological revolution had brought about great changes in the life of the western people. New discoveries in many fields forced people and society to revise radically their understanding of the world. This change was rooted in the Scientific Revolution and the Enlightenment of the previous centuries.

The early 20th century witnessed an astounding burst in scientific activity that challenged the model which has been promoted by the classic physics of Isaac Newton. The new theories espoused by Planck, Einstein, Rutherford and Bohr, shattered the existing faith in the objective reality of matter. Time and space were no longer thought of as absolute, rather, time and space are relative to the observer and linked to a four dimensional space time continuum. These new scientific theories and understandings of the universe changed the view of physical nature and raised the curtain on the Atomic Age. In addition to physics, there were great advances in chemistry and biology that yielded knowledge of polymers, plastics, fertilizers, vitamins, antibiotics, and many others, which resulted in many products that improved life.

1. 1. 3 The Great Depression

Despite the booming industry and material prosperity, there was a sense of unease and restlessness underneath. All culminated in the collapse of the Stock Market in 1929, known as the Crash, which marked the beginning of The Great Economic Depression in the 1930s, which was devastating to Western economies. By 1932, 25% of the British workforce was unemployed, 40% of the German workers, and production in the United States had fallen to 50%. This all created a fertile breeding ground for the totalitarian forces that came to the forefront in some European countries and Japan: Mussolini in Italy, and Adolf Hitler in Germany and Tojo in Japan. These ruthless seizures of power evolved into WWII. Besides, political corruptions, organized crimes, the growth of radical labor force made an already disorderly world even more turbulent.

1.2 Important Figures and Theories

Along with the changes in the material landscape came the changes in the non-material system of belief and behavior.

With the unparalleled increase of productive forces and unprecedented development of science and technology in the latter half of the 19th century, the bourgeoisie began to play less of a social controlling role, granting more freedom to intellectual and ideological development. Some important theories and ideological schools made noticeable progress or were among those being introduced ceaselessly, such as Marxism, Darwinism, Pragmatism, Positivism, Bergson's Intuitionalism, Freud's psycho-analysis and Sartre's Existentialism.

Apart from Darwinism, which was still a big influence over the artists of this period, the three masters of suspicion whose ideas had the greatest impact on the period were the German Karl Marx, the Austrian Sigmund Freud and Friedrich Nietzsche.

1.2.1 Marx and Marxism

Karl Marx (1818 – 1883) was a German philosopher, economist, sociologist, historian, journalist, and revolutionary socialist. His ideas played a significant role in the development of social science and the socialist political movement. He published various books during his lifetime, with the most notable being *The Communist Manifesto* (1848) and *Capital* (1867 - 1894); some of his works were co-written with his friend, the fellow German revolutionary socialist Friedrich Engels.

Marx's theories about society, economics and politics, which are collectively known as Marxism, hold that all societies' progress is made through the dialectic of class struggle. He was heavily critical of the current socio-economic form of society, capitalism, which he called the "dictatorship of the bourgeoisie", believing it to be run by the wealthy middle and upper classes purely for their own benefit, and predicted that, like previous socio-economic systems, it would inevitably produce internal tensions which would lead to its self-destruction and replacement by a new system, socialism. Under socialism, he argued that society would be governed by the working class in what he called the "dictatorship of the proletariat", the "workers state" or "workers democracy". He believed that socialism would, in its turn, eventually be replaced by a stateless, classless society called pure communism. Along with believing in the inevitability of socialism and communism, Marx actively fought for the former's implementation, arguing that both social theorists and underprivileged people should carry out organized revolutionary action to topple capitalism and bring about socio-economic change. Revolutionary socialist governments espousing Marxist concepts took power in a variety of countries in the 20th century, leading to the formation of such socialist states as the Soviet Union in 1922 and the People's Republic of China in 1949. Marx has been described as one of the most influential figures in human history, and in a 1999 BBC poll was voted the "thinker of the millennium" by people from around the world.

1. 2. 2 Sigmund Freud and Psychoanalysis

Sigmund Freud (1856 - 1939) was an Austrian physician and neurologist, the father of psychoanalysis. Major works includes *The interpretation of Dreams*, *Three Contributions to the Sexual Theory*, *The Ego and Id.*

He examined the irrational mind and destabilized the long held belief in the rational nature of humanity. He developed the principles for what became known as psychoanalysis. He argued in his research that the unconscious and inner drives control human behavior. This unconscious control is due to repression of uncomfortable past experiences or memories. Making people aware of their suppressed memories could heal them.

Psychoanalysis of Sigmund Freud is a theory of discussing the pathogeny and therapy of psychosis. The theory of psychoanalysis indicates that our mind likes the iceberg what can be seen above the surface of ocean is just 10% of the iceberg and the most part of the iceberg is deep under the ocean. So do our minds. The unconsciousness is what you are aware of. Then the preconsciousness is our memories and stored knowledge. The unconsciousness is more hidden and deeper in our mind. Then the theory of unconsciousness developed into the tripartite model of the mind: the id, the ego, and the superego. The id is the unconscious part of personality. It contains the lustful, aggressive, and instinct urges. The superego "comprises the norms, values, and ideals that upbringing and education have instilled in us". The id and superego often conflict with each other. The ego faces a threefold challenge: "from the external world, from the libido of id, and from the severity of the superego".

The theory has great influence on literature, especially in the stream of consciousness. In content, influenced by "sublimation" and "psychosis" in Freud's psychoanalysis, writers of the stream of consciousness focus on the excavation of the inner world of man and the people who is mental disordered and crazy; in technique, they adopt free association, symbolization and displacement, which are used in the interpretation of unconsciousness, and the interior monologue used in expressing the thoughts of characters.

1. 2. 3 Friedrich Nietzsche

Friedrich Nietzsche (1844 – 1900) was a German philosopher of the late 19th century who challenged the foundations of traditional morality and Christianity. He was interested in the enhancement of individual and cultural health, and believed in life, creativity, health and the realities of the world we live in, rather than those situated in a world beyond. Central to Nietzsche's philosophy is the idea of "life-affirmation", which involves an honest questioning of all doctrines which drain life's expansive energies, however socially prevalent those views might be. Often referred to as one of the first "existentialist" philosophers, Nietzsche has inspired leading figures in all walks of cultural life, including dancers, poets, novelists, painters, psychologists, philosophers, sociologists and social revolutionaries.

1. 2. 4 Einstein

Albert Einstein (1879 – 1955), German-American theoretical physicist who developed the special and general theories of relativity, won the Nobel Prize for Physics in 1921 for his explanation of the photoelectric effect. Recognized in his own time as one of the most creative intellects in human history, Einstein advanced a series of theories that proposed entirely new ways of thinking about space, time and gravitation. His theories of relativity and gravitation were a profound advance over the old Newtonian, physics and revolutionized scientific and philosophic inquiry.

2 The Connotation of Modernism

The term Modernism applied to the wide range of experimental and avant-garde trends in the arts that emerged from the middle of the 19th century, as artists rebelled against traditional Historicism, and later through 20th century as the necessity of an individual rejecting previous tradition, and by creating individual, original techniques.

Early 20th century avant-garde artists were in the forefront of aggressively challenging traditional and often cherished notions about art and its relations to society. As the old social order collapsed and new ones (such as communism and corporate capitalism) took their places, one of the self-imposed tasks school after school of avant-garde artists embraced was the search for new definitions and uses for art in a radically changed world. The term avant-garde emerged in art after it was in use in politics. This prompted the general public to associate the avant-garde artists with radical political thought and anarchism. While this was so, in contrast, other avant-garde artists in essence withdrew from society and concentrated their attention on art as a unique activity, separated from society at large. These artists pursed an introspective examination of artistic principles and elements (continuing the modernists' goals), resulting in an increasing focus on formal qualities of art.

In general, the term modernism encompasses the activities and output of those who felt the "traditional" forms of art, architecture, literature, religious faith, social organization and daily life were becoming outdated in the new economic, social, and political conditions of an emerging fully industrialized world.

3 Various Schools in Modern Art

Modernist literature embraces several schools, such as Symbolism, Expressionism, Stream of Consciousness, Imagism and Existentialism. For modern painting, there also exist several schools, Fauvism, Expressionism, Cubism, Futurism, Dadaism, Surrealism and Abstract Expressionism.

4 Modernist Literature

Literary Modernism has its origins in the late 19th and early 20th centuries, mainly in Europe and North America, and has reached its height in Europe between 1900 and the middle 1920s. Modernism is characterized by a self-conscious break with traditional styles of poetry and verse. Modernists experimented with literary form and expression, adhering to the modernist maxim to "Make it new". The modernist literary movement was driven by a desire to overturn traditional modes of representation and express the new sensibilities of their time. Modernistic art and literature normally revolved around the idea of individualism, mistrust of institutions (government, religion), and the disbelief of any absolute truths.

Modernist literature attempts to take into account changing ideas about reality developed by Darwin, Freud, Einstein, Nietzsche and others from this developed innovative literary techniques such as stream-of-consciousness, interior monologue, as well as the use of multiple points-of-view. This can reflect doubts about the philosophical basis of realism, or alternatively an expansion of our understanding of what is meant by realism. Therefore, for instance, the use of stream-of-consciousness or interior monologue reflects the need for greater psychological realism. World War I, and the disillusionment that followed, further shaped modernist views of human nature.

Literary Modernism constituted a genuine revolution in Western literature. It rejected traditional Western views on the formal characteristics (or form) of literary art and proposed new ideas on them. Literary Modernism, moreover, defined and explored its own philosophical issues and themes; in this way, it created its own, distinct content. Together with the rejection of traditional Western notions on literary form, this content was what transformed literary Modernism into a new and distinctive way of thinking.

4.1 Symbolism

Symbolism emerged and became a powerful artistic movement in Europe during the last quarter of the nineteenth century. In poetry, the leading figures of Symbolism were Stephane Mallarme and Paul Verlaine.

Symbolist poetry did not provide realistic descriptions of humans' inner world and of the material reality in which we live. Instead, by using metaphorical language and symbols, it tried to evoke the truer, superior reality, hidden behind the world of appearances. As is put by T. S. Eliot, "The only way of expressing emotion in the form of art is by finding an objective correlative; in other words, a set of objects, a situation, a chain of events which shall be the formula of that particular emotion; such that when the external facts, which must terminate in sensory experience, are given, the emotion is immediately evoked."

The key ideas of Symbolism are concluded as following:

—Using concrete images as symbols to express an emotion or an abstract idea, to represent an ideal world.

—The poet is a kind of seer who could see through and beyond the real world to the world of ideal forms and essence.

—Using the method of suggestion to evoke hidden meanings.

—To achieve pure poetry through world relationships: musical quality, image clusters, logical and psychological associations.

—The best form is free verse, or prose poem.

T. S. Eliot, William Butler Yeats, Edgar Allen Poe and Charles Baudelaire are representatives of this school.

4. 1. 1 T. S. Eliot

T. S. Eliot (1888 – 1965) was an American-born English poet, dramatist, literary critic, and modernist. His aesthetic views are listed as following: a poem should be an organic thing in itself, a made object. Once it is finished, the poet will no longer have control of it. It should be judged, analyzed by itself without the interference of the poet's personal influence and other elements.

Modern life is chaotic, futile, fragmentary, so poetry should reflect this fragmentary nature of life and this kind nature of life should be projected, not analyzed.

The poet should draw upon tradition: use the past to serve the present and future (the past, present, future interrelate), borrow from authors remote in time, alien in language, diverse in interest, use the past to underscore what is missing from the present.

His masterpiece, *The Waste Land*, a 434-line modernist poem published in 1922, revealed the spiritual crisis of postwar Europe. It reads like the manifesto of the "lost generation" and established Eliot's position as the leader not only of American poetry, but of a whole generation of writers later to be identified as "Waste Land Painters" like Hemingway and Faulkner.

The Waste Land

The Waste Land consists of five discontinuous segments, each composed of fragments incorporating multiple voices and characters, literary and historical allusions, bits and pieces of contemporary life, myths and legends. The central theme is desperation.

Although it gestured toward religious belief, *The Waste Land* was not an affirmative or religious poem; the desperate quest for regeneration in a cacophonous, desolate landscape remains unfulfilled.

4. 1. 2 Yeats

William Butler Yeats (1865 – 1939) was an Irish poet, dramatis, and one of the foremost figures of the 20th century literature. In 1923, he was awarded a Nobel Prize in Literature for what the Nobel Committee described as "inspired poetry, which in a highly artistic form gives expression to the spirit of a whole nation". He was the first Irishman to win this honor.

Yeats is generally considered to be one of the 20th century's key English language poets. He can be considered a Symbolist poet in that he used allusive imagery and symbolic structures throughout his career. He chose words and assembled them to that in addition to a particular meaning they suggest other abstract thoughts that may seem more significant and resonant. The use of symbols is usually something physical which is used both to be itself and to suggest other, perhaps immaterial, timeless qualities.

The themes of his poetry can be concluded like this: Yeats believed that art and politics were intrinsically linked and used his writing to express his attitudes toward Irish politics, as well as to educate his readers about Irish cultural history. Yeats' devotion to mysticism led to the development of a unique spiritual and philosophical system that emphasized the role of fate and historical determinism, or the belief that events have been preordained. Yeats had rejected Christianity early in his life, but his lifelong study of mythology, theosophy, spiritualism, philosophy, and the occult demonstrate his profound interest in the divine and how it interacts with humanity. Over the course of his life, he created a complex system of spirituality, using the image of interlocking gyres (similar to spiral cones) to map out the development and reincarnation of the soul.

Sailing to Byzantium

Sailing to Byzantium is one of Yeats' most inspired works, and one of the greatest poems of the twentieth century. It uses a journey to Constantinople (Byzantium) as a metaphor for a spiritual journey. Yeats explores his thoughts and musings on how immortality, art, and the human spirit may converge. Through the use of various poetic techniques, Yeats' *Sailing to Byzantium* describes the metaphorical journey of a man pursuing his own vision of eternal life as well as his conception of paradise.

Written in 1926 and included in Yeats' greatest single collection, 1928's *The Tower*, *Sailing to Byzantium* is Yeats' definitive statement about the agony of old age and the imaginative and spiritual work required to remain a vital individual even when the heart is "fastened to a dying animal" (the body). Yeats' solution is to leave the country of the young and travel to Byzantium, where the sages in the city's famous gold mosaics (completed mainly during the sixth and seventh centuries) could become the "singing-masters" of his soul. He hopes the sages will appear in fire and take him away from his body into an existence outside time, where, like a great work of art, he could exist in "the artifice of eternity". In the astonishing final stanza of the poem, he declares that once he is out of his body he will never again appear in the form of a natural thing; rather, he will become a golden bird, sitting on a golden tree, singing of the past ("what is past"), the present (that which is "passing"), and the future (that which is "to come").

4. 1. 3 Edgar Allan Poe

Edgar Allan Poe's (1809 – 1849) position in world literature is secure. His influence is world-wide in modern literature. His aesthetics and conscious craftsmanship, his attack on "the heresy of the didactic" and his call for "the rhythmical creation of beauty" have influenced French symbolism and the devotees of "art' for art's sake". Poe is father of many things, one of which is psychoanalytic criticism, the other being the detective story.

Poe was the first American writer who formulized the technique of the short story. In pursuit of the totality of effect through compression, immediacy and finality, Poe invented the genre of the detective story and developed a new fiction of psychological analysis. Poe has thus often been considered as the father of the modern short story.

All through his life, Poe was a prolific writer of some seventy short stories and a dozen poems. *The Raven* and *To Helen* were his famous poems.

4.2 Imagism

It is a movement in U.S. and English poetry characterized by the use of concrete language and figures of speech, modern subject matter, metrical freedom, and avoidance of romantic or mystical themes, aiming at clarity of expression through the use of precise visual images. It grew out of the Symbolist Movement in 1912 and was initially led by Ezra Pound, Amy Lowell, and Hilda Doolittle. Although as a movement Imagism flourished only briefly, it had considerable influence on the development of form and subject matter in modern poetry.

The Imagist manifesto came out in 1912 showed three Imagist poetic principles: direct treatment of the "thing" (no fuss, frill, or ornament), exclusion of superfluous words (precision and economy of expression), the rhythm of the musical phrase rather than the sequence of a metronome (free verse form and music).

Ezra Pound

Ezra Pound (1885 – 1972) was one of the most important poets and critics of his time and he was regarded as the father of modern American poetry. He is a leading spokesman of the "Imagist Movement", which though short-lived, had a tremendous influence on modern poetry.

He was confident in his belief that the artist was morally and culturally the arbiter and the "saviour" of the race, and he took it upon himself to purify the arts and became the prime mover of a few experimental movements, the aim of which was to dump the old into the dustbin and bring forth something new. To him life was sordid, personal crushing oppression, and culture produced nothing but "intangible bondage". Pound saw in Chinese history and the doctrine of Confucius a source of strength and wisdom with which to counterpoint Western gloom and confusion. He saw a chaotic world that wanted setting to rights, and a humanity, suffering from spiritual death and cosmic injustice, that need saving. He was for the most part of his life trying to offer Confucian philosophy as the one faith which could help to save the west.

In a Station of the Metro

The apparition of these faces in the crowd;

Petals on a wet, black bough.

This poem is probably the most famous of all imagist poems. In two lines it combines a sharp visual image or two juxtaposed images "Petals on a wet, black bough" with an implied meaning. The faces in the dim light of the Metro suggest both the impersonality and haste of city life and the greater transience of human life itself. The word "apparition" is a well-chosen one which has a two-fold meaning. Firstly, it means a visible appearance of something real. Secondly, it builds an image of a ghostly sight, a delusive and unexpected appearance.

Pound uses the fewest possible words to convey an accurate image, which is the principle of the Imagist poetry. This poem looks to be a modern adoption of the haiku form of Japanese poetry which adapts the 3 lines, 17 syllables and where the title is an integral part of the whole. The poem succeeds largely because of its internal rhymes: station/apparition; Metro/petals/wet; crowd/bough. Its form was determined by the experience that inspired it, involving organically rather than being chosen arbitrarily.

4.3 Expressionism

Expressionism in literature, especially drama, flourished in the early 1900s. Expressionist playwrights try to portray life as modified and distorted by their personal interpretation of reality. Characters in expressionist drama tend to be one-sided, standing for single ideas and attitudes. They are placed in situations in which the objects of the outer world are distorted to reveal the tortured minds of the characters or the dramatist. Playwrights achieve these effects with symbolic settings, bizarre lighting, and nonrealistic acting. Eugene O'Neill is a major American expressionist playwright.

The typical trait of Expressionism is to present the world solely from a subjective perspective, distorting it radically for emotional effect in order to evoke moods or ideas. In expressionism the artist tries to present an emotional experience in its most compelling form. The artist is not concerned with reality as it appears but with its inner nature and with the emotions aroused by the subject. To achieve these ends, the subject is frequently caricatured, exaggerated, distorted, or otherwise altered in order to stress the emotional experience in its most intense and concentrated form.

In literature, a common concern of expressionism is with the eruption of irrational and chaotic forces from beneath the surface of a mechanized modern world. Some of its explosive energies issued into Dada, Vorticism, and other avant-garde movements of the 1920s.

4. 3. 1 Eugene O' Neill

Eugene O' Neill (1888 – 1953) was the greatest American dramatist of the first half of the 20th century. He was the first playwright to explore serious themes in the theater and to carry out his continual, vigorous, courageous experiments with theatrical conventions. Specifically, he successfully introduced the European theatrical trends of realism, naturalism, and expressionism to the American stage as devices to express his interest in life and humanity. His success in realistic and expressionistic drama has turned the American drama from the traditions of romantic comedy to a modern mode.

He felt "the discordant, broken, faithless rhythm" of his time and tried to get at the root of human desires and frustration. The tragic sense of modern man being helpless and impotent remained with him all through his career.

He was entitled the Nobel Prize for Literature in 1936 with the official statement: He has been successful in interpreting universal human experience in terms of the drama. The Noble Prize and three Pulitzer Prizes (1920, 1922, 1928) show his achievement and influence at home and abroad. The universal appeal of his plays made him a lively force in the theatre worldwide. He exerted influence upon such playwrights as Tennessee Williams, Edward Albee, Cao Yu.

The Hairy Ape

The Hairy Ape (1922) is an expressionist play which reveals the theme that modern man loses his sense of belonging under technological progress. Humanity is in a predicament by creating a world he does not belong to. The industrial environment is presented as toxic and dehumanizing; the world of the rich, superficial and dehumanized. *The Hairy Ape* displays O'Neill's social concern for the oppressed industrial working class. Despite demonstrating in *The Hairy Ape* his clear belief that the capitalist system persecuted the working man, O'Neill is critical of a socialist movement that can't fulfill individual needs or solve unique problems.

4. 3. 2 Franz Kafka

Franz Kafka (1883 – 1924) is one of the most influential novelists in the 20th century, though becoming famous after his death. Born in Austria, Franz Kafka, has become a legendary figure in the west. His lifetime of obscurity is in sharp contrast with his great reputation of today.

His main period of writing is around the First World War. At that time, economy was facing depression, society was trapped in corruption, and people were poor. Thus, living in this kind of circumstance invoked his deep feeling of strangeness, aloneness and fear for the society. And these kinds of feeling became the eternal thesis of his works.

His works, such as *The Metamorphosis*, *The Trial*, *The Castle* are filled with the themes and archetypes of alienation, physical and psychological brutality, parent-child conflict, characters on a terrifying quest, and mystical transformations.

4.4 Stream of Consciousness

Stream of consciousness which is influenced deeply by Psychoanalysis of Sigmund Freud denotes a literary technique which seeks to describe an individual's point of view by giving the written equivalent of the character's thought processes, which means to attempt to imitate the natural flow of a character's thoughts, feelings, reflections, memories, and mental images as the character experiences them.

The main features of Stream of consciousness are listed as following:

(1) Revealing the action or the plot through the mental processes of the characters rather than through the commentary of an omniscient author;

(2) Character development through revelation of extremely personal or typical thought process rather than through the creation of typical characters in typical circumstances;

(3) Rare correspondence of the action or plot with the real,

chronological time, but rather the moving back and forth through present time to memories of past events and dreams of the future;

(4) Replacing narration, description, and commentary with dramatic interior monologue and free association.

Famous writers to employ this technique in the English language include James Joyce, Virginia Woolf and William Faulkner.

4. 4. 1 James Joyce

James Joyce (1882 – 1941), born into a declining Irish middle class family, received good education, but the rigidity of the religion and its representative effect turned him away from the church to literature.

He felt adamant that universality inheres in particularity, and Dublin is the gateway to the heart of all the cities in the world. Joyce was serious with both his thematic and technical concerns. In thematic terms, he never forgot to promote the spiritual freedom of his native country with his writings. Irish nationalism features prominently in his works. The theme of Irish discontentment and struggle for freedom always appears as a clear narrative thread.

Ulysses

Ulysses is a novel by James Joyce. The complete book was first published in 1922, although parts of it had appeared elsewhere earlier, which was first published in France, because of censorship troubles in the Great Britain and the United States, where the book became legally available in 1933.

Ulysses originated from Greek mythology. The story, using stream-of-consciousness technique, parallels the major events in *Odyssey* (telling Odysseus' journey after Troy War), whose Hero — Odysseus' Latin name is Ulysses. *Ulysses* contained 18 chapters, each of their titles taken from Greek mythology.

It relates to various extended knowledge, such as literature, religion, politics and history, even near 30 kinds of language. Combining author's experience, *Ulysses* is considered as reflection of Joyce's own history, Irish history and the history of mankind.

4. 4. 2 Virginia Woolf

Virginia Woolf (1882 – 1941), was an English novelist and essayist. As a successful innovator in the form of the novel, she is considered a significant force in 20th century fiction. As a novelist, Woolf's primary concern was to represent the flow of ordinary experience. Her emphasis was not on plot or characterization but on a character's consciousness, his thoughts and feelings, which she brilliantly illuminated by the stream of consciousness technique.

Furthermore, she was very much concerned with the rights and position of women, especially of intelligent women and women writers. She actively took part in the struggle for woman's rights of suffrage and rights to work which enabled her to be called as a Feminist.

To the Lighthouse

To the Lighthouse is a truly autobiographical novel with the technique of the stream of consciousness. It is a landmark novel of high modernism, the text, which centers on the Ramsays and their visits to the Isle of Skye in Scotland between 1910 and 1920, skillfully manipulates temporal and psychological elements.

The three sections of the book take place between 1910 and 1920 and revolve around various members of the Ramsay family. The novel spans almost twenty years and exposes the relationships among various members of the Ramsay family and among their visiting friends.

The Lighthouse stands empty as the marks the passage of time and the death of many of the characters. The novel is a meditation on love, loss, and creativity.

To the Lighthouse and its characters often display elements of the Modernist school of thought. Characters such as Mrs. Ramsay disparage Victorian ideals of society and question both the existence of God and the goodness in man. Furthermore, the transience of man is emphasized as a central theme alongside nature as an eternal and sometimes menacing force with the omnipresent potential to consume humanity.

4. 4. 3 William Faulkner

William Faulkner (1897 – 1962), born on September 25, 1897 in New Albany, Mississippi, was an American novelist and short-story writer. He got his first novel *Soldier's Pay* published in 1926, which crowned him for the 1949 Nobel Prize for his powerful and artistically unique contribution to the modern American novel.

He wrote works of psychological drama and emotional depth, typically with long serpentine prose and high, meticulously-chosen diction, also using groundbreaking literary devices such as stream of consciousness, multiple narrations or points of view, and time-shifts within narrative. The best of his fiction, which deal with basic human nature and basic pattern of human behavior, rank among the most enduring works of world literature. In writing about his land about "man in the ageless, eternal struggles", Faulkner speaks for both his people and humanity, and becomes as timeless and spaceless as his stories.

Faulkner was known rather infamously for his drinking problem as well, and throughout his life was known to be an alcoholic.

The Sound and the Fury

The Sound and the Fury is set in the fictional Yoknapatawpha County. The novel centers on the Compson family, former Southern aristocrats who are struggling to deal with the dissolution of their family and its reputation.

The Sound and the Fury literally begins as a "tale / Told by an idiot," as the first chapter is narrated by the mentally disabled Benjy. The novel's central concerns include time, much like Macbeth's "[t] omorrow, and tomorrow"; death, recalling Macbeth's "dusty death"; and nothingness and disintegration, a clear reference to Macbeth's lament that life "[s] ignif [ies] nothing." Additionally, Quentin is haunted by the sense that the Compson family has disintegrated to a mere shadow of its former greatness.

In his soliloquy, Macbeth implies that life is but a shadow of the past and that a modern man, like himself, is inadequately equipped and unable to achieve anything near the greatness of the past. Faulkner reinterprets this idea, implying that if man does not choose to take his own life, as Quentin does, the only alternatives are to become either a cynic and materialist like Jason, or an idiot like Benjy, unable to see life as anything more than a meaningless series of images, sounds, and memories.

4.5 Existentialism

Existentialism is a term applied to the work of a number of philosophers since the 19th century, who, despite large differences in their positions, generally focused on the condition of human existence, and an individual's emotions, actions, responsibilities, and thoughts, or the meaning or purpose of life. Existential philosophers often focused more on what they believed was subjective, such as beliefs and religion, or human states, feelings, and emotions, such as freedom, pain, guilt, and regret, as opposed to analyzing objective knowledge, language, or science.

Existentialism questions why we exist. Existentialists deny the existence of God. Existentialist writers often use prisons and solitary confinement to tell their stories. Often, neither the reader nor the protagonist is aware of what crime has been committed.

4. 5. 1 Camus

Albert Camus (1913 – 1960) was born in Algeria in 1913 and went to France at the age of 25, who is an outstanding representative of French existentialists and won the Nobel Prize for literature in 1956.

In 1940's, he befriended Sartre, the leading figure on existentialism. His work is often associated with existentialism or the philosophy of the absurd, but he rejects such labels.

The Algerian War which began in 1954 presented a moral dilemma for Camus. He identified with pied-noirs, and defended the French government on the grounds that the revolt in Algeria was really an integral part of the "new Arab imperialism". The Algerian War ended in 1962 (two years after his death), which led to the independence of Algeria from France.

He was an advocate against the death penalty and had worked for imprisoned Algerians who faced the death penalty.

The Stranger

This novel implies that we are alienated from the norms of society. We are situated in a world that is foreign to us and the only way to survive is to be assimilated, to accept its system of values, and to act like others do. Otherwise, we will forever be a "stranger" or an alien in our own land.

4. 5. 2 Sartre

Jean-Paul Sartre (1905 – 1980) was a French novelist, playwright, existentialist philosopher, and literary critic. Sartre was awarded the Nobel Prize for literature in 1964, but he declined the honor in protest of the values of bourgeois society.

The Wall

Written prior to Sartre's activism in political causes, *The Wall* was Sartre's personal response to the Spanish Civil War; he wrote it during a period when he felt hopeless about the growing forces of Fascism in Spain. The story also outlines Sartre's philosophy of existentialism. *The Wall*, along with Sartre's existentialist novel *Nausea*, helped solidify Sartre's literary reputation.

Jean-Paul Sartre's *The Wall* reflects his philosophy and personal experiences. He worked for the French resistance and was imprisoned by the Germans during WWII. *The Wall* is told from a first person, stream of consciousness point-of-view, and uses existentialist philosophy, to illuminate the follies of totalitarian governments like Fascism, and Nazism.

5 Modernist Painting

Modernist painting encompasses many new movements in painting since approximately 1860. These movements — Impressionism, Expressionism, Cubism, Futurism, Dada, Surrealism, to name only a few, were very diverse in both their forms and their contents. Most of them, however, were connected, since they grew out of one another.

Perhaps the most fundamental characteristic of these movements was a general tendency towards non-representationalism. Western painting from the Renaissance until the middle of the nineteenth century had been representational. Its main goal had been to create truthful representations of reality from a single perspective.

In sharp contrast, Modernism rejected the traditional aim of Western painting. Instead, Modernist painting turned in the direction of abstraction, of non-representationalism. To different degrees and in various ways, the work of most of the diverse movements of Modernist painting became nonrepresentational. These movements defined for themselves their own, distinct and new aims and objects of representation. But their goals no longer included the production of accurate, single-perspective depictions of reality.

5.1 Impressionism

The Movement that marked the beginning of Modernist painting was Impressionism. It originated in the late 1860s and the 1870s in France. The first exhibition of Impressionist painting was held in 1874 in Paris. The term "Impressionism" was, in fact, coined by the art critic Louis Leroy, after he saw Claude Monet's work *Impression: Sunrise* at the exhibition. Leroy named the new movement after Monet's painting.

A key objective of Impressionist painting was to depict specific moments in time. It sought to represent momentary impressions of the painter's surrounding world. Another important aim was to study the nature, workings, and effects of light. Some Impressionist paintings could be seen as analyses of the operation of light.

5.2 Expressionism

Expressionism superseded Impressionism as the main movement of Modernist painting, around 1900. It was, in fact, partly a reaction against the intellectual and emotional serenity that characterized Impressionism. In contrast to its predecessor, Expressionism emerged as a strongly psychological form of art.

Expressionist painters tried to analyze human psychology. In his portraits, for example, the Austrian artist Oskar Kokoschka endeavored to understand the inner, psychological worlds and experiences of his sitters. Most Expressionists, however, sought to express their feelings in and through their paintings. More than anything else, their works are expressions of their emotions.

5.2.1 Vincent van Gogh

Vincent van Gogh (1853 - 1890) was a pioneer of Expressionism. Van Gogh, in fact, produced his most famous paintings late in his life. Initially, he was a fairly traditional artist. He painted realistic pictures characterized by dark colors.

5.2.2 Edvard Munch

Another key representative of Expressionism was the Norwegian painter Edvard Munch (1863 - 1944). Munch's art was a deeply anguished art. Death and disease afflicted his family throughout his life, and he himself experienced a nervous breakdown. As a result, death, disease, and pain became central themes of his work.

5.3 Cubism

What succeeded Expressionism as the next dominant movement in Modernist painting was Cubism. It was founded by Georges Braque (1882 - 1963) and Pablo Picasso (1881 - 1973) in the first decade of the twentieth century. In contrast to Expressionism, Cubism no longer tried to analyze humans' psychology, or to express emotions. What it did was to introduce into Western painting a new understanding of pictorial representation.

The history of Cubism is usually divided into three phases. These are: Prototype Cubism, Analytical Cubism, and Synthetic Cubism.

What Cubism now did was to bring to Western painting a multiplicity of perspectives. Cubists would try to see an object from many perspectives; then, they would paint fragments from that object, as they were seen from the many perspectives adopted by the painter. This multi-perspectivism was a technique of pictorial representation whose invention constituted a revolution in the history of Western painting.

A crucial new development during the stage of Cubism was the introduction, by Braque and Picasso, of the technique of collage into Modernist painting. Having been introduced into Modernist painting by Cubism, collage subsequently became an important characteristic of Modernist painting.

5.3.1 Picasso

Pablo Picasso (1881 – 1973) was a Spanish painter, draughtsman, and sculptor. He is one of the most recognized figures in 20th-century art. He is best known for co-founding the Cubist movement and for the wide variety of styles embodied in his work. Among most famous Pablo Picasso paintings are the proto-Cubist Les Demoiselles d'Avignon (1907) and Guernica (1937), his portrayal of the German bombing of Guernica during the Spanish Civil War.

Picasso creativity manifested itself in numerous mediums, including oil paintings, sculpture, drawing, and architecture. His revolutionary artistic accomplishments brought him universal renown and immense fortunes throughout his life, making him the best-known figure in twentieth century art.

5.4 Futurism

The first decade of the twentieth century gave birth to another movement in Modernist painting, besides Cubism. This was Futurism. In terms of its fundamental philosophy, Futurism was strongly optimistic. Its representatives looked towards, and welcomed, the future. In essence, Futurism was a celebration of Western modernity. Futurists were especially fascinated by modern technology.

5.5 Dadaism

The second decade of the twentieth century saw the beginning of yet another movement within Modernist painting — Dada. That same decade also witnessed the tragedy of the First World War. Profoundly disillusioned by the War, the founders of Dada rejected the entire established order of Western society. Since, in the eyes of Dadaists, this Western establishment had allowed the tragedy of the War to happen, it deserved condemnation. For Dada, Western art — including Modernist painting — was also a part of the West's established order. Dada, therefore, decisively rejected Western art as well. This renunciation of Western culture was the main intellectual principle of the movement of Dada.

5.6 Surrealism

Following Dada, Surrealism became the main movement of Modernist painting between the two world wars. Intellectually, it was influenced strongly by Sigmund Freud's psychoanalysis. Surrealists shared Freud's view that humans have hidden, primitive drives, which are located in the unconscious part of the human psyche — in what Freud called the "Id." Surrealist painters came to believe that the Id could be a source of creativity and creative energy. Holding this conviction, they tried to invent a new process of artistic creation.

5.7 Fauvism

Fauvism is the style of les Fauves (French for "the wild beasts"), a short-lived and loose group of early twentieth-century Modern artists whose works emphasized painterly qualities and strong color over the representational or realistic values retained by Impressionism. While Fauvism as a style began around 1900 and continued beyond 1910, the movement as such lasted only a few years, 1904 – 1908, and had three exhibitions. The leaders of the movement were Henri Matisse and André Derain.

Henri Matisse (1869 – 1954) was a French artist, known for his use of colour and his fluid and original draughtsmanship. Matisse is commonly regarded, along with Picasso and Marcel Duchamp, as one of the three artists who helped to define the revolutionary developments in the plastic arts in the opening decades of the 20th century, responsible for significant developments in painting and sculpture. He was the leading figure in Fauvism painting. One of his representatives is *Harmony in Red*.

6 Modernist Architecture

Modern architecture is generally characterized by simplification of form and creation of ornament from the structure and theme of the building. It is a term applied to an overarching movement, with its exact definition and scope varying widely. In a broader sense, early modern architecture began at the turn of the 20th century with efforts to reconcile the principles underlying architectural design with rapid technological advancement and the modernization of society. It would take the form of numerous movements, schools of design, and architectural styles, some in tension with one another, and often equally defying such classification.

The concept of modernism would be a central theme in these efforts. Gaining popularity after the Second World War, architectural modernism was adopted by many influential architects and architectural educators, and continues as a dominant architectural style for institutional and corporate buildings into the 21st century.

Modernist architecture emphasizes on function. It attempts to provide for specific needs rather than imitate nature. Notable architects important to the history and development of the modernist movement include Frank Lloyd Wright, Ludwig Mies van der Rohe, Walter Gropius, Le Corbusier, Louis Sullivan, Oscar Niemeyer and Alvar Aalto.

Modernist architecture has these features:

(1) The notion that "Form follows function", meaning that the result of design should derive directly from its purpose

(2) Simplicity and clarity of forms and elimination of "unnecessary detail", meaning little or no ornamentation

(3) Visual expression of structure (as opposed to the hiding of structural elements)

(4) The related concept of "Truth to materials", meaning that the true nature or natural appearance of a material ought to be seen rather than concealed or altered to represent something else

(5) Use of industrially-produced materials; adoption of the machine aesthetic

(6) Particularly in International Style modernism, a visual emphasis on horizontal and vertical lines

Questions for Discussion

1. What has led to people's distrust about the westen world at the end of the 19th century?

2. How do you understand the statement that the development of industrial society in the very beginning of the 20th century resulted in people's moral corruption and meaningless life?

3. Compare the influence of Great Depression and that of the Subprime Crisis in 2008.

4. Comment on the influence of Darwin's theory on people's religious belief in the 20th century.

5. How do you understand the Psychoanalysis theory of Sigmund Freud? Can you use it to illustrate your dreams?

6. What is the influence of Sigmund Freud on modern writing?

7. "Ezra Pound was for the most part of his life trying to offer Confucian philosophy as the one faith which could help to save the west." How can you illustrate the function of Confucian philosophy in saving the west?

8. How did Friedrich Nietzsche differ from Arthur Schopenhauer regarding their philosophical thoughts?

9. How did Eugene O' Neill influence the Chinese writer Cao Yu?